组织行为学

Organizational Behavior

主　编　刘畅唱　阮晓文

哈爾濱工程大学出版社
Harbin Engineering University Press

内容简介

本书为江苏省2020年留学生全英文精品课程建设成果之一，全书分为6个部分，共12章。

第一部分是对组织行为学的整体概述，分别介绍了组织行为学的基本概念（第一章）、组织绩效和组织承诺（第二章）这两个组织最关心的内容。第二部分侧重探讨组织行为学关心的个体特征，包括个性、文化价值观和能力（第三章）。第三部分探讨影响个体工作结果的主要机制，包括动机（第四章），学习和决策制定（第五章）。第四部分探讨工作和组织特征，包括工作满意度（第六章），工作压力（第七章），信任、公正和伦理（第八章）。第五部分探讨群体机制，包括团队（第九章）和领导力（第十章）。第六部分讨论组织机制，包括组织结构（第十一章）和组织文化（第十二章）。

本书可作为高等院校留学生的全英文教学用书，也可作为广大高校组织行为学课程的双语教材使用，还可作为经济管理、人力资源管理、国际商务从业人员的自学用书或培训用书。

图书在版编目(CIP)数据

组织行为学/刘畅唱主编. —哈尔滨：哈尔滨工程大学出版社，2021.5
ISBN 978-7-5661-3047-1

Ⅰ.①组… Ⅱ.①刘… Ⅲ.①组织行为学 Ⅳ.①C936

中国版本图书馆CIP数据核字(2021)第077757号

组织行为学
ZUZHI XINGWEIXUE

选题策划 田 婧
责任编辑 张玮琪
封面设计 李海波

出版发行 哈尔滨工程大学出版社
社　　址 哈尔滨市南岗区东大直街124号
邮政编码 150001
发行电话 0451-82519328
传　　真 0451-82519699
经　　销 新华书店
印　　刷 哈尔滨市石桥印务有限公司
开　　本 787 mm×1 092 mm 1/16
印　　张 14
字　　数 473千字
版　　次 2021年5月第1版
印　　次 2021年5月第1次印刷
定　　价 49.80元

http://www.hrbeupress.com
E-mail:heupress@hrbeu.edu.cn

前　言

组织行为学主要研究个体、群体以及组织结构对组织内部行为的影响，目的是应用这些知识提高组织绩效。组织行为学关注人们在组织中做什么，以及这种行为如何影响组织关心的各种结果，探讨与工作、岗位、出勤、员工流动、生产率、工作绩效和管理有关的行为。可以说，组织行为学探讨的主题与进入或即将进入职场的每一个人息息相关。

组织行为学是工商管理学科的主干课程，也是经济、管理相关专业的必修课程，并且国内双语教学需求的增长和来华留学生数量的上升对教材提出了更高的要求，但相关学科的双语教材很少。

然而，国外原版教材直接引进难免“水土不服”，主要原因有：篇幅较长、辅助材料繁杂、引进内容（法律结构、经济、文化背景）不适用于国内教学等。针对上述实际问题，本书的编写以从事组织行为学双语教学多年的一线教师为主力，其中由刘畅唱负责全文构思、体例安排和部分内容编写；阮晓文对本书结构和部分内容进行了编写和审定。

本书使用对象为国内高校进行组织行为学双语教学的广大师生，也可作为经济管理、人力资源管理、国际商务从业人员的自学用书。

在本书的编写过程中，编者参阅了大量国内外专家、学者的著作、论文和网站资料，吸收和借鉴了其中的精华，在此向这些专家、学者表示感谢。由于编者水平有限，书中不妥之处在所难免，恳请专家和读者批评指正。

编　者

2021 年 4 月

目　　录

Section Ⅰ　Introduction to Organizational Behavior

Section Ⅱ　Individual Characteristics

Section Ⅲ Individual Mechanisms

Section Ⅳ Job and Organization

Section V Group Mechanisms

Section Ⅵ Organization Mechanisms

Section Ⅰ Introduction to Organizational Behavior

Chapter 1 Explaining Organizational Behavior

Imagine that you just ordered a soft drink and a sandwich. The person who served you was abrupt and unpleasant, did not smile, ignored you, did not make eye contact, and continued their conversation with a colleague, instead of attending to your needs. Rather than handing your changes politely, they slapped them on the counter and turned away for small talks. You have entered this restaurant many times, but you have never been treated so rudely. You leave feeling angry, deciding never to return. How can you explain the unusual behavior of the person who served you?

Let's put it this way: if you have a limited understanding of organizational behavior, then you struggle with comprehending of one of the major sets of forces influencing your personality, as well as the world around you, including the society and culture you are immersed in. Organizations draws an impact on everything that you do—filling stomach, finishing your degree, relaxing in a comfy home, or visiting exotic countries. It is by organizations you could have your life unfolded in this modern era. From satisfying instant needs to meeting ultimate life-goals, you depend on help from organizations.

Before we jump into defining what organizational behavior is, consider firstly this following question: who was the single worst coworker you've ever encountered? Search from fellow classmates with whom you've done projects; colleagues from part-time or summer jobs; or peers, subordinates, or supervisors working in your current organization. What did this coworker do that earned him or her such status? Was it some of the behaviors shown in the right column of Table 1 – 1 (or perhaps all of them)? Now, switch to recalling the single best coworker you've ever met. Again, what did this person do to earn "best coworker" status—some or most of the behaviors shown in the left column of Table 1 – 1?

If characteristics of the two types of coworkers profiled in the Table 1 – 1 are close to your real life examples, you probably are asking two questions to yourself now: "Why does the worst coworker act that way?" "Why does the best coworker act the other way?" Once you noticed the reasons why two coworkers act so differently, you might know how to interact with the difficult coworker more efficiently (thereby adding some pleasant values to your collaborations). If you happen to be a manager, you could devise plans for improving attitudes and behaviors in the unit. Such plans might direct screening applicants, training and socializing newcomers, managing evaluations and rewards for performance, and dealing with conflicts among employees. Without understanding why employees act the way they do, it's very difficult to find a way to improve their attitudes and behaviors at work.

Table 1 - 1 The Best of Coworkers, the Worst of Coworkers

The Best	The Worst
Got the job done, without having to be managed or reminded	Did not get the job done, even with a great deal of hand-holding
Adapted when something needed to be changed or done differently	Was resistant to any and every form of change, even when changes were beneficial
Was always a "good sport", even when bad things happened at work	Whined and complained, no matter what was happening
Attended optional meetings or functions to support colleagues	Optional meeting? Was too lazy to make it to some required meetings and functions!
Helped new coworkers or people who seemed to need a hand	Made fun of new coworkers or people who seemed to need a hand
Followed key rules, even when the reasons for them were not apparent	Broke virtually and rule that somehow make his or her work more difficult
Felt an attachment and obligation to the employer for the long haul	Seemed to always be looking for something else, even if it wasn't better
Was first to arrive, last to leave	Was first to leave for lunch, last to return

1.1 Define organizational behavior (OB)

Organizational behavior (OB) is a field of study of the structure and management of organizations, their environments, and the actions and interactions of their individual members and groups. Research on OB are conducted by scholars in university management departments and scientists in business organizations. The research findings are then applied by managers or consultants to check if they help solve real-world challenges. The field of OB formulate theories by drawing concepts from multiple disciplines. For instance, industrial and organizational psychology is primarily the field of inspiration for research on job performance and individual traits. Research on satisfaction, emotions, and team processes relies on social psychology. Team characteristics and organizational structures draws from sociology. Anthropology informs researchers investigating organizational culture. In the end, patterns of motivation, learning, and decision making are further clarified with help from models of economics. Such interdisciplinary nature of OB is what makes this field unique to many students, who might be intrinsically interested and thought-provoked by a particular topic among the wide-scope of directions enlisted in OB.

Because of the diversity in its topics and disciplinary roots, it's easy for students in an OB class to wonder "How does all this stuff fit together?" This textbook answers such question by exploring this field with an integrative model of OB as a structural guidance, shown in Figure 1 - 1. The model is designed as a roadmap for learning organizational behavior. The model shows how the topics in the next 11 chapters all fit together. We should stress that there are other potential ways of combining the 11 topics, and Figure 1 - 1 certainly over simplifies the connections among the topics. Still, we believe the model provides a helpful guide as you move through this course. Figure 1 - 1 includes five different kinds of topics.

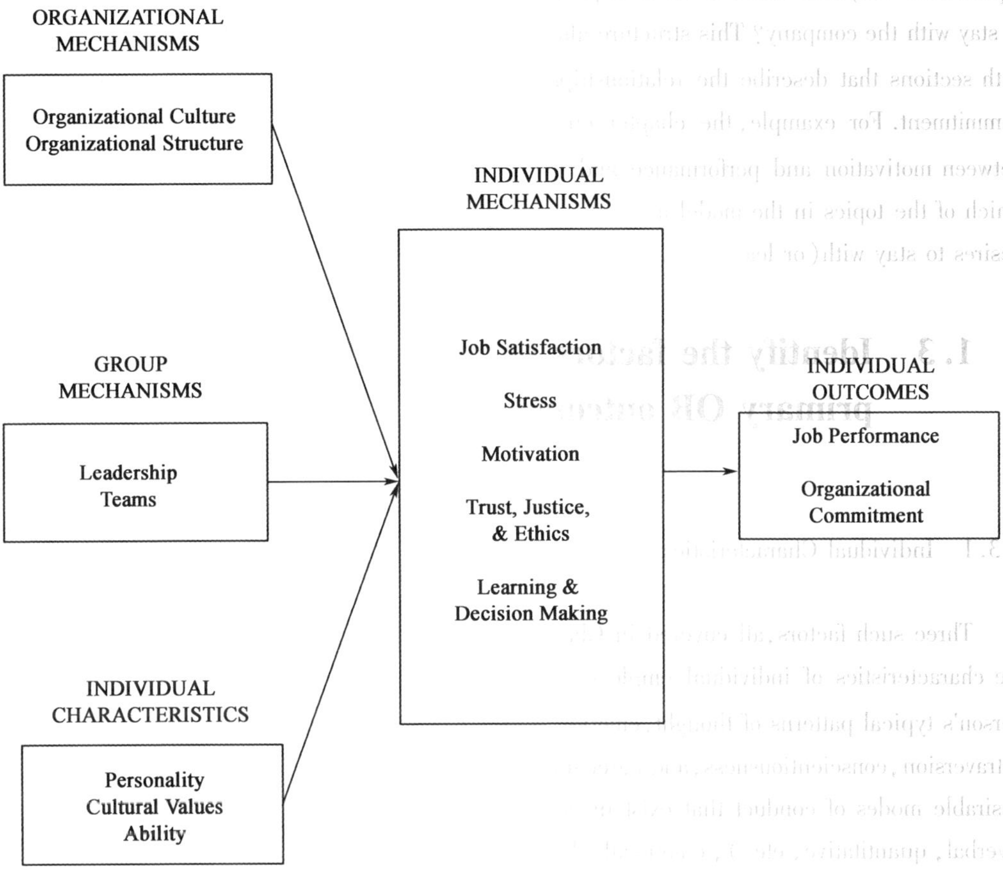

Figure 1 - 1 Integrative Model of Organizational Behavior

1.2 Describe the two primary outcomes in studies of OB

The right-most portion of the model contains the two primary outcomes of interest to organizational behavior researchers (and employees and managers in organizations): job performance and organizational commitment. Most employees have two primary goals for their working lives: to perform their jobs well and to remain a member of an organization that they respect. Likewise, most managers have two primary goals for their employees: to maximize their job performance and to ensure that they stay with the firm for a significant length of time. As described in Chapter 2, there are several specific behaviors that, when taken together, constitute good job performance. There are also several beliefs, attitudes, and emotions that cause an employee to remain committed to an employer.

This book starts by covering job performance and organizational commitment so that you can better understand the two primary organizational behavior goals. We hope that by using performance and commitment as starting points, we can highlight the practical importance of OB topics. After all, what could be more important than having employees who perform well and want to stay with the company? This structure also enables us to conclude the other chapters in the book with sections that describe the relationships between each chapter's topic and performance and commitment. For example, the chapter on motivation concludes by describing the relationships between motivation and performance and motivation and commitment. In this way, you'll learn which of the topics in the model are most useful for understanding your job performance and your desires to stay with (or leave) your company.

1.3 Identify the factors that influence the two primary OB outcomes

1.3.1 Individual Characteristics

Three such factors, all covered in Chapter 3 Personality, Cultural Values and Ability, reflect the characteristics of individual employees. Personality reflects the various traits that explain a person's typical patterns of thought, emotion, and behavior, with commonly studied traits including extraversion, conscientiousness, and agreeableness. Cultural Values reflect the shared beliefs about desirable modes of conduct that exist in certain cultures. Ability describes the cognitive abilities (verbal, quantitative, etc.), emotional skills (other awareness, emotion regulation, etc.), and physical abilities (strength, endurance, etc.) that employees bring to a job. Taken together, these individual characteristics help summarize what employees are like and what employees can do.

1.3.2 Individual Mechanisms

Our integrative model also illustrates a few individual mechanisms that directly affect job performance and organizational commitment. These include job satisfaction, which captures what employees feel when thinking about their jobs and doing their day-to-day work (Chapter 6). Another individual mechanism is stress, which reflects employees' psychological responses to job demands that tax or exceed their capacities (Chapter 7). The model also includes motivation, which captures the energetic forces that drive employees' work effort (Chapter 4). Trust, justice, and ethics reflect the degree to which employees feel that their company does business with fairness, honesty, and integrity (Chapter 8). The final individual mechanism shown in the model is Learning and Decision Making, which deals with how employees gain job knowledge and how they use that knowledge to make accurate judgments on the job (Chapter 5).

1.3.4 Group Mechanisms

Employees do not work alone. Instead, they typically work in one or more work teams led by some formal (or sometimes informal) leader. Like the individual characteristics, these group mechanisms shape satisfaction, stress, motivation, trust, and learning. Chapter 9 describes the qualities that work groups possess, such as their norms, their roles, and the way members depend on one another. Chapter 9 also describes the processes that summarize how groups behave, including topics like cooperation, conflict, and communication. Chapter 10 focuses on the leadership. We start by describing how individuals become leaders in the first place by considering the power and influence dynamics within organizational groups. Then we describe how leaders behave in their leadership roles as they use specific actions to influence others at work.

1.3.5 Organizational Mechanisms

Finally, our integrative model acknowledges that the teams described in the prior section are grouped into larger organizations that themselves affect satisfaction, stress, motivation, and so forth. For example, every company has an organizational structure that dictates how the units within the firm link to (and communicate with) other units (Chapter 11). Sometimes structures are centralized around a decision-making authority, whereas other times, structures are decentralized, affording each unit some autonomy. Every company also has an organizational culture that captures "the way things are" in the organization—shared knowledge about the rules, norms, and values that shape employee attitudes and behaviors (Chapter 12).

1.3.6 Summary

We hope that this integrative model will serve as a guide for where you are in this book, as well as where you've been and where you're going. Some of you will be able to apply the topics in the chapters to your current working life, whether you're working full-time or part-time and whether you occupy a managerial or non-managerial role. Of course, some of you are fulltime students or between jobs now. Regardless of your work status, one thing all of you have in common is that you're students. As it turns out, many of the same concepts that predict success in an organization also predict success in a classroom. We will explore some of those commonalities in our OB for Students feature, which appears in each chapter and illustrates how OB concepts can be applied to improve academic success.

1.4 Understand why firms that are good at OB tend to be more profitable

1.4.1 The resource-based View

The resource-based view suggests that the value of resources depends on several factors (Figure 1 – 2). For example, a resource is more valuable when it is rare. Diamonds, oil, high technology are all expensive precisely because they are rare. Good people are also rare—witness the adage "good people are hard to find". Ask yourself what percentage of the people you have worked with have been talented, motivated, satisfied, and good team players. In some organizations, cities, or job markets, such employees are the exception rather than the rule. If good people really are rare, then the effective management of OB should prove to be a valuable resource.

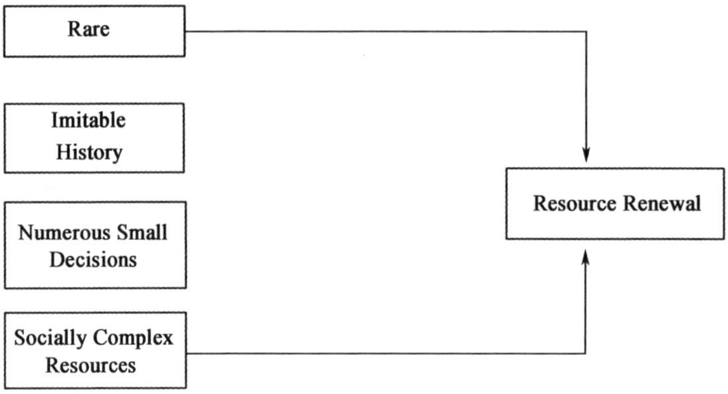

Fig 1 – 2 What Makes a Resource Valuable?

The resource-based view also suggests that a resource is more valuable when it is inimitable, meaning that it cannot be imitated. A new form of technology can help a firm gain an advantage for a short time, but what happens when a competing firm adopts the same technology? Many of a firm's resources can be imitated, though it is sometimes expensive. Manufacturing practices can be copied, building layouts can be mimicked, equipment and tools can be approximated. Good people, in contrast, are much more difficult to imitate. There are three reasons why people are inimitable.

1.4.2 History

People create a history—a collective pool of experience, wisdom, and knowledge that benefits the organization. History cannot be bought. Consider an example from the discount airline industry. Southwest and JetBlue are the market leaders in this industry, profiting from more frequent point-to-point daily schedules routed into less expensive airports. Delta launched its own discount brand-song—to compete in this market, though the brand was ultimately abandoned and folded back into Delta's regular operations. One challenge facing Song was that it was competing, for the first time, in a market in which Southwest had existed for decades. Their respective positions on the "industry learning curve" were quite different.

1.4.3 Numerous Small Decisions

The concept of numerous small decisions captures the idea that people make many small decisions day in and day out, week in and week out. "So what?" you might say, "why worry about small decisions?" Ask yourself how much time elapsed between the arrival of Diet Coke with Lime on grocery store shelves and the arrival of Diet Pepsi Lime. Answer? About two months. Big decisions can be copied; they are visible to competitors and observable by industry experts and analysts. In the case of Song, the company was able to copy one of Jet Blue's signatures—a television for every seat—so that Song passengers were able to watch pay-per-view movies or play video games. However, it would be more difficult to copy one of Southwest's signatures—the playful, whimsical style displayed by flight attendants and service personnel. Officials from Song may not have the opportunity to observe a Southwest flight attendant turning the seatbelt instructions into a comedy routine on a given day or finding a way to make an anxious toddler laugh on a particular flight. Those decisions are invisible to competitors but not to the travelers who make mental notes about their next trip.

1.4.4 Socially Complex Resources

People also create socially complex resources, like culture, trust, and reputation. These resources are termed "socially complex" because it's not always clear how they came to develop, though it is clear which organizations do (and do not) possess them. An upper manager at Song could have exited a Southwest flight convinced that the company would benefit from adopting the competitor's playful and fun culture. But how exactly would that be done? A new culture cannot just be implemented like a change in software systems. It springs from the social dynamics within a given firm at a given point in time.

1.4.5 Research Evidence

In sum, we can build a conceptual argument for why OB might affect an organization's profitability: Good people are both rare and inimitable and therefore serve as a resource that is valuable for creating competitive advantage. Conceptual arguments are helpful, of course, but it would be even better if there were hard data to back them up. Fortunately, it turns out that there is a great deal of research evidence supporting the importance of OB for company performance. Several research studies have been conducted on the topic, each employing a somewhat different approach.

One study focused on 136 non-financial companies who made Initial Public Offerings (IPOs) in 1988.23 firms that undergo an IPO typically have shorter histories and need an infusion of cash to grow or introduce some new technology. The authors of this study examined the prospectus filed by each firm (the Securities and Exchange Commission requires that prospectuses contain honest information, and firms can be liable for any inaccuracies that might mislead investors).

The authors coded each prospectus for information that might suggest OB issues were valued. Examples of valuing OB issues included describing employees as a source of competitive advantage in strategy and mission statements, emphasizing training and continuing education, having a human resources management office; and emphasizing full-time rather than temporary or contract employees. By 1993, 81 of the 136 firms included in the study had survived (60 percent). The key question is whether the value placed on OB predicted which firms did (and did not) survive. The results revealed that firms that valued OB had a 19 percent higher survival rate than firms that did not value OB.

Another study focused on Fortune's "100 Best Companies to Work For" list, which has appeared annually since 1998. These companies include tycoons like Google, Microsoft, Genentech and Nike. If the 100 firms on the list really do have good OB practices, and if good OB practices really do influence firm profitability, then it follows that the 100 firms should be more profitable. To explore this premise, the study went back to the original 1998 list and found a "matching firm" for the companies that were included. The matching firm consisted of the most similar company with respect to industry and size in that particular year, with the added requirement that the company had not appeared on the "100 Best" list. This process essentially created two groups of companies that differ only in terms of their inclusion in the "100 Best". The study then compared the profitability of those two groups of companies. The results revealed that the "100 Best" firms were more profitable than their peers. Indeed, the study's authors noted that an investment portfolio based on the 1998 "100 Best" list would have earned an 82 percent cumulative investment return from 1998 – 2000 compared with only 37 percent for the broader market.

1.4.6 So What's So Hard?

Clearly this research evidence seems to support the conceptual argument that good people constitute a valuable resource for companies. Good OB does seem to matter in terms of company profitability. You may wonder then, "what's so hard?" Why doesn't every company prioritize the effective management of OB, devoting as much attention to it as they do accounting, finance, marketing, technology, physical assets, and so on? Certainly, some companies do a very poor job of managing their people. Why is that?

Work by Jeffrey Pfeffer provides one potential answer. Pfeffer has written extensively about the OB practices that tend to be used by successful organizations. He also has described why more organizations do not use seemingly "commonsense" practices. One reason is that there is no "magic bullet" OB practice—one thing that, in and of itself, can increase profitability. Instead, the effective management of OB requires a belief that several different practices are important, along with a long-term commitment to improving those practices. This premise can be summarized with what might be called the rule of one-eighth: one must bear in mind that one-half of organizations won't believe the connection between how they manage their people and the profits they earn. One-half of those who do see the connection will do what many organizations have done—try to make a single change to solve their problems, not realizing that the effective management of people requires a more comprehensive and systematic approach. Of the firms that make comprehensive changes, probably only about one-half will persist with their practices long enough to derive economic benefits. Since one-half times one-half times one-half equals one-eighth, at best 12 percent of organizations will do what is required to build profits by putting people first.

The integrative model of OB used to structure this book was designed with this rule of one-eighth in mind. High job performance depends not just on employee motivation but also on fostering high levels of satisfaction, effectively managing stress, creating a trusting climate, and committing to employee learning. Failing to do any one of those things could hinder the effectiveness of the other concepts in the model. Of course, that systemic nature reveals another reality of organizational behavior: It is often difficult to "fix" companies that struggle with OB issues. Such companies often struggle in several different areas and on a number of different levels. One such (fictitious) company is spot lighted in our OB on Screen feature, which appears in each chapter and uses well-known movies to demonstrate OB concepts.

1.4.7 How Do We "Know" What We Know About Organizational Behavior?

Now that we've described what OB is and why it's an important topic of study, we now turn to how we "know" what we know about the topic. In other words, where does the knowledge in this textbook come from? To answer this question, we must first explore how people "know" about anything. Philosophers have argued that there are several different ways of knowing things.

- Method of Experience: People hold firmly to some belief because it is consistent with their own experience and observations.
- Method of Intuition: People hold firmly to some belief because it "just stands to reason"—it seems obvious or self-evident.
- Method of Authority: People hold firmly to some belief because some respected official, agency, or source has said it is so.
- Method of Science: People accept some belief because scientific studies have tended to replicate that result using a series of samples, settings, and methods.

Consider the following prediction: Providing social recognition, in the form of public praise and appreciation for good behavior, will increase the performance and commitment of work units. Perhaps you feel that you "know" this claim to be true because you yourself have always responded well to praise and recognition. Or perhaps you feel that you "know" it to be true because it seems like common sense—who wouldn't work harder after a few public pats on the back? Maybe you feel that you "know" it to be true because a respected boss from your past always extolled the virtue of public praise and recognition.

However, the methods of experience, intuition, and authority also might have led you to the opposite belief—that providing social recognition has no impact on the performance and commitment of work units. It may be that public praise has always made you uncomfortable or embarrassed, to the point that you tried to hide especially effective behaviors to avoid being singled out by your boss. Or it may seem logical that social recognition will be viewed as "cheap talk", with employees longing for financial incentives rather than verbal compliments. Or perhaps the best boss you ever worked for never offered a single piece of social recognition in her life, yet her employees always worked their hardest on her behalf.

1.5 Define "theory" and explain its role in the scientific method

From a scientist's point of view, it doesn't really matter what a person's experience, intuition, or authority suggests; the prediction must be tested with data. In other words, scientists don't simply assume that their beliefs are accurate; they acknowledge that their beliefs must be tested scientifically. Scientific studies are based on the scientific method, originated by Sir Francis Bacon in the 1600 s. The scientific method begins with theory, defined as a collection of assertions—both verbal and symbolic—that specify how and why variables are related, as well as the conditions in which they should (and should not) be related. More simply, a theory tells a story and supplies the familiar who, what, where, when, and why elements found in any newspaper or magazine article? Theories are often summarized with theory diagrams, the "boxes and arrows" that graphically depict relationships between variables.

A scientist could build a theory explaining why social recognition might influence the performance and commitment of work units. From what sources would that theory be built? Theories may be built from interviews with employees in a work setting, employees who provide insights into their views about the strengths and weaknesses of social recognition. They also may be built from observations of people at work, in which case scientists take notes, keep diaries, and pore over company documents to find all the elements of a theory story. Alternatively, theories may be built from research reviews, which examine findings of previous studies to look for general patterns or themes.

Although many theories are interesting, logical, or thought provoking, many also wind up being completely wrong. After all, scientific theories once predicted that the earth was fiat and the sun revolved around it. Closer to home, OB theories once argued that money was not an effective motivator and that the best way to structure jobs was to make them as simple and mundane as possible? Theories must therefore be tested to verify that their predictions are accurate. As shown in Figure 1 – 3, the scientific method requires that theories be used to inspire hypotheses. Hypotheses are written predictions that specify relationships between variables. For example, a theory of social recognition could be used to inspire this hypothesis: "Social recognition behaviors on the part of managers will be positively related to the job performance and organizational commitment of their units". This hypothesis states, in black and white, the expected relationship between social recognition and unit effectiveness.

Assume a family member owned a chain of 21 fast-food restaurants and allowed you to test this hypothesis using the restaurants. Specifically, you decided to train the managers in a subset of the restaurants about how to use social recognition as a tool to reinforce behaviors. Meanwhile, you left another subset of restaurants unchanged to represent a control group. You then tracked the total number of social recognition behaviors exhibited by managers over the next nine months by observing the managers at specific time intervals. You measured job performance by tracking drive-through times for the next nine months and used those times to reflect the minutes it takes for a customer to approach the restaurant, order food, pay, and leave. You also measured the commitment of the work unit by tracking employee retention rates over the next nine months.

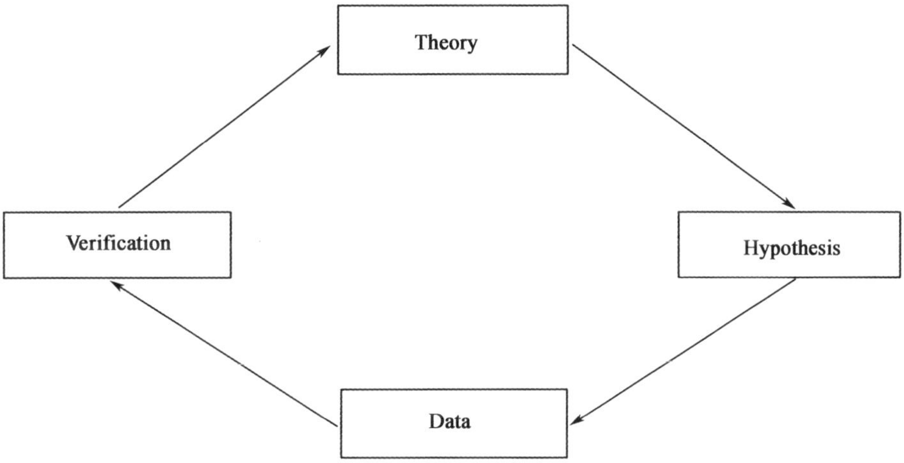

Figure 1 – 3 The Scientific Method

1.6 Takeaways

1. Organizational behavior is a field of study devoted to understanding and explaining the attitudes and behaviors of individuals and groups in organizations. More simply, it focuses on why individuals and groups in organizations act the way they do.

2. The two primary outcomes in organizational behavior are job performance and organizational commitment.

3. A number of factors affect performance and commitment, including individual mechanisms (job satisfaction; stress; motivation; trust, justice, and ethics; learning and decision making),

individual characteristics (personality, cultural values, and ability), group mechanisms (teams, leadership), and organizational mechanisms (organizational structure, organizational culture).

4. The effective management of organizational behavior can help a company become more profitable because good people are a valuable resource. Not only are good people rare, but they are also hard to imitate. They create a history that cannot be bought or copied, they make numerous small decisions that cannot be observed by competitors, and they create socially complex resources such as culture, teamwork, trust, and reputation. Many scientific studies support the relationship between effective organizational behavior and company performance.

5. A theory is a collection of assertions, both verbal and symbolic, that specifies how and why variables are related, as well as the conditions in which they should (and should not) be related. Theories about organizational behavior are built from a combination of interviews, observation, research reviews, and reflection. Theories form the beginning point for the scientific method and inspire hypotheses that can be tested with data.

1.7 Discussion questions

1. Think again about the worst coworker you've ever had—the one who did some of the things listed in Table 1 – 1. Think about what that coworker's boss did (or didn't do) to try to improve his or her behavior. What did the boss do well or poorly? What would you have done differently, and which organizational behavior topics would have been most relevant?

2. Which of the individual mechanisms in Figure 1 – 1 (job satisfaction; stress; motivation; trust, justice, and ethics; learning and decision making) seems to drive your performance and commitment the most? Do you think you're unique in that regard, or do you think most people would answer that way?

3. Create a list of the most successful companies that you can think of. What do these companies have that others don't? Are the things that those companies possess rare and inimitable (Figure 1 – 2)? What makes those things difficult to copy?

4. Think of something that you "know" to be true based on the method of experience, the method of intuition, or the method of authority. Could you test your knowledge using the method of science? How would you do it?

Chapter 2 Performance and Commitment

We begin our journey through the integrative model of organizational behavior with the two primary outcomes in OB: job performance and organizational commitment. Most managers have two primary goals for their employees: they perform their jobs well and remain a member of their current organization. Similarly, most employees have two kinds of questions about their working lives: what does it take to be a good performer and what factors make them want to stay in their current position? Given the importance of these two outcomes, it's critical to understand what performance and commitment represent, and what concepts affect them. This chapter will provide a detailed overview of performance and commitment. In the remainder of this book, you'll work your way through our integrative model to understand the concepts that drive those two important outcomes.

2.1 Define job performance and organizational commitment

Job performance is defined as the value of the set of employee behaviors that contribute, either positively or negatively, to organizational goal accomplishment? Employees who are "good performers" engage in specific behaviors that create positive value for the firm. Employees who are "bad performers" engage in specific behaviors that hinder organizational goal accomplishment. Organizational commitment is defined as the desire on the part of an employee to remain a member of the organization. Employees who are committed to their organization improve the organization's "retention" because they stay around for the long term. Employees who are not committed are more likely to "turn over"—voluntarily quitting their job and ending their membership with the organization. The first half of this chapter will describe the various behaviors that capture an employee's job performance. The second half will then explore the psychological dynamics of commitment, while also describing what happens when employees aren't committed.

2.1.1 Job Performance

The definition of job performance mentioned raises some important questions. Specifically, you might be wondering which employee behaviors fall under the umbrella heading of job performance. In other words, from an employee's perspective, what exactly does it mean to be a good performer? We could probably spend an entire chapter just listing various behaviors that are relevant to job performance. However, those behaviors generally fit into three broad categories. Two categories are task performance and citizenship behavior, both of which contribute positively to the organization. The third category is counterproductive behavior, which contributes negatively to the organization. In our OB on screen feature, you'll find an example of employees who demonstrate various levels of all three aspects of job performance. The sections that follow describe these broad categories of job performance in greater detail.

2.1.2 Task Performance

Task performance includes employee behaviors that are directly involved in the transformation of organizational resources into the goods or services that the organization produces. If you read a description of a job in an employment advertisement online, that description will focus on task performance behaviors—the tasks, duties, and responsibilities that are a core part of the job. Put differently, task performance is the set of explicit obligations that an employee must fulfill to receive compensation and continued employment. For a flight attendant, task performance includes announcing and demonstrating safety and emergency procedures and distributing food and beverages to passengers. For a firefighter, task performance includes searching burning buildings to locate fire victims and operating equipment to put out fires. For an accountant, task performance involves preparing, examining, and analyzing accounting records for accuracy and completeness. Finally, for an advertising executive, task performance includes developing advertising campaigns and preparing and delivering presentations to clients.

2.2 Define task performance and explain how organizations identify key task behaviors

Although the specific activities that constitute task performance differ widely from one job to another, task performance also can be understood in terms of more general categories. One way of categorizing task performance is to consider the extent to which the context of the job is routine or changing. Routine task performance involves well-known responses to demands that occur in a normal, routine, or otherwise predictable way. In these cases, employees tend to act in habitual or programmed ways that vary little from one instance to another. As an example of a routine task activity, you may recall watching an expressionless flight attendant robotically demonstrate how to insert the seatbelt tongue into the seatbelt buckle before your flight takes off. Seatbelts haven't really changed since 1920, so the instructions to passengers tend to be conveyed the same way, repeatedly.

In contrast, adaptive task performance, or more commonly "adaptability" involves employee responses to task demands that are novel, unusual, or, at the very least, unpredictable. For example, on August 2, 2005, Air France Flight 358, carrying 297 passengers and 12 crew members from Paris, France, to Toronto, Canada, skidded off the runway during its landing and into a ravine. Amid smoke and flames, the flight attendants quickly responded to the emergency and assisted three-quarters of the 297 passengers safely off the plane within 52 seconds, before the emergency response team arrived. One minute later, the remaining passengers and 12 crew members were out safely. From this example, you can see that flight attendants' task performance shifted from activities such as providing safety demonstrations and handing out beverages to performing emergency procedures to save passengers' lives. The behaviors involved in adaptability are diverse and have become increasingly important in today's economy.

Now that we've given you a general understanding of task performance behaviors, you might be wondering how organizations identify the sets of behaviors that represent task performance for different jobs. Many organizations identify task performance behaviors by conducting a job analysis. Although there are many ways to conduct a job analysis, most boil down to the following three steps. First, a list of all the activities involved in a job is generated. This list generally results from data from several sources, including observations, surveys, and interviews of employees. Second, each activity on this list is rated by subject matter experts according to things like the importance and frequency of the activity. Subject matter experts generally have experience performing the job or managing people who perform the job and therefore can judge the degree to which specific activities contribute to the organization. Third, activities that are rated highly in terms of their importance and frequency are retained and used to define task performance.

Those retained behaviors often find their way into the measures that managers use to evaluate the task performance of employees. Men's Wearhouse provides a good example of an organization that uses task performance information in this way. The company first gathers information about the employee's on-the-job behavior. After the behavior information is gathered, senior managers provide feedback and coaching to the employee about which types of behaviors he or she needs to change to improve. The feedback is framed as constructive criticism meant to improve an employee's behavior. Put yourself in the place of a Men's Wearhouse wardrobe consultant for a moment. Wouldn't you rather have your performance evaluated based on the behaviors rather than some overall index of sales? After all, those behaviors are completely within your control, and the feedback you receive from your boss will be more informative than the simple directive to "sell more suits next year than you did this year".

When organizations find it impractical to use job analysis to identify the set of behaviors needed to define task performance, they can turn to a database the government has created to help with that important activity. The Occupational Information Network (http://online.onetcenter.org) is an online database that includes, among other things, the characteristics of most jobs in terms of tasks, behaviors, and the required knowledge, skills, and abilities. Of course, O'NET represents only a first step in figuring out the important tasks for a given job. Many organizations ask their employees to perform tasks that their competitors do not, ensuring that their workforce performs jobs in a unique and valuable way. O'NET cannot capture those sorts of unique task requirements—the "numerous small decisions" that separate the most effective organizations from their competitors.

For example, the authors of a book entitled *Nuts* identify "fun" as one of the dominant values of Southwest Airlines. Southwest believes that people are willing to work more productively and creatively in an environment that includes humor and laughter. Consistent with this belief, flight attendant task performance at Southwest includes not only generic flight attendant activities such as those identified by O'NET, but also activities that reflect a sense of humor and playfulness. As an example, effective flight attendants tell jokes over the intercom such as, "We'll be dimming the lights in the cabin, pushing the light-bulb button will turn your reading light on. However, pushing the flight attendant button will not turn your flight attendant on." Thus, though O'NET may be a good place to start, the task information from the database should be supplemented with information regarding behaviors that support the organization's values and strategy.

Citizenship behavior is defined as voluntary employee activities that may or may not be rewarded but that contribute to the organization by improving the overall quality of the setting in which work takes place? Have you ever had a coworker or fellow student who was always willing to help someone who was struggling? Who always attended optional meetings or social functions to support his or her colleagues? Who always maintained a good attitude, even in trying times? We tend to call those people "good citizens" or "good soldiers". High levels of citizenship behavior earn them such titles. Although there are many different types of behaviors that might seem to fit the definition of citizenship behavior, research suggests two main categories that differ according to who benefits from the activity: coworkers or the organization.

2.3 Understand citizenship behavior, and describe some specific examples

The first category of citizenship behavior is the one with which you're most likely to be familiar: interpersonal citizenship behavior (Figure 2 – 1). Such behaviors benefit coworkers and colleagues and involve assisting, supporting, and developing other organizational members in a way that goes beyond normal job expectations. For example, helping involves assisting coworkers who have heavy workloads, aiding them with personal matters, and showing new employees the ropes when they first arrive on the job. Courtesy refers to keeping coworkers informed about matters that are relevant to them. Some employees tend to keep relevant facts and events secret. Good citizens do the opposite; they keep others in the loop because they never know what information might be useful to someone else. Sportsmanship involves maintaining a good attitude with coworkers, even when they've done something annoying or when the unit is going through tough times. Whining and complaining are contagious; good citizens avoid being the squeaky wheel who frequently makes mountains out of molehills.

The second category of citizenship behavior is organizational citizenship behavior (Figure 2 – 1). These behaviors benefit the larger organization by supporting and defending the company, working to improve its operations, and being especially loyal to it. For example, voice involves speaking up and offering constructive suggestions for change. Good citizens react to bad rules or policies by constructively trying to change them as opposed to passively complaining about them? Civic virtue refers to participating in the company's operations at a deeper than normal level by attending voluntary meetings and functions, reading and keeping up with organizational announcements, and keeping abreast of business news that affects the company. Boosterism means representing the organization in a positive way when out in public, away from the office, and away from work. Think of friends you've had who worked for a restaurant. Did they always say good things about the restaurant when talking to you and keep any "kitchen horror stories" to themselves? If so, they were being good citizens by engaging in high levels of boosterism.

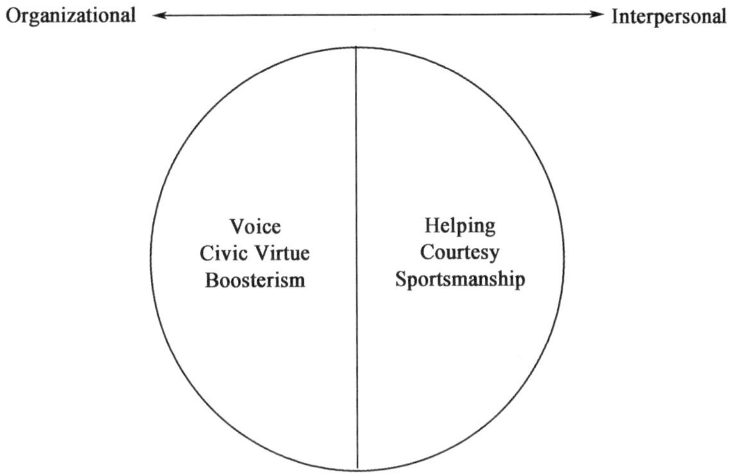

Figure 2 – 1 Types of Citizenship Behaviors

As you've probably realized, citizenship behaviors are relevant in virtually any job, regardless of the particular nature of its tasks, and these behaviors have clear benefits in terms of the effectiveness of work units and organizations. As an example, research conducted in a paper mill found that the quantity and quality of crew output was higher in crews that included more good citizens. Research on 30 restaurants also showed that higher levels of citizenship behavior promoted higher revenue, better operating efficiency, higher customer satisfaction, higher performance quality, less food waste, and fewer customer complaints. Thus, it seems clear that citizenship behaviors have a significant influence on the bottom line.

From an employee's perspective, it may be tempting to discount the importance of citizenship behaviors—to just focus on your own job tasks and leave aside any "extra" stuff. After all, citizenship behaviors appear to be voluntary and optional, whereas task duties are not. However, discounting citizenship behaviors is a bad idea because supervisors do not always view such actions as optional. In fact, research on computer sales people, insurance agents, petrochemical salespeople, pharmaceutical sales managers, office furniture makers, sewing machine operators,

U. S. Air Force mechanics, and first-tour U. S. Army soldiers has shown that citizenship behaviors relate strongly to supervisor evaluations of job performance, even when differences in task performance are also considered. As we discuss in our OB internationally feature, the tendency for supervisors to consider citizenship behaviors in evaluating overall job performance appears to hold even across countries with vastly different cultures. Of course, this issue has a lot of relevance to you, given that in most organizations, supervisors' evaluations of job performance play significant roles in determining pay and promotions. Indeed, employee citizen ship behavior has been found to influence the salary and promotion recommendations people receive, over and above their task performance? Put simply, it pays to be a good citizen.

Counterproductive Behavior

Now we move from the "good soldiers" to the "bad apples". Whereas task performance and citizenship behavior refer to employee activities that help the organization achieve its goals and objectives, other activities in which employees engage do just the opposite. The third broad category of job performance is counterproductive behavior, defined as employee behaviors that intentionally hinder organizational goal accomplishment. The word "intentionally" is a key aspect of this definition; these are things that employees mean to do, not things they accidentally do. Although there are many different kinds of counterproductive behaviors, research suggests that—like task performance and citizenship behavior—they can be grouped into more specific categories.

2.4 Understand counterproductive behavior and describe some specific examples

Property deviance refers to behaviors that harm the organization's assets and possessions. For example, sabotage represents the purposeful destruction of physical equipment, organization processes, or company products. Do you know what a laser disc is? Probably not—and the reason you don't is because of sabotage. A company called Disco Vision (a subsidiary of MCA) manufactured laser discs in the late 1970s, with popular movie titles like Smokey and the Bandit and Jaws retailing for \$15.95. Although this level matches the price of DVDs today, it was far less than the \$50 ~ \$100 needed to buy videocassettes (which were of inferior quality) at the time. Unfortunately, laser discs had to be manufactured in "clean rooms" because specks of dust or debris could cause the image on the TV to freeze, repeat, skip, or drop out. When MCA merged with IBM in 1979, the morale of the employees fell, and counterproductive behaviors began to occur. Specifically, employees sabotaged the devices that measured the cleanliness of the rooms and began eating in the rooms—even "popping" their potato chip bags to send food particles into the air. This sabotage eventually created a 90 percent disc failure rate that completely alienated customers. As a result, despite its much lower production costs and higher quality picture, the laser disc disappeared, and the organizations that supported the technology suffered incredible losses.

Theft represents another form of property deviance and can be just as expensive as sabotage (if not more). Research has shown that up to three-quarters of all employees have engaged in counterproductive behaviors such as theft, and the cost of these behaviors is staggering? For example, one study estimated that 47 percent of store inventory shrinkage was due to employee theft and that this type of theft costs organizations approximately \$14.6 billion per year. Maybe you've had friends who worked at a restaurant or bar and been lucky enough to get discounted (or even free) food and drinks whenever you wanted. Clearly that circumstance is productive for you, but it's quite counterproductive from the perspective of the organization.

Production deviance is also directed against the organization but focuses specifically on reducing the efficiency of work output. Wasting resources is the most common form of production deviance, when employees use too many materials or too much time to do too little work. Manufacturing employees who use too much wood or metal are wasting resources, as are restaurant employees who use too many ingredients when preparing the food. Substance abuse represents another form of production deviance. If employees abuse drugs or alcohol while on the job or shortly before coming to work, then the efficiency of their production will be compromised because their work will be done more slowly and less accurately.

In contrast to property and production deviance, political deviance refers to behaviors that intentionally disadvantage other individuals rather than the larger organization. Gossiping—casual conversations about other people in which the facts are not confirmed as true—is one form of political deviance. Everyone has experienced gossip at some point in time and knows the emotions people feel when they discover that other people have been talking about them. Such behaviors undermine the morale of both friendship groups and work groups. Incivility represents communication that is rude, impolite, discourteous, and lacking in good manners.

Taken one by one, these political forms of counterproductive behavior may not seem particularly serious to most organizations. However, in the aggregate, acts of political deviance can create an organizational climate characterized by distrust and unhealthy competitiveness. Beyond the productivity losses that result from a lack of cooperation among employees, organizations with this type of climate likely cannot retain good employees. Moreover, there is some evidence that gossip and incivility can "spiral"—meaning that they gradually get worse and worse until some tipping point after which more serious forms of interpersonal actions can occur.

Those more serious interpersonal actions may involve personal aggression, defined as hostile verbal and physical actions directed toward other employees. Harassment falls under this heading and occurs when employees are subjected to unwanted physical contact or verbal remarks from a colleague. Abuse also falls under this heading; it occurs when an employee is assaulted or endangered in such a way that physical and psychological injuries may occur. You might be surprised to know that even the most extreme forms of personal aggression are quite prevalent in organizations; one employee is killed by a current or former employee on average each week in the United States? Acts of personal aggression also can be quite costly to organizations. For example, Mitsubishi Motor Manufacturing of America settled a class action sexual harassment lawsuit in 1998 for \$34 million after women at a plant in normal, Illinois, complained of widespread and routine groping, fondling, lewd jokes, lewd behavior, and pornographic graffiti.

Three points should be noted about counterproductive behavior. First, there is evidence that people who engage in one form of counterproductive behavior also engage in others. In other words, such behaviors tend to represent a pattern of behavior rather than isolated incidents. In this sense, there really are bad "apples". Second, like citizenship behavior, counterproductive behavior is relevant to any job. It doesn't matter what the job entails; there are going to be things to steal, resources to waste, and people to be uncivil toward. Third, it is often surprising which employees engage in counterproductive behavior. You might be tempted to guess that poor task performers will be the ones who do these sorts of things, but there is only a weak negative correlation between task performance and counterproductive behavior. Sometimes the best task performers are the ones who can best get away with counterproductive actions because they are less likely to be suspected or blamed.

Organizational Commitment

As a manager or an employee, you'll probably agree that it's nice to work with a coworker who engages in high levels of task performance, frequent instances of citizenship behavior, and little or no counterproductive behaviors. Clearly that's the best case scenario, and only one thing could disrupt that rosy picture: losing that coworker to a competitor. Unfortunately, such a scenario is not far-fetched. One recent survey by the Society for Human Resource Management showed that 75 percent of employees were looking for a new job. Of those job seekers, 43 percent were looking for more money, and 35 percent were reacting to a sense of dissatisfaction with their current employer. Organizations should be worried about these sorts of numbers because the cost of turnover can be very high. Estimates suggest that it costs about 0.5 times the annual salary plus benefits to replace an hourly worker, 1.5 times the annual salary plus benefits to replace a salaried employee, and as much as 5 times the annual salary plus benefits to replace an executive? Why so expensive? Those estimates include various costs, including the administrative costs involved in the separation, recruitment expenses, screening costs, and training and orientation expenses for the new hire. They also include "hidden costs" due to decreased morale, lost organizational knowledge, and lost productivity.

Organizational commitment influences whether an employee stays a member of the organization (is retained) or leaves to pursue another job (turns over). Employees who are not committed to their organizations engage in withdrawal behavior, defined as a set of actions that employees perform to avoid the work situation—behaviors that may eventually culminate in quitting the organization. Some employees may exhibit much more commitment than withdrawal, finding themselves on the green end of the continuum. Leaving aside personal or family issues, these employees are not "retention risks" for the moment. Other employees exhibit much more withdrawal than commitment, finding themselves on the red end of the continuum. These employees are retention risks—teetering on the edge of quitting their jobs. The sections that follow review both commitment and withdrawal in more detail.

One key to understanding organizational commitment is to understand where it comes from. In other words, what creates a desire to remain a member of an organization? To explore this question, consider the following scenario: You've been working full-time for your employer for around five years. The company gave you your start in the business, and you've enjoyed your time there. Your salary is competitive enough that you were able to purchase a home in a good school system, which is important because you have one young child and another on the way. Now assume that a competing firm contacted you while you were attending a conference and offered you a similar position in its company. What kinds of things might you think about? If you created a list to organize your thoughts, what kinds of issues would appear on that list?

2.5 Describe the three types of organizational commitment

One potential list is shown in Table 2 – 1. The left-hand column reflects some emotional reasons for staying with the current organization, including feelings about friendships, the atmosphere or culture of the company, and a sense of enjoyment when completing job duties. These sorts of emotional reasons create affective commitment, defined as a desire to remain a member of an organization due to an emotional attachment to, and involvement with, that organization. Put simply, you stay because you want to. The middle column reflects some cost-based reasons for staying, including issues of salary, benefits, and promotions, as well as concerns about uprooting a family. These sorts of reasons create continuance commitment, defined as a desire to remain a member of an organization because of an awareness of the costs associated with leaving it. In other words, you stay because you need to. The right-hand column reflects some obligation-based reasons for staying with the current organization, including a sense that a debt is owed to a boss, a colleague, or the larger company. These sorts of reasons create normative commitment, defined as a desire to remain a member of an organization due to a feeling of obligation. In this case, you stay because you ought to.

The three types of organizational commitment combine to create an overall sense of psychological attachment to the company. Of course, different people may weigh the three types differently. One person may be very rational and cautious by nature, focusing primarily on continuance commitment when evaluating his or her overall desire to stay. Another person may be more emotional and intuitive by nature, going more on "feel" than on a calculated assessment of costs and benefits. The importance of the three commitment types also may vary over the course of a career. For example, you might prioritize affective reasons early in your work life before shifting your attention to continuance reasons as you start a family or become more established in a community. Regardless of how the three types are prioritized, however, they offer an important insight into why someone might be committed and what an organization can do to make employees feel more committed.

Figure 2 – 2 also shows that organizational commitment depends on more than just "the organization". That is, people aren't always committed to companies; they're also committed to the top management that leads the firm at a given time, the department in which they work, the manager who directly supervises them, or the specific team or coworkers with whom they work most closely, We use the term focus of commitment to refer to the various people, places and things that can inspire a desire to remain a member of an organization. For example, you might choose to stay with your current employer because you are emotionally attached to your work team, worry about the costs associated with losing your company's salary and benefits pack age, and feel a sense of obligation to your current manager. If so, your desire to remain cuts across multiple types of commitment (affective, continuance, and normative) and multiple foci (or focuses) of commitment (work team, company, manager). Now that you're familiar with the drivers of commitment in a general sense, let's go into more depth about each type.

Table 2－1 The Three Types of Organizational Commitment

Affective Commitment	Continuance Commitment	Normative Commitment
Emotion-based Reasons	Cost-based Reasons	Obligation-based Reasons
Some of my best friends work in my office... I'd miss them if I left	I'm due for a promotion soon... will I advance as quickly at the new company	My boss has invested so much time in me, mentoring me, training me, showing me "the ropes."
I really like the atmosphere at my current job... it's fun and relaxed	My salary and benefits get us a nice house in our town... the cost of living is higher in this new area	My organization gave me my start... they hired me when others thought I wasn't qualified
My current job duties are very rewarding... I enjoy coming to work each morning	The school system is good here, my spouse has a good job... we've really "put down roots" where we are	My employer has helped me out of a jam on several occasions... how could I leave now
Staying because you want to	Staying because you need to	Staying because you ought to

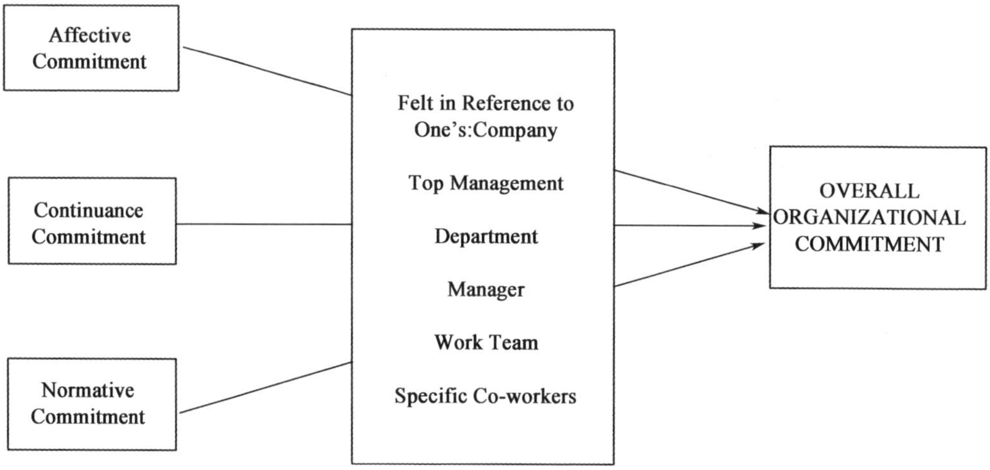

Figure 2－2 Drivers of Overall Organizational Commitment

2.5.1 Affective Commitment

One way to understand the differences among the three types of commitment is to ask yourself what you would feel if you left the organization. Consider the reasons listed in the left-hand column of Table 2 – 1. What would you feel if, even after taking all those reasons into account, you decided to leave your organization to join another one? Answer: You'd feel a sense of sadness. Employees who feel a sense of affective commitment identify with the organization, accept that organization's goals and values, and are more willing to exert extra effort on behalf of the organization.

It's safe to say that if managers could choose which type of commitment they would like to instill in their employees, they would choose affective commitment. Moreover, when a manager looks at an employee and says, "She's committed" or "He's loyal" that manager usually is referring to a behavioral expression of affective commitment. For example, employees who are affectively committed to their employer tend to engage in more interpersonal and organizational citizenship behaviors such as helping, sportsmanship, and boosterism. One meta analysis of 22 studies with more than 6,000 participants revealed a moderately strong correlation between affective commitment and citizenship behavior. (Recall that a meta analysis averages together results from multiple studies investigating the same relationship.) Such results suggest that emotionally committed employees express that commitment by "going the extra mile" whenever they can.

Because affective commitment reflects an emotional bond to the organization, it's only natural that the emotional bonds among coworkers influence it. We can therefore gain a better understanding of affective commitment if we take a closer look at the bonds that tie employees together. Assume you were given a sheet with the names of all the employees in your department or members of your class. Then assume you were asked to rate the frequency with which you communicated with each of those people, as well as the emotional depth of those communications. Those ratings could be used to create a "social network diagram" that summarizes the bonds among employees. Figure 2 – 3 provides a sample of such a diagram. The lines connecting the 10 members of the work unit represent the communication bonds that connect each of them, with thicker lines representing more frequent communication with more emotional depth. The diagram illustrates that some employees are "nodes" with several direct connections to other employees, whereas others remain at the fringes of the network.

The erosion model suggests that employees with fewer bonds will be most likely to quit the organization. If you look at Figure 2 – 3, who's most at risk for turning over? That's right—the employee who only has one bond with someone else (and a relatively weak bond at that). From an affective commitment perspective, that employee is likely to feel less emotional attachment to work colleagues, which makes it easier to decide to leave the organization. Social network diagrams also can help us understand another explanation for turnover. The social influence model suggests that employees who have direct linkages with "leavers" will themselves become more likely to leave. In this way, reductions in affective commitment become contagious, spreading like a disease across the work unit. Think about the damage that would be caused if the central figure in the network (the one who has linkages to five other people) became unhappy with the organization.

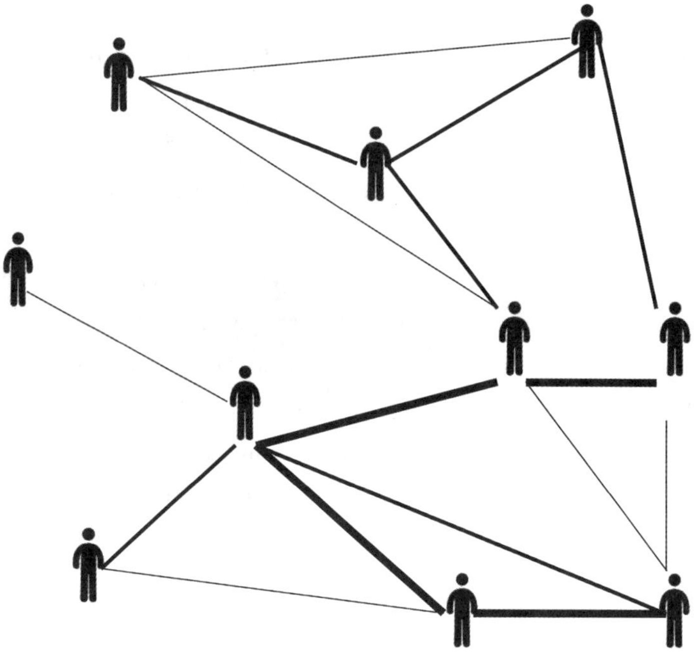

Figure 2 – 3 A Social Network Diagram

Cisco Systems seems to understand the importance of affective commitment. Cisco employees point to the fun workplace culture as a key factor, with company cafes offering movie-themed menus at Academy Awards time or "nerd lunches" during which experts discuss important tech topics. Harley-Davidson also appears to understand the importance of fostering an emotional attachment to the organization. The voluntary turnover rate at the Milwaukee-based motorcycle manufacturer is less than 2 percent, and employee surveys reveal that workers strongly identify with the culture of motorcycle riding. In fact, Harley – Davidson pays some employees to work at biker rallies. These sorts of activities reinforce the emotional bonds between the company and its employees, fostering affective commitment.

2.5.2 Continuance Commitment

Now consider the reasons for staying listed in the middle column of Table 2 – 1. What would you feel if, even after taking all those reasons into account, you decided to leave your organization to join another one? Answer: You'd feel a sense of anxiety. Continuance commitment exists when there is a profit associated with staying and a cost associated with leaving, with high continuance commitment making it very difficult to change organizations because of the steep penalties associated with the switch. One factor that increases continuance commitment is the total amount of investment(in terms of time, effort, energy, etc.) an employee has made in mastering his or her work role or fulfilling his or her organizational duties. Picture a scenario in which you've worked extremely hard for a number of years to finally master the "ins and outs" of working at a particular organization, and now you're beginning to enjoy the fruits of that labor in terms of financial rewards and better work assignments. That effort might be wasted if you moved to another organization(and had to start over on the learning curve).

Another factor that increases continuance commitment is a lack of employment alternatives. If an employee has nowhere else to go, the need to stay will be higher. Employment alternatives themselves depend on several factors, including economic conditions, the unemployment rate, and the marketability of a person's skills and abilities. Of course, no one likes to feel "stuck" in a situation, so it may not be surprising that the behavioral benefits associated with affective commitment do not really occur with continuance commitment. There is no statistical relationship between continuance commitment and citizenship behavior, for example, or any other aspects of job performance. Continuance commitment therefore tends to create more of a passive(as opposed to active) form of loyalty.

Alcon Labs seems to understand the value of continuance commitment. The Texas-based leader in eye care products enjoys a voluntary turnover rate of less than 2 percent. One likely reason for that low rate is the benefits package Alcon offers its employees. For example, Alcon offers a 401(k)-retirement plan in which it matches 240 percent of what employees contribute, up to a total of 5 percent of total compensation. So, for example, if an employee invests $500 toward retirement in each month, Alcon contributes $1,200. That policy more than doubles the most generous rates of other companies, allowing employees to build a comfortable "nest egg" for retirement more quickly. Clearly employees would feel a bit anxious about giving up that benefit if a competitor came calling.

2.5.3 Normative Commitment

Now consider the reasons for staying listed in the right-hand column of Table 2 – 1. What would you feel if, even after taking all those reasons into account, you decided to leave your organization to join another one? Answer: You'd feel a sense of guilt. Normative commitment exists when there is a sense that staying is the "right" or "moral" thing to do. The sense that people should stay with their current employers may result from personal work philosophies or more general codes of right and wrong developed over the course of their lives. They also may be dictated by early experiences within the company, if employees are socialized to believe that long-term loyalty is the norm rather than the exception.

In addition to personal work philosophies or organizational socialization, there seem to be two ways to build a sense of obligation-based commitment among employees. One way is to create a feeling that the employee is in the organization's debt—that he or she owes something to the organization. For example, an organization may spend a great deal of money training and developing an employee. In recognition of that investment, the employee may feel obligated to "repay" the organization with several more years of loyal service. Picture a scenario in which your employer paid your tuition, allowing you to further your education, while also providing you with training and develop mental job assignments that increased your skills. Wouldn't you feel a little guilty if you took the first job opportunity that came your way?

Another possible way to build an obligation-based sense of commitment is by becoming a particularly charitable organization. Did you ever wonder why organizations spend time and money on charitable things—for example, building playgrounds in the local community? Don't those kinds of projects take away from research and development, product improvements, or profits for shareholders? Well, charitable efforts have several potential advantages. First, they can provide good public relations for the organization, potentially generating goodwill for its products and services and helping attract new recruits. Second, they can help existing employees feel better about the organization, creating a deeper sense of normative commitment.

Qualcomm recognizes the value of normative commitment. The California-based firm, specializing in wireless technologies, has a voluntary turnover rate of just over 3 percent. After six Qualcomm employees lost their homes in a forest fire, other Qualcomm employees collected donations and contributed $60,000 to the Red Cross disaster relief fund. Qualcomm matched that contribution and gives 1 ~ 2 percent of its pretax profits to charitable causes each year. Charitable actions are also an important element of Microsoft's culture. Not only does Bill Gates, the founder of the Washington-based software giant, donate a large percentage of his wealth to philanthropic efforts, but his organization matches any charitable contribution made by its employees? These sorts of activities create a sense that employees ought to remain in their current positions.

2.5.4 Withdrawal Behavior

What happens when an employee doesn't feel particularly high levels of affective, continuance, or normative commitment? One likely outcome is that the employee will begin withdrawing from the organization. Such withdrawal might be especially likely when some negative workplace event occurs because organizational commitment can be especially vital in tough times. To paraphrase the old saying, "When the going gets tough, the organization doesn't want you to get going." In tough times, organizations need their employees to demonstrate loyalty, not "get going" right out the door. Of course, it's those same tough times that put an employee's loyalty and allegiance to the test.

Consider the following scenario: You've been working at your company for three years and served on a key product development team for the past several months. Unfortunately, the team has been struggling of late. To enhance the team's performance, the organization has added a new member to the group. This member has a solid history of product development but is, by all accounts, a horrible person with whom to work. You can easily see the employee's talent but find yourself hating every moment spent in the employee's presence. This situation is particularly distressing because the team won't finish its work for another nine months, at the earliest. What would you do in this situation?

2.6 Understand the four primary responses to negative events at work

Research on reactions to negative work events suggests that you might respond in one of four general ways. First, you might attempt to remove yourself from the situation, either by being absent from work more frequently or by voluntarily leaving the organization. This removal is termed exit, defined as an active, destructive response by which an individual either ends or restricts organizational membership. Second, you might attempt to change the circumstances by meeting with the new team member to attempt to work out the situation. This action is termed voice, which was already covered in our discussion of interpersonal citizenship behavior. Voice represents an active, constructive response in which individuals attempt to improve the situation. Third, you might just "grin and bear it"; maintaining your effort level despite your unhappiness. This response is termed loyalty, defined as a passive, constructive response that maintains public support for the situation while the individual privately hopes for improvement. Fourth, you might just go through the motions, allowing your performance to deteriorate slowly as you mentally "check out". This reaction is termed neglect, defined as a passive, destructive response in which interest and effort in the job decline, sometimes neglect can be even more costly than exit because it is not as readily noticed. Employees may neglect their duties for months (or even years) before their bosses catch on to their poor behaviors.

Taken together, the exit voice loyalty neglect frame work captures most of the possible responses to a negative work event, like the addition of a new colleague who makes work more difficult. Where does organizational commitment fit in? Organizational commitment should decrease the likelihood that an individual will respond to a negative work event with exit or neglect (the two destructive responses). At the same time, organizational commitment should increase the likelihood that the negative work event will prompt voice or loyalty (the two constructive responses). Research suggests that factors that promote affective and normative commitment indeed increase the likelihood of voice and loyalty while decreasing the likelihood of exit and neglect.

If we consider employees' task performance levels, together with their organizational commitment levels, we can gain an even clearer picture of how people might respond to negative work events. Consider Table 2 - 2, which depicts combinations of high and low levels of organizational commitment and task performance, Stars possess high commitment and high performance and are held up as role models for other employees. Stars likely respond to negative events with voice because they have the desire to improve the status quo and the credibility needed to inspire change. It's pretty easy to spot the stars in a given unit, and you can probably think about your current or past job experiences and identify the employees who would fit that description. For an example of stars in the world of women's tennis, see our OB in sports feature. Citizens possess high commitment and low task performance but perform many of the voluntary "extra-role" activities that are needed to make the organization function smoothly. Citizens are likely to respond to negative events with loyalty because they may not have the credibility needed to inspire change but possess the desire to remain a member of the organization. You can spot citizens by looking for the people who do the little things—showing around new employees, picking up birthday cakes, ordering new supplies when needed, and so forth.

Table 2 – 2 Four Types of employees

Task Performance			
Organizational Commitment		HIGH	LOW
	HIGH	Stars	Citizens
	LOW	Lone wolves	Apathetics

Source: Griffeth R W, Gaertnerss, Sager J K. Taxonomic Model of Withdrawal Behaviors: The Adaptive Response Model[J]. Human Resource Management Review, 1999, 9: 577 – 90.

Lone wolves possess low levels of organizational commitment but high levels of task performance and are motivated to achieve work goals for themselves, not necessarily for their company. They are likely to respond to negative events with exit. Although their performance would give them the credibility needed to inspire change, their lack of attachment prevents them from using that credibility constructively. Instead, they rely on their performance levels to make them marketable to their next employer. To spot lone wolves, look for the talented employees who never seem to want to get involved in the conflicts or squabbles within a unit. Finally, apathetics possess low levels of both organizational commitment and task performance and merely exert the minimum level of effort needed to keep their jobs. Apathetics should respond to negative events with neglect because they lack the performance needed to be marketable and the commitment needed to engage in acts of citizenship.

It's clear from this discussion that exit and neglect represent withdrawal behavior, which we' ve described as the flipside of organizational commitment. How common is withdrawal behavior within organizations? Quite common, as it turns out. One study clocked employees' on-the-job behaviors over a two-year period and found that only about 51 percent of their time was actually spent working! The other 49 percent was lost to late starts, early departures, long coffee breaks, personal matters, and other forms of withdrawal. As a manager, wouldn't you like to feel like there was more than a coin flip's chance that your employees were working during a given day?

2.7 Describe examples of psychological withdrawal and physical withdrawal, and explain how they relate to one another

Withdrawal comes in two forms: psychological (or neglect) and physical (or exit). Psychological withdrawal consists of actions that provide a mental escape from the work environment. When an employee is engaging in psychological withdrawal, "the lights are on, but nobody's home." Some business articles refer to psychological withdrawal as "warm-chair attrition" meaning that employees have essentially been lost even though their chairs remain occupied. How big of a problem is psychological withdrawal? A recent Gallup poll revealed that more than 70 percent of employees feel "disengaged" from their work (suggesting that the 51 percent work time result discussed previously may be optimistic!).

Psychological withdrawal comes in a number of shapes and sizes. The least serious is daydreaming, when an employee appears to be working but is distracted by random thoughts or concerns. Socializing refers to the verbal chatting about non-work topics that goes on in cubicles and offices or at the mailbox or vending machines. Looking busy indicates an intentional desire on the part of the employee to look like he or she is working, even when not performing work tasks? Sometimes employees decide to reorganize their desks or go for a stroll around the building, even though they have nowhere to go. (Those who are very good at managing impressions do such things very briskly and with a focused look on their faces!) When employees engage in moonlighting, they use work time and resources to complete something other than their job duties, such as assignments for another job.

Perhaps the most widespread form of psychological withdrawal among white collar employees is cyberloafing—using Internet, e-mail, and instant messaging access for their personal enjoyment rather than work duties. One recent survey of more than 3,000 employees from 750 different organizations revealed that employees spend around 40 percent of their workday responding to personal e-mails or surfing the Web. Ninety-seven percent of those surveyed admitted to using the Internet primarily for personal rather than work use. To see for yourself, go for a stroll around any office and count how many screens you see set to ESPN. com, Amazon. com, eBay, the iTunes store, travel sites, stock-watch sites, and (when the boss is clearly not looking) job hunting sites. At the end of 2003, one estimate suggested that cyberloafing had cost the U. S. economy $250 billion in lost productivity, Some employees view cyberloafing as a way of "balancing the scales" when it comes to personal versus work time. For example, one participant in a cyberloafing study noted, "It is alright for me to use the Internet for personal reasons at work. After all, I do work overtime without receiving extra pay from my employer." Although such views are quite reasonable, other employees view cyberloafing as a means of retaliating against negative work events. One participant in the same study noted, "My boss is not the appreciative kind; I take what I can whenever I can. Surfing the net is my way of hitting back."

Physical withdrawal consists of actions that provide a physical escape, whether short term or long term, from the work environment. Physical withdrawal also comes in a number of shapes and sizes. Tardiness reflects the tendency to arrive at work late (or leave work early). Of course, tardiness can sometimes be unavoidable, as when employees have car trouble or must fight through bad weather, but it often represents a calculated desire to spend less time at work. Long breaks involve longer than normal lunches, soda breaks, coffee breaks, and so forth that provide a physical escape from work. Ben Hamper's classic book *Rivet-head: Tales of the Assembly Line* is filled with examples of General Motors manufacturing employees taking excessively long breaks. For example, employees would routinely take turns covering for one another on the assembly line for half a shift so that they could spend several hours sleeping in their cars or at home, running errands, or even drinking beer at local bars. Sometimes such breaks stretch into missing meetings, which means employees neglect important work functions while away from the office. As a manager, you'd like to be sure that employees who leave for lunch are going to come back, but sometimes, that's not a safe bet!

Absenteeism occurs when employees miss an entire day of work. Of course, people stay home from work for a variety of reasons, including illness and family emergencies. There is also a rhythm to absenteeism. For example, employees are more likely to be absent on Mondays or Fridays. Moreover, streaks of good attendance create a sort of pressure to be absent, as personal responsibilities build until a day at home becomes irresistible. That type of absence can sometimes be functional because people return to work with their "batteries recharged". Group and departmental norms also affect absenteeism by signaling whether an employee can get away with missing a day here or there without being noticed. These issues aside, a consistent pattern of absenteeism, month in and month out, is a symptom of the kind of low commitment that concerns most managers. Should absenteeism (in the form of missed classes) concern instructors as well? See our OB for Students feature to find out.

Finally, the most serious form of physical withdrawal is quitting—voluntarily leaving the organization. As with the other forms of withdrawal, employees can choose to "turn over" for a variety of reasons. The most frequent reasons include leaving for more money or a better career opportunity; dissatisfaction with supervision, working conditions, or working schedule; family factors; and health. Note that many of those reasons reflect avoidable turnover, meaning that the organization could have done something to keep the employee, perhaps by offering more money, more frequent promotions, or a better work situation. Family factors and health, in contrast, usually reflect unavoidable turnover that doesn't necessarily signal a lack of commitment on the part of employees.

Regardless of their reasons, some employees choose to quit after engaging in a very thorough, careful, and reasoned analysis. Typically some sort of "shock"? whether it be a critical job change or a negative work experience, jars employees enough that it triggers the thought of quitting in them. Once the idea of quitting has occurred to them, employees begin searching for other places to work, compare those alternatives to their current job, and—if the comparisons seem favorable—

quit. This process may take days, weeks, or even months as employees grapple with the decision. In other cases, though, a shock may result in an impulsive, knee-jerk decision to quit, with little or no thought given to alternative jobs (or how those jobs compare to the current one). Of course, sometimes a shock never occurs. Instead, an employee decides to quit as a result of a slow but steady decrease in happiness until a "straw breaks the camel's back" and voluntary turnover results.

There are 10 different behaviors that employees can perform to psychologically or physically escape from a negative work environment. A key question becomes: "How do all those behaviors relate to one another?" Consider the following testimonials from uncommitted (and admittedly fictional) employees:

- "I can't stand my job, so I do what I can to get by. Sometimes I'm absent, sometimes I socialize, sometimes I come in late. There's no real rhyme or reason to it; I just do whatever seems practical at the time."
- "I can't handle being around my boss. I hate to miss work, so I do what's needed to avoid being absent. I figure if I socialize a bit and spend some time surfing the Web, I don't need to ever be absent. But if I couldn't do those things, I'd definitely have to stay home... a lot."
- "I just don't have any respect for my employer anymore. In the beginning, I'd daydream a bit during work or socialize with my colleagues. As time went on, I began coming in late or taking a long lunch. Lately I've been staying home altogether, and I'm starting to think I should just quit my job and go somewhere else."

Each of these statements sounds like something that an uncommitted employee might say. However, each statement makes a different prediction about the relationship between the withdrawal behaviors. The first statement summarizes the independent forms model of withdrawal, which argues that the various withdrawal behaviors are uncorrelated with one another, occur for different reasons, and fulfill different needs on the part of employees. From this perspective, knowing that an employee cyberloafs tells you nothing about whether that employee is likely to be absent. The second statement summarizes the compensatory forms model of withdrawal, which argues that the various withdrawal behaviors negatively correlate with one another—that doing one means you're less likely to do another. The idea is that any form of withdrawal can compensate for, or neutralize, a sense of dissatisfaction, which makes the other forms unnecessary. From this perspective, knowing that an employee cyberloafs tells you that the same employee probably isn't going to be absent. The third statement summarizes the progression model of withdrawal, which argues that the various withdrawal behaviors are positively correlated: The tendency to daydream or socialize leads to the tendency to come in late or take long breaks, which leads to the tendency to be absent or quit. From this perspective, knowing that an employee cyberloafs tells you that the same employee is probably going to be absent in the near future.

Which of the three models seems most logical to you? Although all three make some sense, the progression model has received the most scientific support. Studies tend to show that the withdrawal behaviors are positively correlated with one another. Moreover, if you view the behaviors as a causal sequence moving from left(daydreaming) to right(quitting), the behaviors that are closest to each other in the sequence tend to be more highly correlated. For example, quitting is more closely related to absenteeism than to tardiness because absenteeism is right next to it in the withdrawal progression. These results illustrate that withdrawal behaviors may begin with very minor actions but eventually can escalate to more serious actions that may harm the organization.

2.8 Takeaways

1. Job performance is the set of employee behaviors that contribute to organizational goal accomplishment. Organizational commitment is the desire on the part of an employee to remain a member of the organization.

2. Task performance includes employee behaviors that are directly involved in the transformation of organizational resources into the goods or services that the organization produces. Organizations gather information about relevant task behaviors using job analysis.

3. Citizenship behaviors are voluntary employee activities that may or may not be rewarded but that contribute to the organization by improving the overall quality of the setting in which work takes place. Examples of citizenship behavior include helping, courtesy, sportsmanship, voice, civic virtue, and boosterism.

4. Counterproductive behaviors are employee behaviors that intentionally hinder organizational goal accomplishment. Examples of counterproductive behavior include sabotage, theft, wasting resources, substance abuse, gossiping, incivility, harassment, and abuse.

5. There are three types of organizational commitment. Affective commitment occurs when an employee wants to stay and is influenced by the emotional bonds between employees. Continuance commitment occurs when an employee needs to stay and is influenced by salary, benefits, and other economic factors. Normative commitment occurs when an employee feels that he or she ought to stay and is influenced by an organization investing in its employees or engaging in charitable efforts.

6. Employees can respond to negative work events in four ways: exit, voice, loyalty, and neglect. Exit is a form of physical withdrawal in which the employee either ends or restricts organizational membership. Voice is an active and constructive response by which employees attempt to improve the situation. Loyalty is passive and constructive; employees remain supportive while hoping the situation improves on its own. Neglect is a form of psychological withdrawal in which interest and effort in the job decrease.

7. Examples of psychological withdrawal include daydreaming, socializing, looking busy, moonlighting, and cyberloafing. Examples of physical withdrawal include tardiness, long breaks, missing meetings, absenteeism, and quitting. Consistent with the progression model, withdrawal behaviors tend to start with minor psychological forms before escalating to more major physical varieties.

2.9 Discussion questions

1. Describe a job in which citizenship behaviors would be especially critical to an organization's functioning and one in which citizenship behaviors would be less critical. What is it about a job that makes citizenship more important?

2. Figure 2 – 4 classifies productive deviance and political deviance as more minor in nature than property deviance and personal aggression. When might those types of counterproductive behavior prove especially costly?

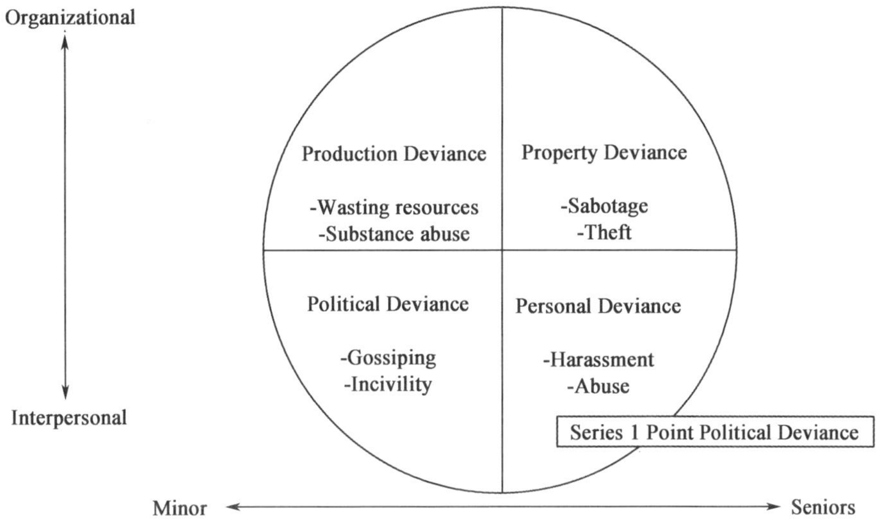

Figure 2 – 4 Types of Counterproductive Behaviors

3. Which type of organizational commitment (affective, continuance, or normative) do you think is most important to the majority of employees? Which do you think is most important to you?

4. Consider times when you've reacted to a negative event with exit, voice, loyalty, or neglect. What was it about the situation that caused you to respond the way you did? Do you usually respond to negative events in the same way, or does your response vary across the four options?

5. Can organizations use a combination of monitoring and punishment procedures to reduce psychological and physical withdrawal? How might such programs work from a practical perspective? Do you think they would be effective?

Section Ⅱ
Individual Characteristics

Chapter 3 Personality, Cultural Values and Ability

Employees can be described, evaluated, and differentiated in a variety of ways, on several dimensions. For example, employees can be described based on their personality. Personality refers to the structures, propensities, and traits inside a person that explain his or her characteristic patterns of thought, emotion, and behavior. Personality creates a person's social reputation—the way he or she is perceived by friends, family, coworkers, and supervisors. Employees also can be described on the basis of their cultural values. Cultural values reflect the shared beliefs about desirable end states or modes of conduct in a given culture. These shared values influence the traits, thoughts, feelings, and behaviors of the individuals who grow up in, or experience, a given culture. Finally, employees can be described based on their ability. Ability refers to the relatively stable capabilities employees possess that allow them to perform a particular range of related activities. In contrast to skills, which can be improved over time with training and experience, ability is relatively stable.

3.1 Define personality, cultural values and ability

Taken together, these sorts of "individual differences" can tell us a lot about people, with personality capturing what people are like, ability capturing what people can do, and cultural values capturing where people are from (in a cultural sense). Indeed, we rely on these individual differences whenever we try to describe one person to another. For example, think about the last time a new coworker joined your work unit. Perhaps you described that coworker as organized, polite, and somewhat shy. Each of those adjectives is an aspect of personality. Or maybe you described him or her as smart and quick, both of which reflect aspects of ability. After spending more time around your new coworker, you might notice that he or she is especially attentive to group norms and feels uncomfortable questioning the opinions of "higher-ups". Both tendencies may be expressions of key cultural values that have shaped the employee's thoughts, feelings, and behaviors. The sections to follow review personality, cultural values, and ability in more detail.

Personality

Even though we sometimes describe people as having "a good personality", personality is actually a collection of multiple specific traits. Traits are defined as recurring regularities or trends in people's responses to their environment. When we described your coworker as organized, polite, and shy, we used three specific personality traits. Of course, it takes more than three traits to describe a person's personality, and we can typically offer a laundry list of adjectives to describe friends, coworkers, and family members. How long could that list potentially be? Well, personality researchers note that the third edition of Webster's Unabridged Dictionary contains 1,710 adjectives that can be used to describe someone's traits! Fortunately, it turns out that most adjectives are variations of five broad "factors" or "dimensions" that can be used to summarize our personalities. Those five personality dimensions include conscientiousness, agreeableness, neuroticism, openness to experience, and extraversion. Collectively, these dimensions have been dubbed the Big Five. Table 3 – 1 lists the traits that can be found within each of the Big Five dimensions. We acknowledge that it can be hard to remember the particular labels for the Big Five dimensions, and we only wish there was some acronyms that could make the process easier.

Table 3 – 1 Trait Adjectives Associated with the Big Five

C	A	N	O	E
Conscientiousness	Agreeableness	Neuroticism	Openness	Extraversion
Dependable Organized Reliable Ambitious Hardworking Persevering	Kind Cooperative Sympathetic Helpful Courteous Warm	Nervous Moody Emotional Insecure Jealous Unstable	Curious Imaginative Creative Complex Refined Sophisticated	Talkative Sociative Passionate Assertive Bold Dominant
NOT	NOT	NOT	NOT	NOT
Careless Sloppy Inefficient Negligent Lazy Irresponsible	Critical Antagonistic Callous Selfish Rude Cold	Calm Steady Relaxed At ease Secure Contented	Uninquisitive Conventional Conforming Simple Unartistic Traditional	Quiet Shy Inhibited Bashful Reserved Submissive

3.2 Understand the Big Five dimensions of personality

3.2.1 Conscientiousness

Conscientious people are dependable, organized, reliable, ambitious, hardworking, and persevering. It's difficult, if not impossible, to envision a job in which those traits will not be beneficial. That's not a claim we make about all of the Big Five because some jobs require high levels of agreeableness, extraversion, or openness, while others demand low levels of those same traits. We don't want to spoil the "how important is personality?" discussion that concludes in this chapter, but suffice it to say that conscientiousness has the biggest influence on job performance of any of the Big Five. Of course, the key question therefore becomes: why is conscientiousness so valuable?

One reason can be found in the general goals that people prioritize in their working life. Conscientious employees prioritize accomplishment striving, which reflects a strong desire to accomplish task-related goals as a means of expressing personality. People who are accomplishment strivers have a built-in desire to finish work tasks, channel a high proportion of their efforts toward those tasks, and work harder and longer on task assignments. As evidence of their accomplishment-striving nature, one research study showed that conscientious salespeople set higher sales goals for themselves than un-conscientious salespeople and were more committed to meeting those goals. Another study of salespeople showed that conscientious salespeople's organizational skills were particularly valuable during their first year of employment, and their ambitious nature became more critical as they gained tenure and experience.

A third research study provides particularly compelling evidence regarding the benefits of conscientiousness. The study used data from the University of California, Berkeley's Intergenerational Studies, which collected data about a set of children in the late 1920s and early 1930s. Those researchers gathered personality data using interviews and assessments of the children by trained psychologists. Follow-up studies collected data on the same sample as they reached early adulthood, middle age, and late adulthood. This last time period included assessments of career success, which included ratings of annual income and occupational prestige. The results of the study showed that childhood conscientiousness was strongly correlated with ratings of career success five decades later! In fact, those conscientiousness effects were roughly twice as strong as the effects of the other Big Five dimensions.

3.2.2 Agreeableness

Agreeable people are warm, kind, cooperative, sympathetic, helpful, and courteous. Agreeable people prioritize communion striving, which reflects a strong desire to obtain acceptance in personal relationships as a means of expressing personality. Put differently, agreeable people focus on "getting along", not necessarily "getting ahead". Unlike conscientiousness, agreeableness is not related to performance across all jobs or occupations. Why not? The biggest reason is that communion striving is beneficial in some positions but detrimental in others. For example, managers often need to prioritize the effectiveness of the unit over a desire to gain acceptance. In such cases, effective job performance may demand being disagreeable in the face of unreasonable requests or demands.

Of course, there are some jobs in which agreeableness can be beneficial. The most obvious example is service jobs—jobs in which the employee has direct, face-to-face, or verbal contact with a customer. How many times have you encountered a customer service person who is cold, rude, or antagonistic? Did you tend to buy the company's product after such experiences? Research suggests that agreeable employees have stronger customer service skills. One reason for their effectiveness in customer service environments is that they are reluctant to react to conflict with criticism, threats, or manipulation. Instead, they tend to react to conflict by walking away, adopting a "wait-and-see" attitude, or giving in to the other person.

3.2.3 Extraversion

Extraverted people are talkative, sociable, passionate, assertive, bold, and dominant (in contrast to introverts, who are quiet, shy, and reserved). Like agreeableness, extraversion is not necessarily related to performance across all jobs or occupations. However, extraverted people prioritize status striving, which reflects a strong desire to obtain power and influence within a social structure as a means of expressing personality. Extraverts care a lot about being successful and influential and direct their work efforts toward "moving up" and developing a strong reputation. Indeed, research suggests that extraverts are more likely to emerge as leaders in social and task-related groups, They also tend to be rated as more effective in a leadership role by the people who are following them. One potential reason for these findings is that people tend to view extraverts, who are more energetic and outgoing, as more "leaderlike" than introverts.

In addition to being related to leadership emergence and effectiveness, research suggests that extraverts tend to be happier with their jobs. Later in Chapter 6 Job Satisfaction we will categorize people's day-to-day moods along two dimensions: pleasantness and engagement. Extraverted employees tend to be high in what's called positive affectivity—a dispositional tendency to experience pleasant, engaging moods such as enthusiasm, excitement, and elation. That tendency to experience positive moods across situations explains why extraverts tend to be more satisfied with their jobs. Research now acknowledges that employees' genes have a significant impact on their job satisfaction and that much of that genetic influence is due to extraversion (and neuroticism, as discussed next). For example, one study of identical twins reared apart showed that twins' job satisfaction levels were significantly correlated, even when the twins held jobs that were quite different in terms of their duties, their complexity, and their working conditions. In fact, this study suggested that around 30 percent of the variation in job satisfaction is due to genetic factors such as personality.

Other research suggests that extraverts have more to be happy about than just their jobs. One study asked students to complete a "life event checklist" by indicating whether various events had happened to them in the preceding four years. The results showed that extraversion was associated with more positive events such as joining a club or athletic team, going on vacation with friends, getting a raise at work, receiving an award for nonacademic reasons, and getting married or engaged. Other studies have linked extraversion to the number of same sex peers, number of dating partners, frequency of alcohol consumption, and frequency of attending parties. However, extraverts spend so much time doing those things that they wind up having less frequent interactions with their family. Even parents of extraverts enjoy a phone call home now and again!

3.2.4 Neuroticism

Neurotic people are nervous, moody, emotional, insecure, and jealous. Occasionally you may see this Big Five dimension called by its flip side: "emotional stability" or "emotional adjustment". If conscientiousness is the most important of the Big Five from the perspective of job performance, neuroticism is the second most important. There are few jobs for which the traits associated with neuroticism are beneficial to on-the-job behaviors. Instead, most jobs benefit from employees who are calm, steady, and secure.

Whereas extraversion is synonymous with positive affectivity, neuroticism is synonymous with negative affectivity—a dispositional tendency to experience unpleasant moods such as hostility, nervousness, and annoyance. That tendency to experience negative moods explains why neurotic employees often experience lower levels of job satisfaction than their less neurotic counterparts. Along with extraversion, neuroticism explains much of the impact of genetic factors on job satisfaction. Research suggests that the negative affectivity associated with neuroticism even influences more general life satisfaction, such that neurotic people tend to be less happy with their lives in general.

Neuroticism is also strongly related to locus of control, which reflects whether people attribute the causes of events to themselves or to the external environment. Neurotic people tend to hold an external locus of control, meaning that they often believe that the events that occur around them are driven by luck, chance, or fate. Less neurotic people tend to hold an internal locus of control, meaning that they believe that their own behavior dictates events. Table 3 – 2 provides more detail about the external versus internal distinction. The table includes a number of beliefs that are representative of an external or internal viewpoint, including beliefs about life in general, work, school, politics, and relationships. If you tend to agree more strongly with the beliefs in the left column, then you have a more external locus of control. If you tend to agree more with the right column, your locus is more internal.

Table 3 – 2 External and Internal Locus of Control

People with an External Locus of Control tend to believe:	People with Internal Locus of Control tend to believe:
Many of the unhappy things in people's lives are partly due to bad luck	People's misfortunes result from the mistakes they take
Getting a good job depends mainly on being in the right place at the right time	Becoming successful is a matter of hard work; luck has little or nothing to do with it
Many times, exam questions tend to be so unrelated to course work that study is really useless	In the case of the well-prepared student, there is rarely if ever such a thing as an unfair test

Table 3 – 2(continued)

This world is run by the few people in power, and there is not much the little guy can do about it	The average citizen can have an influence in government decisions
There's not much use in trying too hard to please people; if they like you, they like you	People are lonely because they don't try to be friendly

How important is locus of control? One meta-analysis of 135 different research studies showed that an internal locus of control was associated with higher levels of job satisfaction and job performance. A second meta-analysis of 222 different research studies showed that people with an internal locus of control enjoyed better health, including higher self-reported mental well-being, fewer self-reported physical symptoms, lower blood pressure, and lower stress hormone secretion. Internals also enjoyed more social support at work than externals and sensed that they had a stronger relationship with their supervisors. They viewed their jobs as having more beneficial characteristics such as autonomy and significance and fewer negative characteristics such as conflict and ambiguity. In addition, those with an internal locus of control earned a higher salary than those with an external locus.

3.2.5 Openness to Experience

The final dimension of the Big Five is openness to experience. Open people are curious, imaginative, creative, complex, refined, and sophisticated. Of all the Big Five, openness to experience has the most alternative labels. Sometimes it's called "inquisitiveness" or "intellectualness" or even "culture" (not in the national culture sense—rather, in the "high culture" sense of knowing fine wine, art, and classical music). Much like agreeableness and extraversion, the traits associated with openness are beneficial in some jobs but not others. As a result, openness is not related to job performance across all occupations.

What jobs benefit from high levels of openness? Generally speaking, jobs that are very fluid and dynamic, with rapid changes in job demands. Research shows that open employees excel in learning and training environments because their curiosity gives them a built-in desire to learn new things. They also tend to be more adaptable and quicker to identify when the "old way of doing things" is no longer effective, excelling at the search for a new and better approach. In fact, conscientious employees are sometimes less effective than open employees in such environments because their persevering nature sometimes prevents them from abandoning "tried-and-true" task strategies.

Openness to experience is also more likely to be valuable in jobs that require high levels of creativity, defined as the capacity to generate novel and useful ideas and solutions. The relationship between openness and creativity can be seen in Figure 3 – 1. Together with cognitive ability (discussed later in this chapter), openness to experience is a key driver of creative thought, as smart and open people excel at the style of thinking demanded by creativity. Creative thought then results in creative behavior when people come up with new ideas, create fresh approaches to problems, or suggest new innovations that can help improve the workplace. The creativity benefits of openness likely explain why highly open individuals are more likely to migrate into artistic and scientific fields, in which novel and original products are so critical.

Figure 3 - 1 Openness to Experience and Creativity

3.2.6 Cultural Values

Now that we've described a number of personality traits, we turn our attention to the cultural values that can affect the expression of those traits. To some extent, cultural values provide countries with their own distinct personalities. For example, we can say that Australian people, on average, value the traits associated with extraversion more than Chinese people. We also can say that Swiss people, on average, value the traits associated with openness more than Irish people. Such statements are based on research that reveals consistent between nation differences on various personality traits. Of course, that doesn't mean that all Australian, Chinese, Swiss, and Irish citizens have exactly the same personality—merely that certain cultures tend to have higher levels of certain traits.

3.3 Understand Hofstede's dimensions of cultural values

3.3.1 Hofstede's dimensions

Although it's possible to describe nations on values relevant to the Big Five, as we just did, there are other values that are more commonly used to categorize nations. Many of those values are derived from a landmark study in the late 1960s and early 1970s by Geert Hofstede, who analyzed data about 88,000 IBM employees from 72 countries in 20 languages. His research showed that employees working in different countries tended to prioritize different values, and those values clustered into several distinct dimensions. Those dimensions are summarized in Table 3 - 3 and include individualism-collectivism, power distance, uncertainty avoidance, masculinity - femininity, and short-term vs. long-term orientation. The table also includes cultures that tend to be high on a given dimension.

Table 3 – 3　Hofstede's Dimensions of Cultural Values

Individualism	Collectivism
The culture is a loosely knit social framework in which people take care of themselves and their immediate family	The culture is a tight social framework in which people take care of the members of a broader ingroup and act loyal to it
United States, the Netherlands, France	Indonesia, China, West Africa
Power Distance	
LOW	HIGH
The culture prefers that power be distributed uniformly where possible, in a more egalitarian fashion	The culture accepts the fact that power is usually distributed unequally within organizations
United States, Germany, the Netherlands	Russia, China, Indonesia
Uncertainty Avoidance	
LOW	HIGH
The culture tolerates uncertain and ambiguous situations and values unusual ideas and behaviors	The culture feels threatened by uncertain and ambiguous situations and relies on formal rules to create stability
United States, Indonesia, the Netherlands	Japan, Russia, France
Masculinity – Femininity	
MASCULINITY	FEMININITY
The culture values stereotypically male traits such as assertiveness and the acquisition of money and things.	The culture values stereotypically female traits such as caring for others and caring about quality of life
United States, Japan, Germany	The Netherlands, Russia, France
Short-term vs. Long-term Orientation	
SHORT TERM	LONG TERM
The culture stresses values that are more past- and present-oriented such as respect for tradition and fulfilling obligations	The culture stresses values that are more future-oriented such as persistence, prudence, and thrift
United States, Russia, West Africa	China, Japan, the Netherlands

The table reveals that citizens of the United States tend to be high on individualism, low on power distance, low on uncertainty avoidance, high on masculinity, and high on short-term orientation; while China is mostly the opposite: high on collectivism, high on power distance, and high on long-term orientation. Why is this description important to know? Because, for instance, it illustrates the adjustments that American employees and American businesses may need to make when doing business in other cultures. Differences in cultural values can create differences in reactions to change, conflict management styles, negotiation approaches, and reward preferences. Failing to understand those differences can compromise the effectiveness of multinational groups and organizations. Such problems are particularly likely if employees are high in ethnocentrism, defined as a propensity to view one's own cultural values as "right" and those of other cultures as "wrong".

Of Hofstede's five dimensions, individualism – collectivism has received the most research attention, by a wide margin. Much of this research has focused on the individualism – collectivism of individual people rather than nations, sometimes referred to as "psychological individualism" or "psychological collectivism". This focus on individuals rather than nations is understandable, given that some experts estimate that only 60 percent of the citizens in a collective culture actually hold collective cultural values themselves. Studies of psychological collectivism have revealed that collective employees identify deeply with relevant ingroups such as family members, close friends, or work teams. They prefer to interact with those ingroups, care for the members of those ingroups, and accept and prioritize ingroup norms and goals.

3.3.2 Ability

Besides personality and cultural values, employees can be characterized according to what they're innately good at. Some employees excel at physical tasks, possessing exceptionally high levels of strength, stamina, and coordination. Other employees are especially good at cognitive tasks, with an aptitude for reading, mathematics, or logic and reasoning sorts of activities. Still other employees have emotional talents, being able to read the emotions of others while controlling the expression of their own emotions. Of course, training and practice can increase an employee's performance at these sorts of tasks. Still, employees who are genetically gifted in a given ability will always have a "higher ceiling" when it comes to performing particular tasks at an exceptionally high level. The sections to follow discuss cognitive ability and emotional ability in more detail. (We'll leave out a full discussion of physical abilities, given that cognitive and emotional aptitudes are more critical in most of the jobs that you'll hold.)

Cognitive abilities are capabilities related to the acquisition and application of knowledge in problem solving. Cognitive abilities are very relevant in jobs involving the use of information to make decisions and solve problems. Chances are good that your cognitive abilities have been tested several times throughout your life. For example, almost all children in the United States take standardized tests of intelligence at some point during elementary school. Although you might not remember taking one of these, you probably do remember taking the Scholastic Assessment Test (SAT). And though you probably only thought about the SAT as a test that would have a major impact on where you could and could not go to college, the SAT is actually a test of cognitive ability.

You might also remember that the SAT included a variety of different questions; some tested your ability to do math problems, whereas other questions assessed your ability to complete sentences and make analogies. The different types of questions reflect the several specific types of cognitive ability that contribute to effectiveness on intellectual tasks. Table 3 – 4 lists many of these cognitive ability types, along with their specific facets and some jobs in which they are thought to be important.

Table 3 – 4 Types and Facets of Cognitive Ability

Type	More Specific Facet	Jobs Where Relevant
Verbal	Oral and Written Comprehension: Understanding written and spoken words and sentences Oral and Written Expression: Communicating ideas by speaking or writing so that others can understand	Business executives, police, fire, and ambulance dispatchers; clinical psychologist
Quantitative	Number Facility: Performing basic math operations quickly and correctly Mathematical Reasoning: Selecting the right method or formula to solve a problem	Treasurers, financial managers, mathematical technicians, statisticians
Reasoning	Problem Sensitivity: Understanding when there is a problem or when something may go wrong Deductive Reasoning: Applying general rules to specific problems Inductive Reasoning: Combining specific information to for general conclusions Originality: Developing new ideas	Anesthesiologists, surgeons, business executives, fire inspectors, judges, police detectives, forensic scientists, cartoonists, designers
Spatial	Spatial Orientation: Knowing where one is relative to objects in the environment Visualization: Imaging how something will look after it has been rearranged	Pilots, drivers, boat captains, photographers, set designers, sketch artists
Perceptual	Speed and Flexibility of Closure: Making sense of information and finding patters Perceptual Speed: Comparing information or objects with remembered information or objects	Musicians, fire fighter, police officers, pilots, mail clerks, inspectors

3.4 Describe the dimensions of cognitive ability

Verbal ability refers to various capabilities associated with understanding and expressing oral and written communication. Oral comprehension is the ability to understand spoken words and sentences, and written comprehension is the ability to understand written words and sentences. Although these two aspects of verbal ability would seem highly related—that is, people who have high oral comprehension would tend to have high written comprehensive, and vice versa—it's not difficult to think of people who might be high on one ability but low on the other. As an example, it has been reported that as a result of his dyslexia, Tom Cruise has poor written comprehension and can only learn his lines after listening to them on tape.

Two other verbal abilities are oral expression, which refers to the ability to communicate ideas by speaking, and written expression, which refers to the ability to communicate ideas in writing. Again, though it might seem that these abilities should be highly related, they are not necessarily. You may have taken a class with a professor who has published several well-regarded books and articles but had a very difficult time expressing concepts and theories to students effectively. Although there could be many reasons, one possible explanation is that the professor had high ability in terms of written expression but low ability in terms of oral expression.

Verbal abilities are most important in jobs in which effectiveness depends on understanding and communicating ideas and information to others. The effectiveness of business executives depends on their ability to consider information from reports and other executives and staff, as well as their ability to articulate a vision and strategy that promotes employee understanding. As another example, consider how important the verbal abilities of a 9-1-1 dispatcher might be if a loved one suddenly became ill and stopped breathing one evening.

Quantitative ability refers to two types of mathematical capabilities. The first is number facility, which is the capability to do simple math operations (adding, subtracting, multiplying, and dividing). The second is mathematical reasoning, which refers to the ability to choose and apply formulas to solve problems that involve numbers. If you think back to the SAT, you can probably remember problems such as the following: "There were two trains 800 miles apart, and they were traveling toward each other on the same track. The first train began traveling at noon and averaged 45 miles per hour. The second train started off two hours later. At what speed did the second train average if the two trains smashed into each other at 10:00 p. m. of the same day?"

Although number facility may be necessary to solve this problem, mathematical reasoning is crucial because the test taker needs to know which formulas to apply. Although most of us wish that problems like this would be limited to test-taking contexts (especially this particular problem), there are countless situations in which quantitative abilities are important. For example, consider the importance of quantitative ability in jobs involving statistics, accounting, and engineering. Quantitative abilities may be important in less complex, lower-level jobs as well. Have you ever been at a fast-food restaurant or convenience store when the cash register wasn't working and the clerk couldn't manage to count out change correctly or quickly? If you have, you witnessed a very good example of low quantitative ability, and perhaps some very annoyed customers.

Reasoning ability is a diverse set of abilities associated with sensing and solving problems using insight, rules, and logic. The first reasoning ability, problem sensitivity, is the ability to sense that there's a problem right now or likely to be one in the near future. Anesthesiology is a great example of a job for which problem sensitivity is crucial. Before surgeries, anesthesiologists give drugs to patients so that surgical procedures can take place without the patients experiencing pain. However, during the surgery, patients can have negative reactions to the drugs that might result in the loss of life. So the ability of the anesthesiologist to sense when something is wrong even before the problem is fully apparent can be a life or death matter.

The second type of reasoning ability is called deductive reasoning. This ability, which refers to the use of general rules to solve problems, is important in any job in which people are presented with a set of facts that need to be applied to make effective decisions. The job of a judge requires deductive reasoning because it centers on making decisions by applying the rules of law to make verdicts. In contrast, inductive reasoning refers to the ability to consider several specific pieces of information and then reach a more general conclusion regarding how those pieces are related. Every episode of the CBS show CSI is filled with inductive reasoning. Crime scene investigators, like Gil Grissom, are experts at considering things like the blood-splatter patterns, bruises, abrasions, DNA, fibers, and fingerprints to reach conclusions about causes of death and possible perpetrators.

Finally, originality refers to the ability to develop clever and novel ways to solve problems. Larry Page and Sergey Brin, the two founders of Google, provide good examples of originality. They not only developed the search software that gave Google a competitive advantage, but they also created the first completely new advertising medium in nearly half a century. They also refuse to follow conventional wisdom when it comes to managerial practices and business decisions. Clearly, originality is important in a wide variety of occupations, but in some jobs, originality is the most critical ability. For example, a cartoonist, designer, writer, or advertising executive without originality would find it difficult to be successful.

There are two main types of spatial abilities. The first is called spatial orientation, which refers to having a good understanding of where one is relative to other things in the environment. A tourist with high spatial organization would have no trouble finding her way back to her hotel on foot after a long day of sightseeing, even without a map or help from anyone on the street. The second spatial ability is called visualization, which is the ability to imagine how separate things will look if they were put together in a particular way. If you're good at imagining how a room would look if it were rearranged, or if your friends are impressed that you can buy things that go together well, chances are that you would score high on visualization.

Perceptual abilities generally refer to being able to perceive, understand, and recall patterns of information. More specifically, speed and flexibility of closure refers to being able to pick out a pattern of information quickly in the presence of distracting information, even without all the information present. This ability is easy to understand if you've ever seen the CBS show Numbers. In the show, Charlie Eppes helps the FBI solve crimes by using his genius to discover patterns in data and information. In the series premiere, for example, Charlie used the metaphor of a sprinkler to describe his unique ability, noting, "Say I couldn't see the sprinkler; from the pattern of the drops, I could calculate its precise location." Related to this ability is perceptual speed, which refers to being able to examine and compare numbers, letters, and objects quickly. If you can go into the produce section of a supermarket and choose the best tomatoes faster than the people around you, chances are you have high perceptual speed. Effectiveness in jobs in which people need to proofread documents, sort things, or categorize objects depends a lot on perceptual speed.

If you've read the preceding sections thoughtfully, you probably considered where you stand on the different types of cognitive abilities. In doing so, you also may have reached the conclusion that you are higher on some of these abilities and lower on others. Maybe you think of yourself as being smart in verbal abilities but not as smart in quantitative abilities. In fact, most people score more similarly across their cognitive abilities than they realize. People who are high on verbal abilities also tend to be high on reasoning, quantitative, spatial, and perceptual abilities, and people who are low on verbal abilities tend to be low on the other abilities. Although this consistency might not apply to everyone, it applies often enough that researchers have been trying to understand why this occurs for well over 100 years.

The most popular explanation for the similarity in the levels of different cognitive abilities within people is that there is a general cognitive ability—sometimes called "g" or the "g factor"—that underlies or causes all of the more specific cognitive abilities we have discussed so far. This overlap of all depicted abilities generates g factor, which exists because each of the specific abilities depends somewhat on the brain's ability to process information effectively. So, because some brains are capable of processing information more effectively than others, some people tend to score higher across the specific abilities, whereas others tend to score lower.

Most of us know someone who is very smart from a cognitive ability standpoint, but at the same time, the person just can't manage to be effective in real-world situations that involve other people. Sometimes such individuals are held back by their personality, as it may be that extreme introversion or neuroticism is hindering them in certain social situations. However, research has begun to examine whether there is a type of ability that influences the degree to which people tend to be effective in social situations. Although there has been some debate among these researchers, many believe that there is indeed an ability that affects social functioning, called emotional intelligence. Emotional intelligence is defined in terms of four different but related abilities.

3.5 Describe the dimensions of emotional ability

The first type of emotional intelligence is self-awareness, or the appraisal and expression of emotions within oneself. This facet refers to a person'ability to understand the types of emotions he or she is experiencing, the willingness to acknowledge them, and the capability to express them naturally. As an example, someone who is low in this aspect of emotional intelligence might not admit to himself or show to anyone else that he is feeling somewhat anxious during the first few days of a new job. These types of emotions are perfectly natural in this job context, and ignoring them might increase the stress of the situation. Ignoring those emotions also might send the wrong signal to new colleagues, who might wonder, "why isn't the new hire more excited about his new job?"

The second facet of emotional intelligence is called other-awareness, or the appraisal and recognition of emotion in others. As the name of this facet implies, it refers to a person's ability to recognize and understand the emotions that other people are feeling. People who are high in this aspect of emotional intelligence not only are sensitive to the feelings of others but also can anticipate the emotions that people will experience in different situations. In contrast, people who are low in this aspect of emotional intelligence do not effectively sense the emotions that others are experiencing, and if the emotions are negative, this inability could result in the person doing something that worsens the situation. As a specific example, have you ever had a professor who could not sense that students in class did not understand the material being presented in a lecture? When that professor continued to press on with the overheads, oblivious to the fact that the students were becoming even more confused, it was poor other-awareness in action.

The third facet of emotional intelligence, emotion regulation, refers to being able to recover quickly from emotional experiences. As an example of this aspect of emotional intelligence, consider the possible responses of someone who is listening to NPR while driving to work and is cut off by an aggressive driver who, as she passes by, throws a beer can and shouts an obscenity. If this person is able to regulate his emotions effectively, he would be able to recover quickly from the initial anger and shock of the encounter. He would be able to get back to whatever he was listening to on the radio, and by the time he got to work, the incident would likely be all but forgotten. However, if this person was not able to regulate his emotions effectively, he might lose his temper, tailgate the aggressive driver, and then ram into her rusted-out 1968 Ford pickup at the next stoplight. We hope it is obvious to you that the former response is much more appropriate than the latter, which could prove quite costly to the individual. Although this example highlights the importance of regulating negative emotions, we should also point out that this aspect of emotional intelligence applies to positive emotions. Consider the response of someone who is told that she is about to receive a significant pay raise. If this person is unable to regulate her own emotions effectively, she might feel joyous and giddy the rest of the day and, consequently, not be able to accomplish any more work.

The fourth aspect of emotional intelligence is the use of emotions. This capability reflects the degree to which people can harness emotions and employ them to improve their chances of being successful in whatever they are seeking to do. To understand this facet of emotional intelligence, consider a writer who is struggling to finish a book but is under a serious time crunch because of the contract with the publisher. If the writer was high in this aspect of emotional intelligence, she would likely psych herself up for the challenge and encourage herself to work hard through any bouts of writer's block. In contrast, if the writer is low in this aspect of emotional intelligence, she might begin to doubt her competence as a writer and think about different things she could do with her life. Because these behaviors will slow progress on the book even further, the number and intensity of self-defeating thoughts might increase, and ultimately, the writer might withdraw from the task entirely.

Although you may appreciate how emotional intelligence can be relevant to effectiveness in a variety of interpersonal situations, you might be wondering whether knowledge of emotional intelligence can be useful to managers in their quest to make their organizations more effective. It turns out there is growing evidence that the answer to this question is "yes". In fact, the U. S. Air Force studied recruiters and found that those recruiters who were high in some aspects of emotional intelligence were three times more likely to meet recruiting quotas than recruiters who scored lower in the same aspects of emotional intelligence. Recruiters with high emotional intelligence were more effective because they projected positive emotions and could quickly sense and appropriately respond to recruits'concerns. Because these capabilities made recruiting easier, there was less pressure to meet performance quotas, which translated into fewer hours at the office, higher satisfaction, and ultimately higher retention. In fact, after the Air Force began requiring new recruiters to pass an emotional intelligence test, turnover among new recruiters dropped from 25 percent to 2 percent. Given that, on average, it costs about $30, 000 to train a new recruiter, this lower turnover translated into about $2.75 million in savings a year. To give you an example of how the testing of emotional intelligence operates, the following lists sample questions from a popular emotional intelligence test (Mayer-Salvoyer-Caruso Emotional Intelligence Test):

Question 1: What mood might be helpful to feel when meeting in-laws for the very first time (slight tension, surprise or joy)?

Question 2: Tom felt anxious, and he became a bit stressed when he thought about all the work he needed to do. When his supervisor brought him an additional project, how did he feel (overwhelmed, depressed, ashamed, self-conscious, jittery)?

Question 3: Debbie just came back from vacation. She was feeling peaceful and content. How well would each action preserve her mood?

Action 1: She started to make a list of things at home that she needed to do.

Action 2: She began thinking about where and when she would go on her next vacation.

Action 3: She decided it was best to ignore the feeling since it wouldn't last anyway.

Now that we've described all the personality traits, cultural values, and ability facets that can be used to describe and differentiate employees, the key question becomes: "Which of them are most strongly related to performance and commitment?" Well, it should come as no surprise, based on our earlier discussion, that two individual characteristics stand apart from the rest when it comes to relationships with performance and commitment: general cognitive ability and conscientiousness. In fact, a good rule of thumb to emphasize in virtually any hiring situation is to look at "g" and "c" (where "g" stands for general cognitive ability and "c" stands for conscientiousness).

3.6 Understand how ability and personality affect job performance and organizational commitment

Cognitive ability is a strong predictor of job performance—in particular, the task performance aspect. Across all jobs, smarter employees fulfill the requirements of their job descriptions more effectively than less smart employees. In fact, of all the variables discussed in this book, none has a stronger correlation with task performance than general cognitive ability. Thousands of organizations, and many that are quite well known, assess cognitive ability in an effort to select the best candidates available for specific jobs. The use of cognitive ability tests for this purpose appears to be reasonable, given that scores on such tests have a strong positive correlation with measures of performance across different types of jobs.

So, what explains why general cognitive ability relates to task performance? People who have higher general cognitive ability tend to be better at learning and decision making. They are able to gain more knowledge from their experiences at a faster rate, and, as a result, they develop a bigger pool of knowledge regarding how to do their jobs effectively. There are, however, three important caveats that we should mention. First, cognitive ability tends to be more strongly correlated with task performance than citizenship behavior or counterproductive behavior. An increased amount of job knowledge helps an employee complete job tasks, but it does not necessarily affect the choice to help a coworker or refrain from breaking an important rule. Second, the positive correlation between cognitive ability and performance is even stronger in jobs that are complex or situations that demand adaptability. Third, people may do poorly on a test of general cognitive ability for reasons other than a lack of cognitive ability. As an example, people who come from economically disadvantaged backgrounds may do poorly on such tests, not because they lack the underlying cognitive ability but because they may not have had the learning opportunities needed to provide the appropriate responses.

In contrast to relationships with job performance, research has not supported a significant linkage between cognitive ability and organizational commitment. On the one hand, we might expect a positive relationship with commitment because people with higher cognitive ability tend to perform more effectively, and therefore, they might feel they fit well with their job. On the other hand, we might expect to see a negative relationship with commitment because people with higher cognitive ability possess more job knowledge, which increases their value on the job market and in turn the likelihood that they would leave for another job. In the end, knowing how smart an employee is telling us very little about the likelihood that he or she will remain a member of the organization.

Conscientiousness has a moderate correlation with task performance, partly because conscientious employees have higher levels of motivation than other employees. They are more self-confident, perceive a clearer linkage between their effort and their performance, and are more likely to set goals and commit to them. For these reasons, conscientiousness is a key driver of what's referred to as typical performance, reflecting performance in the routine conditions that surround daily job tasks. General cognitive ability, in contrast, is the stronger driver of maximum performance, reflecting performance in brief, special circumstances that demand a person's best effort.

Conscientious employees are also more likely to engage in citizenship behaviors. Why? One reason is that conscientious employees are so punctual and have such good work attendance that they are simply more available to offer "extra mile" sorts of contributions. Another reason is that they engage in so much more work-related effort that they have more energy to devote to citizenship behaviors. Finally, conscientious employees are less likely to engage in counterproductive behaviors, for two major reasons. First, they tend to have higher levels of job satisfaction, making it less likely that they'll feel a need to retaliate against their organization. Second, even if they do perceive some slight injustice, their dependable and reliable nature should prevent them from violating organizational norms by engaging in negative actions.

Conscientious employees tend to be more committed to their organization. They are less likely to engage in day-to-day psychological and physical withdrawal behaviors because such actions go against their work habits. They are also significantly less likely to voluntarily leave the organization. Why? One reason is that the persevering nature of conscientious employees prompts them to persist in each course of action for long periods of time. That persistence can be seen in their daily work effort, but it extends to a sense of commitment to the organization as well. Another reason is that conscientious employees are better at managing stress, perceiving lower levels of key stressors, and being less affected by them at work.

3.7 Takeaways

1. Personality refers to the traits and propensities inside a person that explain his or her characteristic patterns of thought, emotion, and behavior. It also refers to a person's social reputation—the way he or she is perceived by others. Cultural values are shared beliefs about desirable end states or modes of conduct in each culture that influence the expression of traits. Ability refers to the relatively stable capabilities of people to perform a particular range of related activities.

2. The Big Five include conscientiousness (e. g., dependable, organized, reliable), agreeableness (e. g., warm, kind, cooperative), neuroticism (e. g., nervous, moody, emotional), openness to experience (e. g., curious, imaginative, creative), and extraversion (e. g., talkative, sociable, passionate).

3. Hofstede's dimensions of cultural values include individualism – collectivism, power distance, uncertainty avoidance, masculinity-femininity, and short-term vs. long-term orientation.

4. Cognitive abilities include verbal ability, quantitative ability, reasoning ability, spatial ability, and perceptual ability. General mental ability, or g, underlies all of these more specific cognitive abilities.

5. Emotional intelligence includes four specific kinds of emotional skills: self-awareness, other awareness, emotion regulation, and use of emotions.

6. General cognitive ability has a strong positive relationship with job performance, due primarily to its effects on task performance. In contrast, general cognitive ability is not related to organizational commitment. Conscientiousness has a moderate positive relationship with job performance and a moderate positive relationship with organizational commitment. It has stronger effects on these outcomes than the rest of the Big Five.

3.8 Discussion questions

1. Consider the duties that you perform in your current job, or the last job that you held. Rank in order the Big Five dimensions from most important to least important in terms of their ability to help you succeed in that environment. Why did you rank them that way?

2. Consider the profile of the United States on Hofstede's cultural values, as shown in Table 3 – 3. Do you personally feel like you fit the profile, or do your values differ in some respects? If you served as an expatriate, meaning you were working in another country, which cultural value differences would be most difficult for you to deal with?

3. Think of a job that requires very high levels of certain cognitive abilities. Can you think of a way to redesign that job so that people who lack those abilities could still perform the job effectively?

4. Think of experiences you've had with people who demonstrated unusually high or low levels of emotional intelligence. Then consider how you would rate them in terms of their cognitive abilities. Do you think that emotional intelligence "bleeds over" to affect people's perceptions of cognitive ability?

Section Ⅲ
Individual Mechanisms

Chapter 4 Motivation

4.1 Define motivation

Few OB topics matter more to employees and managers than motivation. How many times have you wondered to yourself, "Why can't I get myself going today?" Or how many times have you looked at a friend or coworker and wondered, "Why are they working so slowly right now?" Both questions are asking about "motivation" which derived from the Latin word for movement, movere. Those Latin roots nicely capture the meaning of motivation, as motivated employees simply move faster and longer than unmotivated employees. More formally, motivation is defined as a set of energetic forces that originates both within and outside an employee, initiates work-related effort, and determines its direction, intensity, and persistence. Motivation is after all a critical consideration—in addition to the other variables in our integrative model, job performance is strongly related to motivation and ability (discussion of ability for more on such issues in Chapter 3).

The first part of the motivation definition illustrates that motivation is not one thing but rather a set of distinct forces. Some of those forces are internal to the employee, such as a sense of self-confidence, whereas others are external to the employee, such as the goals an employee is given. The next part of that definition illustrates that motivation determines several facets of an employee's work effort. These facets are summarized in Figure 4 – 1, which depicts a scenario in which your boss has given you an assignment to work on. Motivation determines what employees do at a given moment—the direction in which their effort is channeled. Every moment of the workday offers choices between task and citizenship sorts of actions, or withdrawal and counterproductive sorts of actions. For example, when it's 1 p. m., 5 minutes after lunch, do you keep working on the assignment your boss gave you, or do you browse news on your cell phone? It is after direction of efforts being decided, when motivation goes on determine how hard. Once the direction of effort has been decided, motivation goes on to determine how hard an employee works—the intensity of effort—and for how long—the persistence of effort. We all have friends or coworkers who work extremely hard, but for only 5 minutes. We also have friends or coworkers who work extremely long hours but always seem to be functioning at half-speed. Neither of those groups of people would be described as extremely motivated.

There are a number of theories and concepts that attempt to explain why some employees are more motivated than others. The sections that follow review those theories and concepts in some detail. Most of them are relevant to each of the three motivation components described in Figure 4 – 1. However, some of them are uniquely suited to explaining the direction of effort, whereas others do a better job of explaining the intensity and persistence of effort.

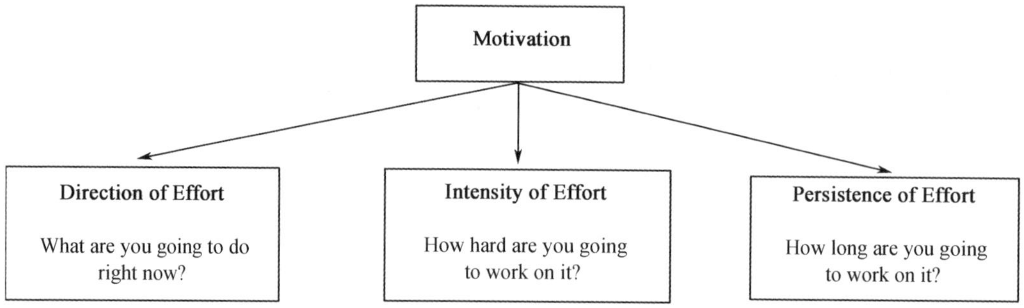

Figure 4 – 1 Motivation and Effort

Expectancy Theory

What makes you decide to direct your effort to work assignments rather than taking a break or wasting time? Or what makes you decide to be a "good citizen" by helping a colleague or attending some optional company function? Expectancy theory describes the cognitive process that employees go through to make choices among different voluntary responses. Drawing on earlier models from psychology, expectancy theory argues that employee behavior is directed toward pleasure and away from pain or, more generally, toward certain outcomes and away from others? How do employees make the choices that take the min the "right direction"? The theory suggests that our choices depend on three specific beliefs that are based in our past learning and experience: expectancy, instrumentality, and valence. These three beliefs are summarized in Figure 4 – 2, and we review each of them in turn.

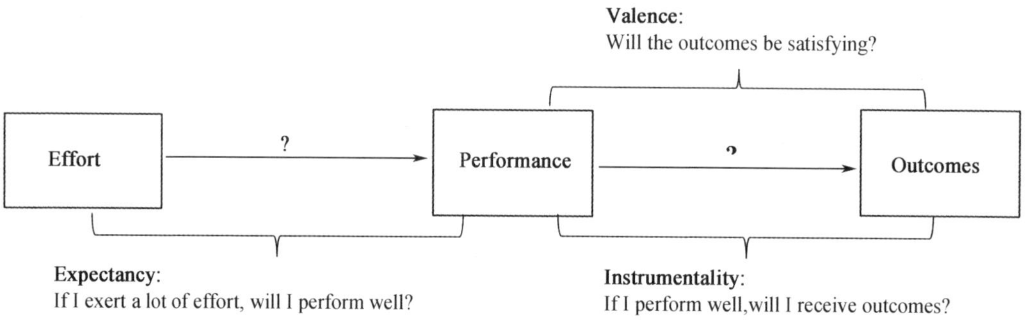

Figure 4 – 2 Expectancy Theory

4.2 Describe expectancy theory and the three beliefs that help determine how work effort is directed

Expectancy represents the belief that exerting a high level of effort will result in the successful performance of some task. More technically, expectancy is a subjective probability, ranging from 0 (no chance!) to 1 (a mortal lock!) that a specific amount of effort will result in a specific level of performance (abbreviated E→P). Think of a task at which you're not particularly good, such as writing romantic poetry. You may not be very motivated to write romantic poetry because you don't believe that your effort, no matter how hard you try, will result in a poem that "moves" your significant other. As another example, you'll be more motivated to work on the assignment described in Figure 4 - 1 if you're confident that trying hard will allow you to complete it successfully.

What factors shape our expectancy for a particular task? One of the most critical factors is self-efficacy, defined as the belief that a person has the capabilities needed to execute the behaviors required for task success. Think of self-efficacy as a kind of self-confidence or a task-specific version of self-esteem. Employees who feel more "efficacious" (that is, self-confident) for a particular task will tend to perceive higher levels of expectancy—and therefore be more likely to choose to exert high levels of effort. Why do some employees have higher self-efficacy for a given task than other employees? Figure 4 - 3 can help explain such differences.

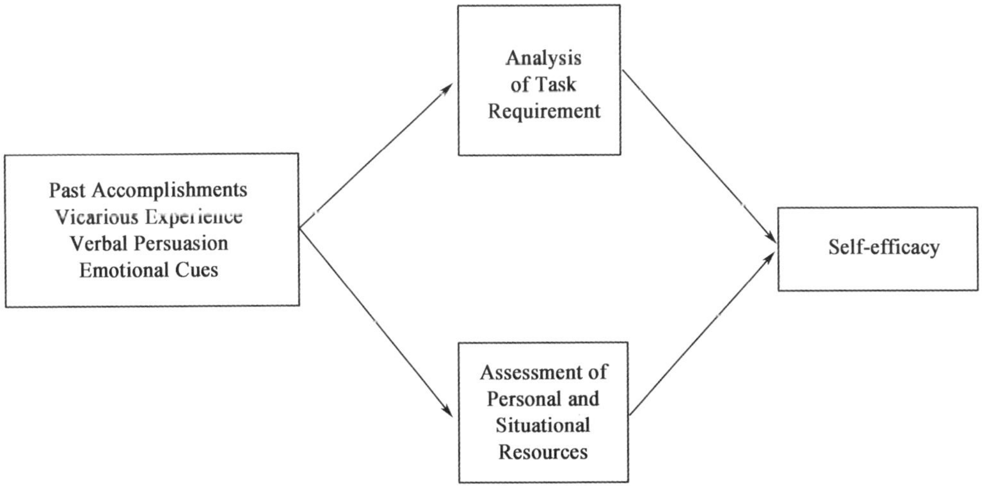

Figure 4 - 3 Sources of Self-efficacy

When employees consider efficacy levels for a given task, they first consider their past accomplishments—the degree to which they have succeeded or failed on similar sorts of tasks in the past. They also consider vicarious experiences by considering their observations and discussions with others who have performed such tasks. Self-efficacy is also dictated by verbal persuasion because friends, coworkers, and leaders can persuade employees that they can "get the job done". Finally, efficacy is dictated by emotional cues, in that feelings of fear or anxiety can create doubts about task accomplishment, whereas pride and enthusiasm can bolster confidence levels. Taken together, these efficacy sources shape analyses of how difficult the task requirements are and how adequate an employee's personal and situational resources will prove to be. They also explain the content of most "halftime speeches" offered by coaches during sporting events. Such speeches commonly include references to past comebacks or victories (past accomplishments), pep talks about how good the team is (verbal persuasion), and cheers to rally the troops (emotional cues).

Instrumentality represents the belief that successful performance will result in some outcome (s). More technically, instrumentality is a set of subjective probabilities, each ranging from 0 (no chance!) to 1 (a mortal lock!) that successful performance will bring a set of outcomes (abbreviated P→O). The term "instrumentality" makes sense when you consider the meaning of the adjective "instrumental". We say something is "instrumental" when it helps attain something else—for example, reading this chapter is instrumental for getting a good grade in an OB class (at least, we hope so!). Unfortunately, evidence indicates that many employees don't perceive high levels of instrumentality in their workplace. One survey of more than 10,000 employees in 2005 revealed that 60 percent viewed seniority as the key determinant of their pay. Those that viewed successful performance as the key driver: only 35 percent.

Valence reflects the anticipated value of the outcomes associated with performance (abbreviated V). Valences can be positive ("I would prefer having outcome X to not having it"), negative ("I would prefer not having outcome X to having it"), or zero ("I'm bored... are we still talking about outcome X?"). Salary increases, bonuses, and more informal rewards are typical examples of "positively valenced" outcomes, whereas disciplinary actions, demotions, and terminations are typical examples of "negatively valenced" outcomes. In this way, employees are more motivated when successful performance helps them attain attractive outcomes such as bonuses, while helping them avoid unattractive outcomes such as termination.

What exactly makes some outcomes more "positively valenced" than others? In general, outcomes are deemed more attractive when they help satisfy needs. Needs can be defined as cognitive groupings or clusters of outcomes that are viewed as having critical psychological or physiological consequences. Although scholars once suggested that certain needs are "universal" across people, it is likely that different people have different "need hierarchies" that they use to evaluate potential outcomes. For instance, the need of self actualization (able to perform tasks appealing to one's purpose) is ranked well above or after fulfilling the need for existence (sufficiency of food, shelter, safety, and protection), according to Maslow's motivational hierarchy.

Table 4-1 lists some of the most commonly considered outcomes in studies of motivation. Outcomes that are deemed particularly attractive are likely to satisfy a few different needs. For example, praise can signal that interpersonal bonds are strong (satisfying relatedness needs) while also signaling competence (satisfying esteem needs). Note also that some of the outcomes in Table

4 - 1 result from other people acknowledging successful performance, whereas others are self-generated, originating in task performance itself. The former set creates extrinsic motivation—motivation that is controlled by some contingency that depends on task performance. The latter set creates intrinsic motivation—motivation that is felt when task performance serves as its owner ward. Extrinsic and intrinsic motivation together represent an employee's "total motivation" level.

Table 4 - 1 Extrinsic and Intrinsic Outcomes

Extrinsic Outcomes	Intrinsic Outcomes
Pay	Enjoyment
Bonuses	Interestingness
Promotions	Accomplishment
Benefits and perks	Knowledge gain
Spot awards	Skill development
Praise	Personal expression
Job security	(Lack of) Boredom
Support	(Lack of) Anxiety
(Lack of) Disciplinary actions	(Lack of) Frustration

You might wonder which of the outcomes in the table are most attractive to employees. That's a difficult question to answer, given that different employees emphasize different needs, but two things are clear. First, the attractiveness of outcomes varies across cultures. For example, good performance on a project in an American company might earn a "spot award" such as an expensive watch or a trip to Las Vegas. However, a moped would likely be deemed more attractive in congested areas like India or China, and trips to alcohol- and gambling-intensive areas are taboo in parts of Asia and the Middle East. Second, research suggests that employees underestimate how powerful a motivator pay is to them. When employees rank the importance of outcomes like those in Table 4 - 1, they often put pay in fifth or sixth place. However, research studies show that financial incentives almost always have a stronger impact on motivation than other sorts of outcomes.

Why can pay and bonuses be so motivational? One reason is that money, like many of the outcomes in Table 4 - 1, is relevant to multiple needs. For example, money can help satisfy existence needs by helping employees buy food, afford a house, and save for retirement. However, money also conveys a sense of esteem by sending the signal that employees are competent and well regarded. In fact, research suggests that people differ in how they view the meaning of money—the degree to which they view money as having symbolic, not just economic, value. The symbolic value of money can be summarized in at least three dimensions: achievement (i. e., money symbolizes success), respect (i. e., money brings respect in one's community), and freedom (i. e., money provides opportunity).

Who is more likely to view money from these more symbolic perspectives? Some research suggests that men are more likely to view money as representing achievement, respect, and freedom than are women. Research also suggests that employees with higher salaries are more likely to view money in achievement-related terms. Younger employees are less likely to view money in a positive light, relative to older employee. Differences in education do not appear to impact the meaning of money, however.

(1) Motivational Force

According to expectancy theory, the direction of effort is dictated by three beliefs: expectancy (E→ P), instrumentality (P → O), and valence (V). More specifically, the theory suggests that the total "motivational force" to perform a given action can be described using the following formula:

$$\text{Motivational Force} = E \rightarrow P \times \sum[(P \rightarrow O) \times V]$$

The $\sum$ symbol in the equation signifies that instrumentalities and valences are judged with various outcomes in mind, and motivation increases as successful performance is linked to more and more attractive outcomes. Note the significance of the multiplication signs in the formula: Motivational force equals zero if any one of the three beliefs is zero. In other words, it doesn't matter how confident you are if performance doesn't result in any outcomes. Similarly, it doesn't matter how well performance is evaluated and rewarded if you don't believe you can perform well.

(2) Goal-Setting Theory

So, returning to the choice shown in Figure 4 – 1, let's say that you feel confident you can perform well on the assignment your boss gave you and that you also believe successful performance will bring valued outcomes. Now that you've chosen to direct your effort to that assignment, two critical questions remain: How hard will you work, and for how long? To shed some more light on these questions, you stop by your boss's office and ask her, "So, when exactly do you need this done?" After thinking about it for a while, she concludes, "Just do your best". After returning to your desk, you realize that you're still not sure how much to focus on the assignment, or how long you should work on it before turning to something else.

4.3 Understand the two qualities that make goals strong predictors of task performance, according to goal-setting theory

Goal-setting theory views goals as the primary drivers of the intensity and persistence of effort. Goals are defined as the objective or aim of an action and typically refer to attaining a specific standard of proficiency, often within a specified time limit. More specifically, the theory argues that assigning employees specific and difficult goals will result in higher levels of performance than assigning no goals, easy goals, or "do-your-best" goals. Why are specific and difficult goals more effective than do-your-best ones? After all, doesn't "your best" imply the highest possible levels of effort? The reason is that few people know what their "best" is (and even fewer managers can tell whether employees are truly doing their "best"). Assigning specific and difficult goals gives people a number to shoot for—a "measuring stick" that can be used to tell them how hard they need to work and for how long. So, if your boss had said, "Have the assignment on my desk by 10:30 a. m. on Tuesday, with no more than two mistakes", you would have known exactly how hard to work and for how long.

Of course, a key question then becomes, "What's a difficult goal?" When goals are easy, there's no reason to work your hardest or your longest, so task effort is lower. As goals move from moderate to difficult, the intensity and persistence of effort become maximized. At some point, however, the limits of a person's ability get reached, and self-efficacy begins to diminish. At that point, goals move from difficult to impossible, and employees feel somewhat helpless when attempting to achieve them. At that point, effort and performance inevitably decline. So, a difficult goal is one that stretches an employee to perform at his or her maximum level while still staying within the boundaries of his or her ability.

Why exactly do specific and difficult goals have positive effects? Figure 4-5 presents goal-setting theory in more detail to understand that question better. First, the assignment of a specific and difficult goal shapes people's own self-set goals—the internalized goals that people use to monitor their own task progress. In the absence of an assigned goal, employees may not even consider what their own goals are, or they may self-set relatively easy goals that they're certain to meet. As a self-set goal becomes more difficult, the intensity of effort increases, and the persistence of effort gets extended. However, goals have another effect; they trigger the creation of task strategies, defined as learning plans and problem-solving approaches used to achieve successful performance. In the absence of a goal, it's easy to rely on trial and error to figure out how best to do a task. Under the pressure of a measuring stick, however, it becomes more effective to plan out the next move.

Figure 4-5 also includes three variables that specify when assigned goals will have stronger or weaker effects on task performance. In the jargon of theory diagrams, these variables are called "moderators". Rather than directly affecting other variables in the diagram, moderators affect the strength of the relationships between variables. One moderator is feedback, which consists of updates on employee progress toward goal attainment. Imagine being challenged to beat a friend's score on the Halo 3 video game but then not being told what exactly your score was as you were playing. How would you know how hard to try? Another moderator is task complexity, which reflects how complicated the information and actions involved in a task are, as well as how much the task changes. In general, the effects of specific and difficult goals are almost twice as strong on simple tasks as on complex tasks, though the effects of goals remain beneficial even in complex cases. Goal setting at Wyeth, the New Jersey-based pharmaceuticals company, illustrates the value of goals for complex tasks (after all, what's more complicated than chemistry?). When Robert Ruffolo was appointed the new chief of R&D six years ago, he was concerned about the low number of new drug compounds being generated by Wyeth's labs. To improve task performance, he gave scientists a goal of discovering 12 new drug compounds every year, up from the 4 compounds they were previously averaging, with bonuses contingent on reaching the goals. Wyeth's scientists have reached the goal every year since, and the goal was upped to 15 compounds in 2006.

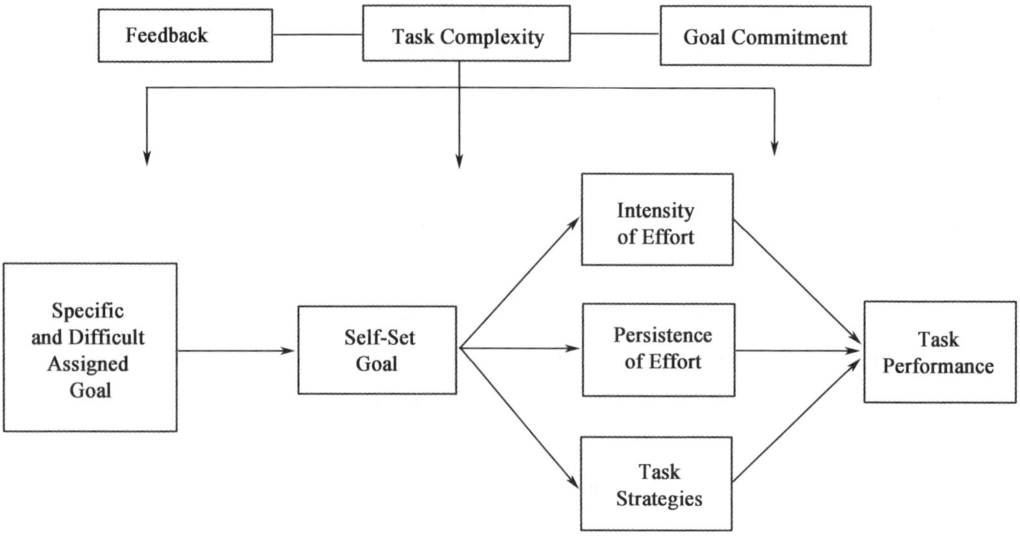

Figure 4 – 5 Goal-Setting Theory

The final moderator shown in Figure 4 – 5 is goal commitment, defined as the degree to which a person accepts a goal and is determined to try to reach it. When goal commitment is high, assigning specific and difficult goals will have significant benefits for task performance. However, when goal commitment is low, those effects become much weaker. The importance of goal commitment raises the question of how best to foster commitment when assigning goals to employees. Research suggests that commitment can be fostered in several ways, including tying rewards to goal achievement, making goals public, providing supportive supervision, and allowing employees to participate in the goal-setting process.

Equity Theory

Returning to our running example in Figure 4 – 1, imagine that at this point, you've decided the direction of work is toward the assignment your boss gave you, and you've been told that it is due by Tuesday at 10:30 a. m. and cannot have any more than two mistakes in it. That's a specific and difficult goal, so Internet Explorer hasn't been launched in a while, and you haven't even thought about checking your e-mail. In short, you've been working very hard for a few hours, until the guy from across the hall pops his head in. You tell him what you're working on, and he nods sympathetically, saying, "Yeah, the boss gave me a similar assignment that sounds just as tough. I think she realized how tough it was though, because she said I could use the company's playoff tickets if I finish it on time." Playoff tickets? Looks like it's time to check that e-mail after all.

Unlike the first two theories, equity theory acknowledges that motivation doesn't just depend on your own beliefs and circumstances but also on what happens to other people? More specifically, equity theory suggests that employees create a "mental ledger" of the outcomes (or rewards) they get from their job duties? What outcomes might be part of your mental ledger? That's completely up to you and depends on what you find valuable, though pay, benefits, status symbols, perks, and satisfying supervision are typically critical. Equity theory further suggests that employees create a mental ledger of the inputs (or contributions and investments) they put into their job duties. Again, the composition of your mental ledger is completely specific to you, but many employees focus on effort, performance, skills, education, experience, and seniority.

4.4 Describe what it means to be equitably treated according to equity theory and how employees respond when they feel a sense of inequity

So, what exactly do you do with these mental tallies of outcomes and inputs? Equity theory argues that you compare your ratio of outcomes and inputs to the ratio of some comparison other—some person who seems to provide an intuitive frame of reference for judging equity. There are three general possibilities that can result from this "cognitive calculus". The first possibility is that the ratio of outcomes to inputs is balanced between you and your comparison other. In this case, you feel a sense of equity, and you're likely to maintain the intensity and persistence of your effort. This situation would have occurred if you have been offered playoff tickets, just like your colleague.

The second possibility is that your ratio of outcomes to inputs is less than your comparison other's ratio. According to equity theory, any imbalance in ratios triggers equity distress—an internal tension that can only be alleviated by restoring balance to the ratios. In an under reward case, the equity distress likely takes the form of negative emotions such as anger or envy. One way to stop feeling those emotions is to try to restore the balance in some way. We name two ways to restore such balance. You could be constructive and proactive by talking to your boss and explaining why you deserve better outcomes. Such actions would result in the growth of your outcomes, restoring balance to the ratio. Of course, anger often results in actions that are destructive rather than constructive, and research shows that feelings of under reward inequity are among the strongest predictors of counterproductive behaviors such as employee theft (see Chapter 8 on Trust, Justice, and Ethics for more on this issue). More relevant to this chapter, another means of restoring balance is to shrink your inputs by lowering the intensity and persistence of effort. Remember, it's not the total outcomes or inputs that matter in equity theory—it's only the ratio.

The third possibility is that your ratio of outcomes to inputs is greater than your comparison other's ratio. Equity distress again gets experienced, and the tension likely creates negative emotions such as guilt or anxiety. Balance could be restored by shrinking your outcomes (taking less money, giving some thing back to the comparison other), but the theory acknowledges that such actions are unlikely in most cases. Instead, the more likely solution is to increase your inputs in some way. You could increase the intensity and persistence of your task effort or decide to engage in more "extra mile" citizenship behaviors. At some point though, there may not be enough hours in the day to increase your inputs any further. An alternative (and less labor-intensive) means of increasing your inputs is to simply rethink them—to reexamine your mental ledger to see if you may have "undersold" your true contributions. On second thought, maybe your education or seniority is more critical than you realized, or maybe your skills and abilities are more vital to the organization. This cognitive distortion allows you to restore balance mentally, without altering your behavior in any way.

These mechanisms make it clear that judging equity is a very subjective process. Recent data from a Salary. com report highlight that very subjectivity. A survey of 1, 500 employees revealed that 65 percent of the respondents planned to look for a new job in the next three months, with 57 percent doing so because they felt underpaid. However, Salary. com estimated that only 19 percent of those workers really were underpaid, considering their relevant inputs and the current market conditions. In fact, it was estimated that 17 percent were being overpaid by their companies! On the one hand, that subjectivity is likely to be frustrating to most managers in charge of compensation. On the other hand, it's important to realize that the intensity and persistence of employees' effort is driven by their own equity perceptions, not anyone else's. Some organizations grapple with concerns about equity by emphasizing pay secrecy. One survey indicated that 36 percent of companies explicitly discourage employees from discussing pay with their colleagues, and surveys also indicate that most employees approve of pay secrecy.

Now we return, for one last time, to our running example in Figure 4 – 1. When last we checked in, your motivation levels had suffered because you learned your coworker was offered the company's playoff tickets for successfully completing a similar assignment. As you browse the Web in total "time-wasting mode", you begin thinking about all the reasons you hate working on this assignment. Even aside from the issue of goals and rewards, you keep coming back to this issue: you would never have taken on this project by choice. More specifically, the project itself doesn't seem very meaningful, and you doubt that it will have any real impact on the functioning of the organization.

4.5 Describe psychological empowerment and the four beliefs that determine how empowered employees feel

Those sentiments signal a low level of psychological empowerment, which reflects an energy rooted in the belief that work tasks contribute to some larger purpose. Psychological empowerment represents a form of intrinsic motivation, in that merely performing the work tasks serves as its own reward and supplies many of the intrinsic outcomes shown in Table 4 – 1. The concept of psychological empowerment has much in common with our discussion of "satisfaction with the work itself " in Chapter 6. That discussion illustrated that jobs with high levels of variety, significance, and autonomy can be intrinsically satisfying. Models of psychological empowerment argue that a similar set of concepts can make work tasks intrinsically motivating. Four concepts are particularly important: meaningfulness, self-determination, competence, and impact.

Meaningfulness captures the value of a work goal or purpose relative to a person's own ideals and passions. When a task is relevant to a meaningful purpose, it becomes easier to concentrate on the task and get excited about it. You might even find yourself cutting other tasks short so you can devote more time to the meaningful one or thinking about the task outside of work hours. In contrast, working on tasks that are not meaningful brings with a sense of emptiness and detachment. As a result, you might need to mentally force yourself to keep working on the task. Managers can instill a sense of meaningfulness by articulating an exciting vision and fostering a non-cynical climate where employees are free to express passion without criticism. For their part, employees can build their own sense of meaningfulness by identifying and clarifying their own passions. What exactly makes them excited and fulfilled at work, and how can they seek out more opportunities to feel that way?

Self-determination reflects a sense of choice in the initiation and continuation of work tasks. Employees with high levels of self-determination can choose what tasks to work on, how to structure those tasks, and how long to pursue those tasks. That sense of self-determination is a strong driver of intrinsic motivation because it allows employees to pursue activities that they themselves find meaningful and interesting. Managers can instill a sense of self-determination in their employees by delegating work tasks, rather than micro-managing them, and by trusting employees to come up with their own approach to certain tasks. For their part, employees can gain more self-determination by earning the trust of their bosses and negotiating for the latitude that comes with that increased trust.

Competence captures a person's belief in his or her capability to perform work tasks successfully. Competence is identical to the self-efficacy concept reviewed previously in this chapter. Employees with a strong sense of competence (or self-efficacy) believe they can execute the particular behaviors needed to achieve success at work. Competence brings with it a sense of pride and mastery that is itself intrinsically motivating. Managers can instill a sense of competence in their employees by providing opportunities for training and knowledge gain, expressing positive feedback, and providing challenges that are an appropriate match for employees' skill levels. Employees can build their own competence by engaging in self-directed learning, seeking out feedback from their managers, and managing their own workloads.

Impact reflects the sense that a person's actions "make a difference"—that progress is being made toward fulfilling some important purpose. Phrases such as "moving forward", "being on track" and "getting there" convey a sense of impact. The polar opposite of impact is "learned helplessness"—the sense that it doesn't matter what a person does, nothing will make a difference. Here, phrases such as "stuck in a rut" "at a standstill" or "going nowhere" become more relevant. Managers can instill a sense of impact by celebrating milestones along the journey to task accomplishment, particularly for tasks that span a long time-frame. Employees can attain a deeper sense of impact by building the collaborative relationships needed to speed task progress and initiating their own celebrations of "small wins" along the way.

Designing Compensation Systems

Many of the concepts contained in expectancy theory, goal-setting theory, equity theory, and psychological empowerment can be used to describe effective (and ineffective) compensation systems. After all, compensation is one of the organization's most powerful tools for motivating its employees. Table 4 – 2 provides an overview of many of the elements used in typical compensation systems. We use the term "element" in the table to acknowledge that most organizations use a combination of multiple approaches to compensate their employees. Two points must be noted about Table 4 – 2. First, the descriptions of the elements are over simplistic; the reality is that each of the elements can be implemented and executed in a variety of ways. Second, the elements are designed to do more than just motivate. For example, plans that put pay "at risk" rather than creating increases in base salary are geared toward control of labor costs. As another example, plans that reward unit or organizational performance are designed to reinforce collaboration, information sharing, and monitoring among employees, regardless of their impact on motivation levels.

One way of judging the motivational impact of compensation plan elements is to consider whether the elements provide difficult and specific goals for channeling work effort. Merit pay and profit-sharing offer little in the way of difficult and specific goals because both essentially challenge employees to make next year as good (or better) than this year. In contrast, lump-sum bonuses and gainsharing provide a forum for assigning difficult and specific goals; the former does so at the individual level and the latter at the unit level. Partly for this reason, both types of plans have been credited with improvements in employee productivity.

Table 4 – 2　Compensation Plan Elements

Element	Description
Individual-focused	
Pierce rate	A specific is paid for each unit produced, each unit sold, or each service provided
Merit rate	An increase to base salary is made in accordance with performance evaluation ratings
Lump-sum bonuses	A bonus is received for meeting individual goals, but not change is made to base salary. The potential bonus represents "at risk" pay that must be re-earned each year. Base salary may be lower in cases in which potential bonuses may be large

Table 4 –2(continued)

Element	Description
Recognition awards	Tangible awards (such as gift cards, merchandise, trips, plaques), or intangible awards (praises) are given on an impromptu basis to recognize achievement
Unit-focused	
Gainsharing	A bonus is received for meeting unit goals(department goals, plant goals, business unit goals) for criteria controllable by employees(labor costs, use of materials, quality). No change is made to base salary. The potential bonus represents "at risk" pay that must be re-earned each year. Base salary may be lower in cases in which potential bonuses may be large
Organization-focused	
Profit-sharing	A bonus is received when the publicly reported earnings of a company exceed some minimum level, with the magnitude of the bonus contingent on the magnitude of the profits. No change is made to base salary. The potential bonus represents "at risk" pay that must be re-earned each year. Base salary may be lower in cases in which potential bonuses may be large

Another way of judging the motivational impact of the compensation plan elements is to consider the correspondence between individual performance levels and individual monetary outcomes. After all, that correspondence influences perceptions of both instrumentality and equity. Profit sharing, for example, is unlikely to have strong motivational consequences because an individual employee can do little to improve the profitability of the company, regardless of his or her job performance. Instrumentality and equity are more achievable with gain sharing because the relevant unit is smaller, and the relevant outcomes are more controllable. Still, the highest instrumentality and equity levels will typically be achieved through individual-focused compensation elements. Piece-rate plans can create stronger performance-outcome contingencies but are difficult to apply outside of manufacturing, sales, and service contexts. Merit pay represents the most common element of organizational compensation plans, yet the pay increase for top performers(5. 6 percent on average) is only modestly greater than the pay increase for poor performers (2. 5 percent on average). Why such a small difference? One reason is that many managers give lenient ratings to avoid upsetting employees. To combat such trends, Yahoo, the California-based Internet company, has instituted a "stacked ranking" system to determine compensation, in which managers rank all the employees within their unit from top to bottom. Employees at the top end of those rankings then receive higher bonuses than employees at the bottom end. Although such practices raise concerns about employee morale and excessive competitiveness, research suggests that such forced distribution systems can boost the performance of a company's workforce, especially for the first few years after their implementation.

Does motivation have a significant impact on the two primary outcomes in our integrative model of OB—does it correlate with job performance and organizational commitment? Answering that question is somewhat complicated because motivation is not just one thing but rather a set of energetic forces.

4.6 Understand how motivation affects job performance and organizational commitment

Turning first to job performance, literally thousands of studies support the relationships between the various motivating forces and task performance. The motivating force with the strongest performance effect is self-efficacy/competence because people who feel a sense of internal self-confidence tend to outperform those who doubt their capabilities. Difficult goals are the second most powerful motivating force; people who receive such goals outperform the recipients of easy goals. The motivational force created by high levels of valence, instrumentality, and expectancy is the next most powerful motivational variable for task performance. Finally, perceptions of equity have a somewhat weaker effect on task performance.

Less attention has been devoted to the linkages between motivation variables and citizenship and counterproductive behavior. With respect to the former, employees who engage in more work-related effort would seem more likely to perform "extra-mile" sorts of actions because those actions themselves require extra effort. The best evidence in support of that claim comes from research on equity. Specifically, employees who feel a sense of equity on the job are more likely to engage in citizenship behaviors, particularly when those behaviors aid the organization. The same employees are less likely to engage in counterproductive behaviors because such behaviors often serve as a retaliation against perceived inequities.

As with citizenship behaviors, the relationship between motivation and organizational commitment seems straightforward. After all, the psychological and physical forms of withdrawal that characterize less-committed employees are themselves evidence of low levels of motivation. Clearly employees who are daydreaming, coming in late, and taking longer breaks are struggling to put forth consistently high levels of work effort. Research on equity and organizational commitment offers the dearest insights into the motivation-commitment relationship. Specifically, employees who feel a sense of equity are moreemotionally attached to their firms and feel a stronger sense of obligation to remain.

4.7 Takeaways

1. Motivation is defined as a set of energetic forces that originates both within and outside an employee, initiates work-related effort, and determines its direction, intensity, and persistence.

2. Expectancy theory describes the cognitive process that employees go through to make choices among different voluntary behaviors. Effort is directed toward behaviors when effort is

believed to result in performance (expectancy), performance is believed to result in outcomes (instrumentality), and those outcomes are anticipated to be valuable (valence).

3. Goal-setting theory describes the impact of assigned goals on the intensity and persistence of effort. Goals become strong drivers of motivation and performance when they are difficult and specific. Specific and difficult goals affect performance by increasing self-set goals and task strategies. Those effects occur more frequently when employees are given feedback, tasks are not too complex, and goal commitment is high.

4. Rewards are equitable when a person's ratio of outcomes to inputs matches those of some relevant comparison other. A sense of inequity triggers equity distress. Under-reward inequity typically results in lower levels of motivation or higher levels of counterproductive behavior. Over-reward inequity typically results in cognitive distortion, in which inputs are reevaluated in a more positive light.

5. Psychological empowerment reflects an energy rooted in the belief that tasks are contributing to some larger purpose. Psychological empowerment is fostered when work goals appeal to employees' passions (meaningfulness), employees have a sense of choice regarding work tasks (self-determination), employees feel capable of performing successfully (competence), and employees feel they are making progress toward fulfilling their purpose (impact).

6. Motivation has a strong positive relationship with job performance and a moderate positive relationship with organizational commitment. Of all the energetic forces subsumed by motivation, self-efficacy/competence has the strongest relationship with performance.

4.8 Discussion questions

1. Which of the outcomes in Table 4 – 1 are most appealing to you? Are you more attracted to extrinsic outcomes or intrinsic outcomes? Do you think that your preferences will change as you get older?

2. Assume that you were working on a group project and that one of your teammates was nervous about speaking in front of the class during the presentation. Drawing on Figure 4 – 3, what exactly could you do to make your classmate feel more confident?

3. How do you tend to respond when you experience over-reward and under-reward inequity?

4. Think about a job that you've held in which you felt very low levels of psychological empowerment. What could the organization have done to increase empowerment levels?

Chapter 5 Learning and Decision Making

There is perhaps no more familiar sight on a construction site than to see the large, bright-yellow trucks, engines, and tools produced by Caterpillar, the world's leading manufacturer of construction and mining equipment, diesel and natural gas engines, and industrial gas turbines, based in Peoria, Illinois. What you likely don't know though is that this Fortune 100 company has one of the largest and most effective systems of knowledge sharing in the world. This ability to share and harness knowledge has played a large role in its ability to double in size during the past three years. As Caterpillar CEO Jim Owens recently said, "Learning is essential to our aspiration to be a great company."

One reason learning is so important to Caterpillar is the fact that intellectual capital accounts for almost 85 percent of its value (as opposed to only 30 percent 30 years ago). To feed this intellectual capital, in 2,000, the company formed "Caterpillar University", through which employees acquired traditional training opportunities and more than 3,000 online courses, in languages dealing with job tasks, business-unit opportunities, and discretionary learning. However, the real heart of what makes Caterpillar different than most companies is its "Knowledge Network". This extensive intranet-based social network organized around "communities of practice", hold platform for knowledge sharing among 100,000 employees spread out over 300 manufacturing operations in 40 countries. This process of knowledge sharing, which is driven primarily by employees (no top-down oversight), has achieved a record-setting return on investment for Caterpillar and sets it apart from its competitors and most other companies when it comes to learning.

5.1 Define learning and decision making

Caterpillar is extremely concerned about knowledge transfer because learning and decision making are so important in organizations. Learning reflects relatively permanent changes in an employee's knowledge or skill that result from experience. The more employees learn, the more they bring to the table when they come to work. Why is learning so important? Because it has a significant impact on decision making, which refers to the process of generating and choosing from a set of alternatives to solve a problem. The more knowledge and skills employees possess, the more likely they are to make accurate and sound decisions. The risk, at Caterpillar and other organizations, is that less experienced employees will lack the knowledge base needed to make the right decisions when stepping into new roles.

One reason inexperience can be so problematic is that learning is not necessarily easy. Have you ever watched experts perform their jobs? How is it that someone becomes an expert? It takes a significant amount of time to become proficient at most complex jobs. It takes most employees anywhere from three months to a year to perform at a satisfactory level. To develop high levels of expertise takes significantly longer. This difficulty makes it even more important for companies to find a way to improve learning and decision making by their employees.

Bill Buford, a journalist interested in becoming a chef, was hired by Mario Batali's world-renowned restaurant Babbo in New York. At some point early in his tenure in the kitchen, he realized he was in over his head while he stood and watched other, more experienced cooks work at an unbelievably frantic pace. He knew right then that he had a decision to make:

"*I was at a go-forward-or-backward moment. If I went backward, I'd be saying, 'Thanks for the visit, very interesting, that's sure not me.' But how to go forward? There was no place for me. These people were at a higher level of labor. They didn't think. Their skills were so deeply inculcated they were available to them as instincts. I didn't have skills of that kind and couldn't imagine how you'd learn them. I was aware of being poised on the verge of something: a long, arduous, confidence-bashing, profoundly humiliating experience.*"

In this situation, Buford realized that his coworkers had more expertise than he did. Expertise refers to the knowledge and skills that distinguish experts from novices and less experienced people. Research shows that the differences between experts and novices is almost always a function of learning as opposed to the more popular view that intelligence or other innate differences make the difference. Although learning cannot be directly seen or observed, we can tell when people have learned by observing their behaviors. It is those behaviors that can be used to tell experts from novices, and it is changes in those behaviors that can be used to show that learners are gaining knowledge. Although it's sometimes easy for employees to mimic a behavior once or twice, or get lucky with a few key decisions, true learning only occurs when changes in behavior become relatively permanent and are repeated over time. Understanding why some employees prove better at this than others requires understanding what exactly employees learn and how they do it.

5.2 Describc the types of knowledge that employees can gain as they learn and build expertise

Employees learn two basic types of knowledge, both of which have important implications for organizations. Explicit knowledge is the kind of information you are likely to think about when you picture someone sitting down at a desk to learn. It's information that is relatively easily communicated and a large part of what companies teach during training sessions. Although such information is necessary to perform well, it winds up being a relatively minor portion of all that you need to know.

Tacit knowledge, in contrast, is what employees can typically learn only through experience.

It's not easily communicated but could very well be the most important aspect of what we learn in organizations. In fact, it's been argued that up to 90 percent of the knowledge contained in organizations occurs in tacit form. Did you ever get to be so good at something that you had the ability to do it but couldn't really explain it to someone else? That's a common way to explain tacit knowledge. It's been described as the "know-how" "know-what" and "know-who" types of knowledge. The short answer is that we learn through "who" acquired solely through experience. Table 5 – 1 lists the qualities that help explain the differences between explicit and tacit knowledge. Some would go as far as to say that explicit knowledge is what everyone can find and use, but tacit knowledge is what separates experts from common people.

Table 5 – 1 Characteristics of Explicit and Tacit Knowledge

Explicit Knowledge	Tacit Knowledge
Easily transferred through written or verbal communication	Very difficult, if not impossible, to articulate to others
Readily available to most	Highly personal in nature
Can be learned through books	Based on experience
Always conscious and accessible information	Sometimes holders don't even recognize that they possess it
General information	Typically job-and/or situation-specific

5.3 Explain the methods by which employees learn in organizations

5.3.1 Methods of Learning

Tacit and explicit knowledge are extremely important to employees and organizations. As an employee, it's hard to build a high level of tacit knowledge without some level of explicit knowledge to build off of. From an organization's perspective, the tacit knowledge its employees accumulate may be the single most important strategic asset a company possesses. The question then becomes: How do employees learn these reinforcement (rewards and punishments), observation, and experience.

5.3.2 Reinforcement

We've known for a long time that managers use various methods of reinforcement to induce desirable or reduce undesirable behaviors by their employees.

Originally known as operant conditioning, B. F. Skinner was the first to pioneer the notion that we learn by observing the link between our voluntary behavior and the consequences that follow it. Research has continually demonstrated that people will exhibit specific behaviors if they are rewarded for doing so. Not surprisingly, we tend to repeat behaviors that result in consequences that we like and to not exhibit behaviors that result in consequences we don't like. Figure 5 – 1 shows this operant conditioning process.

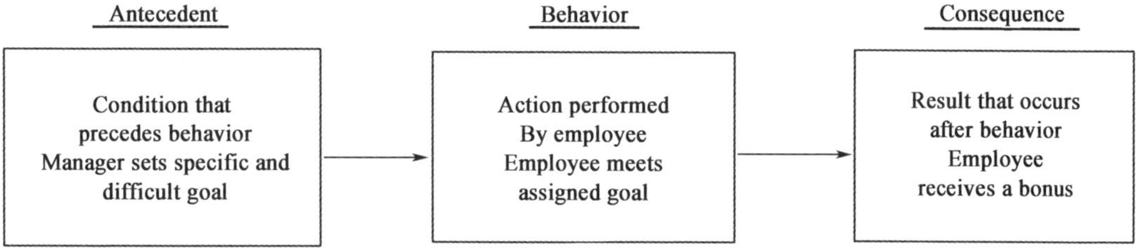

Figure 5 – 1 Operant Conditioning Components

In that model, you can see that there are antecedents or events that precede or signal certain behaviors, which are then followed by consequences. Antecedents in organizations are typically goals, rules, instructions, or other types of information that help show employees what is expected of them. Although antecedents are useful for motivational reasons, it is primarily the consequences of actions that drive behavior. This entire process of reinforcement is a continuous cycle, and the repetition of behaviors is strengthened to the degree that reinforcement continues to occur. There are four specific consequences typically used by organizations to modify employee behavior, known as the contingencies of reinforcement. Figure 5 – 2 summarizes these contingencies. It's important to separate these contingencies into what they are designed to do, namely, increase desired behaviors or decrease unwanted behaviors.

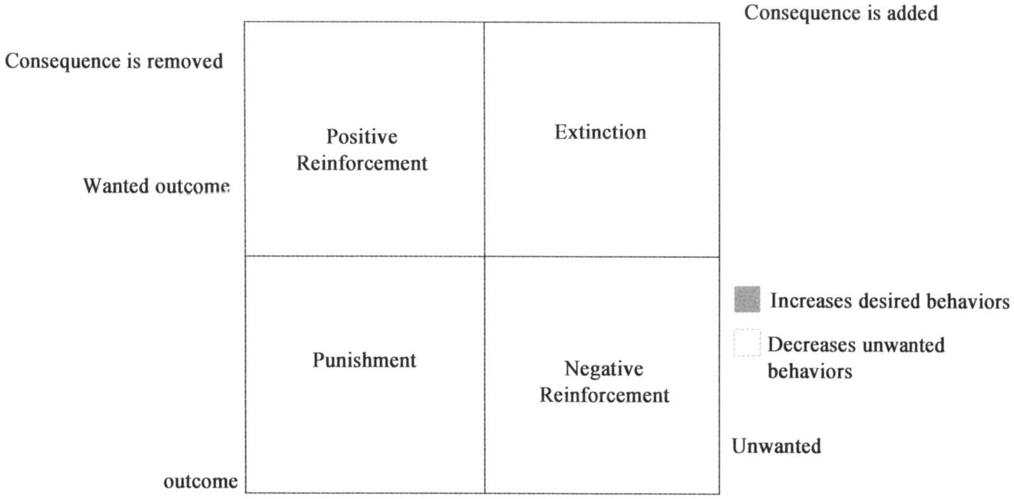

Figure 5 – 2 Contingencies of Reinforcement

Two contingencies of reinforcement are used to increase desired behaviors. Positive reinforcement occurs when a positive outcome follows a desired behavior. It is perhaps the most common type of reinforcement and the type we think of when an employee receives some type of "reward." Increased pay, promotions, praise from a manager or coworkers, and public recognition would all be considered positive reinforcement when given as a result of an employee exhibiting wanted behaviors. Negative reinforcement occurs when an unwanted outcome is removed following a desired behavior. Have you ever performed a task for the specific reason of not getting yelled at? If so, you learned to perform certain behaviors through the use of negative reinforcement. It is important to remember that even though the word "negative" has a sour connotation to it, it is designed to increase desired behaviors.

The next two contingencies of reinforcement are designed to decrease undesired behaviors, Punishment occurs when an unwanted outcome follows an unwanted behavior. Punishment is exactly what it sounds like. In other words, the employee is given something he or she doesn't like as a result of performing a behavior that the organization doesn't like. Suspending an employee for showing up to work late, assigning job tasks generally seen as demeaning for not following safety procedures, or even firing an employee for gross misconduct are all examples of punishment. Extinction occurs when there is the removal of a consequence following an unwanted behavior. The use of extinction to reinforce behavior can be purposeful or accidental. Perhaps an employee receives attention from coworkers when he or she acts in ways that are somewhat childish at work. Finding a way to remove the attention would be a purposeful act of extinction. Similarly though, perhaps an employee works late every now and then to finish up job tasks when work gets busy, but his or her manager stops acknowledging that hard work. Desired behavior that is not reinforced will diminish over time. In this way, a manager who does nothing to reinforce good behavior is actually decreasing the odds that it will be repeated!

In general, positive reinforcement and extinction should be the most common forms of reinforcement used by managers to create learning among their employees. Positive reinforcement doesn't have to be in the form of material rewards to be effective. There are many ways for managers to encourage wanted behaviors. Offering praise, providing feedback, public recognition, and small celebrations are all ways to encourage employees and increase the chances they will continue to exhibit desired behaviors. At the same time, extinction is an effective way to stop unwanted behaviors. Both contingencies deliver their intended results, but perhaps more important, they do so without creating feelings of animosity and conflict. Although punishment and negative reinforcement will work, they tend to bring other, detrimental consequences along with them.

5.3.3 Observation

In addition to learning through reinforcement, social learning theory argues that people in organizations have the ability to learn through the observation of others. In fact, many would argue that social learning is the primary way by which employees gain knowledge in organizations. Think about where you are most likely to get your cues while working in an organization. When possible, chances are good you'll look around at other employees to figure out the appropriate behaviors on your job. Not only do employees have the ability to see the link between their own behaviors and their consequences, they also can observe the behaviors and consequences of others. When employees observe the actions of others, learn from what they observe, and then repeat the observed behavior, they are engaging in behavioral modeling.

In fact, because tacit knowledge is so difficult to communicate, modeling might be the single best way to acquire it. For that reason, modeling is a continual process that is used at all levels of many organizations. Kellogg's, the Michigan-based cereal company, groomed current CEO David Mackay for two years by allowing him to observe and model an interim, experienced CEO prior to taking over the helm. Mackay shadowed the CEO and observed board-room proceedings to gain the insider experience that the Kellogg's board felt he was lacking. Needless to say, choosing a good model is important, and not all models are good ones. Salomon Brothers, the New York-based investment bank, learned this lesson the hard way when employees began to model the unethical behaviors of their managers and leaders.

5.4 Describe what steps organizations take to foster learning

How can organizations proactively take advantage of these methods of learning to boost employee expertise and, ultimately, improve decision making? One approach is to rely on which represents a systematic effort by organizations to facilitate the learning of job-related knowledge and behavior. Organizations spent over \$55.8 billion and approximately \$1,273 per learner on formal training and development costs in 2006. Estimates suggest that organizations spend three to six times that amount on informal, observational, and on the job training. A full discussion of all the types of training companies offer is beyond the scope of this section, but suffice it to say that companies are using many different methods to help their employees acquire explicit and tacit knowledge. Technological changes are altering the way those methods are delivered, as instructor-led classroom training has declined while online self-study programs have increased. These technological changes are occurring on university campuses as well. Indeed, some of you may be working in a virtual classroom right now!

As evidenced in our opening example, another form of knowledge transfer that's being used by companies more frequently is communities of practice. Communities of practice are groups of employees who work together and learn from one another by collaborating over an extended period. Many companies are utilizing this newer form of informal social learning. Communities of practice introduce their own unique complications, but the potential of their ability to transfer knowledge through employees is significant.

Goal Orientation. Before we leave this section, it's important to recognize that people learn somewhat differently according to their predispositions or attitudes toward learning and performance. These differences are reflected in an individual's goal orientation, which captures the kinds of activities and goals that they prioritize. Some people have what is known as a learning orientation, according to which building competence is deemed more important than demonstrating competence. "Learning-oriented" persons enjoy working on new kinds of tasks, even if they fail during their early experiences. Such people view failure in positive terms—as a means of increasing knowledge and skills in the long run. For others, the demonstration of competence is deemed a more important goal than the building of competence. That demonstration of competence can be motivated by two different thought processes. Those with a performance-prove orientation focus on demonstrating their competence so that others think favorably of them. Those with a performance-avoid orientation focus on demonstrating their competence so that others will not think poorly of them. In either case, "performance-oriented" people tend to work mainly on tasks at which they're already good at, preventing them from failing in front of others. Such individuals view failure in negative terms—as an indictment of their ability and competence.

Research has shown that a learning goal orientation improves self-confidence, feedback-seeking behavior, learning strategy development, and learning performance. Research on the two performance orientations is more mixed. Although focusing on performance should improve performance-based outcomes, research shows that isn't necessarily the case. Overall, a performance-prove orientation tends to be a mixed bag, producing varying levels of performance and outcomes.

5.5 Describe the two methods that employees use to make decisions

How do employees take explicit and tacit knowledge; however it's gained, and turn that knowledge into effective decision making? Sometimes that process is very straightforward. Programmed decisions are decisions that become somewhat automatic because a person's knowledge allows him or her to recognize and identify a situation and the course of action that needs to be taken. As shown in Figure 5 – 3, experts often respond to an identified problem by realizing that they've dealt with it before. That realization triggers a programmed decision that is implemented and then evaluated according to its ability to deliver the expected outcome. For experts who possess high levels of explicit and tacit knowledge, many decisions they face are of this programmed variety. That's not to say that the decisions are necessarily easy. It simply means that their experience and knowledge allow them to see the problems more easily and recognize and implement solutions more quickly.

To experts, this kind of decision making sometimes comes across as intuition or a "gut feeling". Intuition can be described as emotionally charged judgments that arise through quick, nonconscious, and holistic associations. Because of their tacit knowledge, experts sometimes cannot put into words why they know that a problem exists, why a solution will work, or how they accomplished a task. They just "know". Of course, the difficulty arises in knowing when to trust that "gut instinct" and when not to. As a general rule of thumb, you should probably ask yourself how much expertise you have in that on which you are making a judgment. In other words, don't go laying down your life savings on a spin of the roulette wheel in Vegas because your intuition tells you "red"! Effective intuition results when people have a certain amount of tacit knowledge.

When a situation arises that is new, complex, and not recognized, it calls for a non-programmed decision on the part of the employee. Organizations are complex and changing, environments, and many workers are faced with uncertainty on a daily basis. In these instances, employees have to make sense of their environment, understand the problems they are faced with, and come up with solutions to overcome them. As a rule of thumb, as employees move up the corporate ladder, a larger percentage of their decisions become less and less programmed. How should decision making proceed in such contexts? The rational decision-making model presented on the right side of Figure 5 – 3 offers a step-by-step approach to making decisions that maximize outcomes by examining all available alternatives. This model only becomes relevant when people don't recognize a problem as one they have dealt with before.

The rational decision-making model assumes that people are, of course, perfectly rational. However, problems immediately arise when we start to examine some of the assumptions the model makes about human decision makers. The model assumes there is a clear and definite problem to solve and that people have the ability to identify what that exact problem is. It also assumes that decision makers have perfect information that they know and are able to identify the available alternatives and the outcomes that would be associated with those alternatives. The model further assumes that time and money are generally not issues when it comes to making a decision, that decision makers always choose the solution that maximizes value, and that they will act in the best interests of the organization. Given all these assumptions, perhaps we shouldn't label the model as "rational" after all!

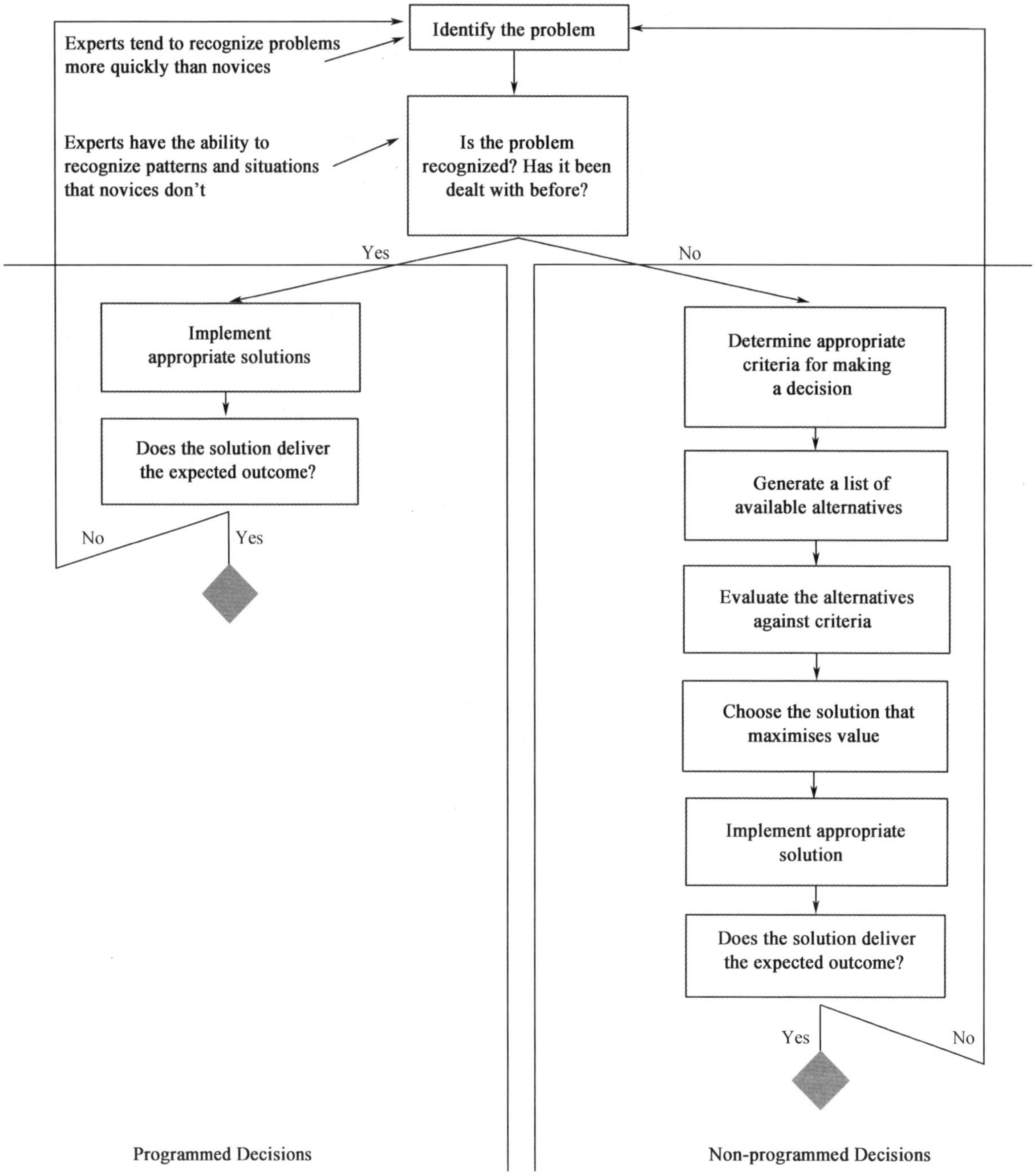

Figure 5 – 3　Programmed and Non-programmed Decisions

5.6 Understand the decision-making problems that can prevent employees from translating their learning into accurate decisions

Because employees don't always make rational decisions, it's easy to second-guess decisions after the fact. Many decisions made inside organizations look good at the time and were made with perfectly good justifications to support them but turn out to have what are perceived as "bad results" The reality, however, is that it's a lot easier to question decisions in hindsight. As Warren Buffet, CEO of Berkshire Hathaway, is often quoted as saying, "In the business world, the rearview mirror is always clearer than the windshield." Our responsibility here is not to rehash all the poor decisions employees and managers have made (and there are many of them!) but rather to detail some of the most common reasons for bad decision-making—in other words, when are people most likely to falter in terms of the rational decision-making model and why?

5.6.1 Limited Information

Although most employees perceive themselves as rational decision makers, the reality is that they are all subject to bounded rationality. Bounded rationality is the notion that decision makers simply do not have the ability or resources to process all available information and alternatives to make an optimal decision. A comparison of bounded rationality and rational decision making is presented in Table 5 – 2. This limit results in two major problems for making decisions. First, people have to filter and simplify information to make sense of their complex environment and the myriad of potential choices they face. This simplification leads them to miss information when perceiving problems, generating and evaluating alternatives, or judging the results. Second, because people cannot possibly consider every single alternative when making a decision, they satisfice. Satisficing means decision makers select the first acceptable alternative considered.

Table 5 – 2 Rational Decision Making vs. Bounded Rationality

To be rational decision makers, we should...	Bounded rationality says we are likely to...
Identify the problem by thoroughly examining the situation and considering all interested parties	Boil the problem down to something that is easily understood
Develop an exhaustive list of alternatives to consider all solutions	Come up with a few solutions that tend to be straightforward, familiar, and similar to what is currently being done
Evaluate all the alternatives simultaneously	Evaluate each alternative as soon as we think of it

Table 5 –2(continued)

To be rational decision makers, we should...	Bounded rationality says we are likely to...
Use accurate information to evaluate alternatives	Use distorted and inaccurate information during the evaluation process
Pick the alternative that maximizes value	Pick the first acceptable alternative (satisfice)

In addition to choosing the first acceptable alternative, decision makers tend to come up with alternatives that are straight-forward, familiar, and not that different from what they're already doing. When you and another person are deciding where to go out for dinner tonight, will you sit down and list every restaurant available to you within a certain mile limit? Of course not. You'll start listing off alternatives, generally starting with the closest and most familiar, until both parties arrive at a restaurant that is acceptable to them. Making decisions this way is no big deal when it comes to deciding where to go for dinner because the consequences of a poor decision are minimal. However, many managers make decisions that have critical consequences for their employees and their customers. In those cases, making a decision without thoroughly looking into the alternatives becomes a problem!

5.6.2 Faulty Perceptions

As decision makers, employees are forced to rely on their perceptions to make decisions. Perception is the process of selecting, organizing, storing, and retrieving information about the environment. Although perceptions can be very useful because they help us make sense of the environment around us, they can often become distorted versions of reality. Perceptions can be dangerous in decision making because we tend to make assumptions or evaluations based on them. Selective perception is the tendency for people to see their environment only as it affects them and as it is consistent with their expectations. Has someone ever told you, "You only see what you want to see"? If a relative, spouse, or significant other said that to you, chances are good it probably wasn't the best experience. That person was likely upset that you did not perceive the environment (or what was important to them) the same way he or she did. Selective perception affects our ability to identify problems, generate and evaluate alternatives, and judge outcomes. In other words, we take "shortcuts" when we process information. In the following paragraphs, we'll discuss some of the ways in which we take perceptual shortcuts when dealing with people and situations.

Another example of faulty perceptions is caused by the way we cognitively organize people into groups. Social identity theory holds that people identify themselves by the groups to which they belong and perceive and judge others by their group memberships. There is a substantial amount of research that shows that we like to categorize people on the basis of the groups to which they belong. These groups could be based on demographic information (gender, race, religion, hair color), occupational information (scientists, engineers, accountants), where they work (GE, Halliburton, Microsoft), what country they are from (Americans, French, Chinese), or any other subgroup that makes sense to the perceiver. You might categorize students on campus by whether they are a member of a fraternity or sorority. Those inside the Greek system categorize people by which fraternity or sorority they belong to. And people within a certain fraternity might group their own members based on whom they hang out with the most. There is practically no end to the number of subgroups that people can come up with.

When confronted with situations of uncertainty that require a decision on our part, we often use heuristics—simple, efficient rules of thumb that allow us to make decisions more easily. In general, heuristics are not bad. In fact, they lead to correct decisions more often than not. However, heuristics can also bias us toward inaccurate decisions at times. Consider this example from one of the earliest studies on decision-making heuristics: "Consider the letter R. Is R more likely to appear in the first position of a word or the third position of a word?" If your answer was the first position of a word, you answered incorrectly and fell victim to one of the most frequently talked about heuristics. The availability bias is the tendency for people to base their judgments on information that is easier to recall. It is significantly easier for almost everyone to remember words in which R is the first letter as opposed to the third. The availability bias is why more people are afraid to fly than statistics would support. Every single plane crash is plastered all over the news, making plane crashes more available in memory than successful plane landings. Aside from the availability bias, there are many other biases that affect the way we make decisions. Regardless of how often we fall victim to the biases, being aware of potential decision errors can help us make them less frequently.

5.6.3 Faulty Attributions

Another category of decision-making problems centers on how we explain the actions and events that occur around us. Research on attributions suggests that when people witness a behavior or outcome, they make a judgment about whether it was internally or externally caused. For example, when a coworker of yours named Joe shows up late to work and misses an important group presentation, you'll almost certainly make a judgment about why that happened. You might attribute Joe's outcome to internal factor—for example, suggesting that he is lazy or has a poor work ethic. Or you might attribute Joe's outcome to external factors—for example, suggesting that there was unusually bad traffic that day or that other factors prevented him from arriving on time.

The fundamental attribution error argues that people have a tendency to judge others' behaviors as due to internal factors. This error suggests that you would likely judge Joe as having low motivation, poor organizational skills, or some other negative internal attribute. What if you yourself had showed up late? It turns out that we're less harsh when judging ourselves. The self-serving bias occurs when we attribute our own failures to external factors and our own successes to internal factors. Interestingly, evidence suggests that attributions across cultures don't always work the same way.

One model of attribution processes suggests that when people have a level of familiarity with the person being judged, they'll use a more detailed decision framework. This model is illustrated in Figure 5 –4. To return to our previous example, if we want to explore why Joe arrived late to work, we can ask three kinds of questions:

Consensus: Did others act the same way under similar situations? In other words, did others arrive late on the same day?

Distinctiveness: Does this person tend to act differently in other circumstances? In other words, does Joe show compliance to responsibility when it comes to other appointments other than this one?

Consistency: Does this person always do this when performing this task? In other words, has Joe arrived late for work before?

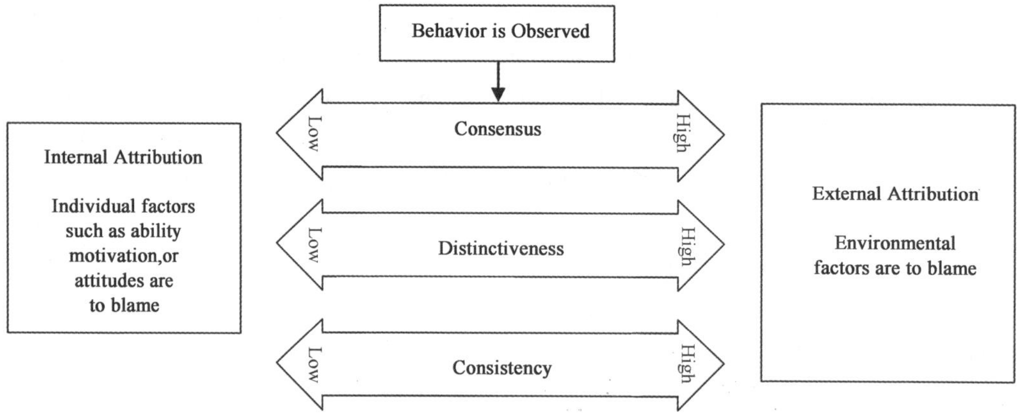

Figure 5 –4 Consensus, Distinctiveness, and Consistency

The way in which these questions are answered will determine if an internal or external attribution is made. An internal attribution such as laziness or low motivation for Joe will occur if there is low consensus (others arrived on time), low distinctiveness (Joe is irresponsible with other commitments as well), and high consistency (Joe has arrived late before). An external attribution such as bad traffic or a power outage will occur if there is high consensus (others arrived late), high distinctiveness (Joe is responsible with other commitments), and low consistency (Joe has never come late to work before).

5.6.4 Escalation of Commitment

Our last category of decision-making problems centers on what happens as a decision begins to go wrong. Escalation of commitment refers to the decision to continue to follow a failing course of action. The expression "throwing good money after bad" captures this common decision-making error. An enormous amount of research shows that people have a tendency, when presented with a series of decisions, to escalate their commitment to previous decisions, even in the face of obvious failures. Why do decision makers fall victim to this sort of error? They may feel an obligation to stick with their decision to avoid looking incompetent. They also may want to avoid admitting that they made a mistake. Those escalation tendencies become particularly strong when decision makers have invested a lot of money into the decision and when the project in question seems quite close to completion.

One recent example of escalation of commitment is United Airlines' abandonment of the automated baggage-handling system at the Denver International Airport. When it opened in 1995 (after a two-year delay), the baggage-handling system with 26 miles of track designed to haul baggage across three terminals was supposed to be the single most advanced baggage-handling system in the world. However, though it was originally scheduled to cost $186 million, a series of delays and technological problems caused the cost of the system to skyrocket by $1 million per day. Because of a series of technological issues, the system never really worked very well. In fact, United was the only airline in the airport willing to use it. It took 10 years and many mangled and lost suitcases before United finally "cut its losses" in 2005, saving itself $1 million a month in maintenance fees.

5.7 Understand how learning affects job performance and organizational commitment

Does learning have a significant impact on the two primary outcomes in our integrative model of OB—does it correlate with job performance and organizational commitment? In fact, learning does influence job performance. Why? The primary reason is that learning is moderately correlated with task performance. It's difficult to fulfill job duties if the employee doesn't possess adequate levels of job knowledge. In fact, there are reasons to suggest that the moderate correlation depicted in the figure is actually an underestimate of learning's importance.

That's because most of the research linking learning to task performance focuses on explicit learning, which is more practical to measure. It's difficult to measure tacit knowledge because of its unspoken nature, but clearly such knowledge is relevant to task performance. Learning seems less relevant to citizenship behavior and counterproductive behavior however, given that those behaviors are often less dependent on knowledge and expertise.

Learning is only weakly related to organizational commitment. In general, having higher levels of job knowledge is associated with slight increases in emotional attachment to the firm. It is true that companies that have a reputation as organizations that value learning tend to receive higher-quality applicants for jobs. However, there is an important distinction between organizations that offer learning opportunities and employees who take advantage of those opportunities to actually gain knowledge. Moreover, it may be that employees with higher levels of expertise become more highly valued commodities on the job market, thereby reducing their levels of continuance commitment.

5.8 Takeaways

1. Learning is a relatively permanent change in an employee's knowledge or skill that results from experience. Decision making refers to the process of generating and choosing from a set of alternatives to solve a problem.

2. Employees gain both explicit and tacit knowledge as they build expertise. Explicit knowledge is easily communicated and available to everyone. Tacit knowledge, however, is something employees can only learn through experience.

3. Employees learn new knowledge through reinforcement and observation of others. That learning also depends on whether the employees are learning-oriented or performance-oriented.

4. Through various forms of training, companies can give employees more knowledge and a wider array of experiences that they can use to make decisions.

5. Programmed decisions are decisions that become somewhat automatic because a person's knowledge allows him or her to recognize and identify a situation and the course of action that needs to be taken. Many task-related decisions made by experts are programmed decisions. Non-programmed decisions are made when a problem is new, complex, or not recognized. Ideally, such decisions are made by following the steps in the rational decision-making model.

6. Employees are less able to translate their learning into accurate decisions when they struggle with limited information, faulty perceptions, faulty attributions, and escalation of commitment.

7. Learning has a moderate positive relationship with job performance and a weak positive relationship with organizational commitment.

5.9 Discussion questions

1. In your current or past workplaces, what types of tacit knowledge did experienced workers possess? What did this knowledge allow them to do?

2. Given your occupational choice, how do you expect to learn what you need to know when you start working? Do you expect the company to provide you with these opportunities, or will you have to seek them out on your own?

3. Do you consider yourself a "rational" decision maker? For what types of decisions are you determined to be the most rational? What types of decisions are likely to cause you to behave irrationally?

4. Given your background, which of the decision-making biases listed in the chapter do you most struggle with? What could you do to overcome those biases to make more accurate decisions?

Section Ⅳ
Job and Organization

Chapter 6 Job Satisfaction

6.1 Define job satisfaction

Job satisfaction is defined as a pleasurable emotional state resulting from the appraisal of one's job or job experiences. In other words, it represents how you feel about your job and what you think about your job. Employees with high job satisfaction experience positive feelings when they think about their duties or take part in task activities. Employees with low job satisfaction experience negative feelings when they think about their duties or take part in their task activities. Unfortunately, workplace surveys suggest that satisfied employees are becoming more and more rare. For example, a recent survey showed that just 49 percent of Americans are satisfied with their jobs, down from 58 percent a decade ago. The survey also revealed that only 20 percent are satisfied with their employer's promotion and reward policies and 33 percent with their pay. Reversing such trends requires a deeper understanding of exactly what drives job satisfaction levels.

So what explains why some employees are more satisfied than others? At a general level, employees are satisfied when their job provides the things that they value, Values are those things that people consciously or subconsciously want to seek or attain. Think about this question for a few moments: What do you want to attain from your job; that is, what things might you want your job to give you? A good wage? A sense of achievement? Colleagues who are fun to be around? If you had to make a list of the things you value with respect to your job, most or all of them would likely be shown in Table 6 – 1. This table summarizes the values assessed in the five most general categories. Many of those values deal with the things that your work can give you, such as good pay or the chance for frequent promotions. Other values pertain to the context that surrounds your work, including whether you have a good boss or good coworkers. Still other values deal with the work itself, like whether your job tasks provide you with freedom or a sense of achievement.

6.2 Describe values and how they affect job satisfaction

Value-percept Theory

Values play a key role in explaining job satisfaction. Value-percept theory argues that job satisfaction depends on whether you perceive that your job supplies the things that you value. This theory can be summarized with the following equation:

$$\text{Dissatisfaction} = (V_{want} - V_{have}) \times (V_{importance})$$

In this equation, V_{want} reflects how much of a value an employee wants, V_{have} indicates how much of that value the job supplies, and $V_{importance}$ reflects how important the value is to the employee. Big differences between wants and haves create a sense of dissatisfaction, especially when the value in question is important. Note that the difference between V_{want} and V_{have} gets multiplied by importance, so existing discrepancies get magnified for important values and minimized for trivial values. As an example, say that you were evaluating your pay satisfaction. You want to be earning around \$70, 000 a year but are currently earning \$50, 000 a year, so there's a \$20, 000 discrepancy. Does that mean you feel a great deal of pay dis satisfaction? Only if pay is one of the most important values to you from Table 6 – 1. If pay isn't that important, you likely don't feel much dissatisfaction.

Table 6 – 1 Commonly Assessed Work Values

Categories	Specific Values
Pay	High salary Secure salary
Promotions	Frequent promotions Promotions based on ability
Supervision	Good supervisory relations Praise for good work
Coworkers	Enjoyable coworkers Responsible coworkers
Work itself	Utilization of ability Freedom and independence Intellectual stimulation Creative expression Sense of achievement
Altruism	Helping others Moral causes
Status	Prestige Power over others Fame
Environment	Comfort Safety
Key Question: Which of these things are most important to you?	

Source: Dawis R V. Vocational Interests, Values, and Preferences [M].//Handbook of Industrial and Organizational Psychology, 2ed. Dunnette M D, Hough L M. Palo Alto, CA: Consulting Psychologists Press, 1991: 834 – 71.

6.3 List the specific facets that individuals often use to evaluate their job satisfaction

Value – percept theory also suggests that people evaluate job satisfaction according to specific "facets" of the job. After all, a "job" isn't one thing—it's a collection of tasks, relationships, and rewards. The most common facets that employees consider in judging their job satisfaction appear in Figure 6 – 1. The figure includes the "want vs. have" calculations that drive satisfaction with pay, promotions, supervision, coworkers, and the work itself. The figure also shows how satisfaction with those five facets adds together to create "overall job satisfaction". Employees might be satisfied for all kinds of reasons. One person may be satisfied because she's in a high-paying job and working for a good boss. Another person may be satisfied because he has good coworkers and enjoyable work tasks. You may have noticed that a few of the values in Table 6 – 1—such as working for moral causes and gaining fame and prestige—are not represented in Figure 6 – 1. This omission is because those values are not relevant in all jobs, unlike pay, promotions, and so forth. For a discussion of values and satisfaction in the world of sports, see our OB in Sports feature.

The first facet in Figure 6 – 1, pay satisfaction, refers to employees' feelings about their pay, including whether it is as much as they deserve, secure, and adequate for both normal expenses and luxury items. Like the other facets, pay satisfaction is based on a comparison of the pay that employees want and the pay they receive. Although more money is almost always better, most employees base their desired pay on a careful examination of their job duties and the pay given and to comparable colleagues. Henceforth, non-millionares can be very satisfied with their payments (good news for many of us.) For example, employees at Bright Horizons, a Massachusetts-based provider of child-care and early education programs, are provided with an average salary of around $50,000. They generally experience higher pay satisfaction other colleagues in child-care industry, since such industry is known for low wages.

Promotion satisfaction, referring to workers' attitudes and feelings towards the organization's establishment and execution of promotion policies, which considers frequency and fairness of promotions, and whether they are based on ability. However, unlike pay, some employees may not want frequent promotions because promotions bring more responsibility and increased work hours. Many other employees value promotions and deem them opportunities for personal growth, higher wage and more prestige. QuikTrip, the Oklahoma-based chain of gas and convenience stores, does a good job fostering promotion satisfaction on the part of its employees. "Promote from within" is a key motto in the company, and all 400-plus of its managers worked their way up from entry-level positions.

Supervision satisfaction relates to satisfaction with supervisor. Good supervisor-subordinated relationship is fostered partially by characteristics of the employer, whether he/she is competent, polite, and serves as a good communicator (rather than lazy, annoying, and too distant). Most employees ask two questions about their supervisors: (1) "Can they help me attain the things that I value?" and(2) "Are they generally likable?" The first question depends on whether supervisors provide rewards for good performance, help employees obtain necessary resources, and protect employees from unnecessary distractions. The second question depends on whether supervisors have good personalities, as well as values and beliefs similar to the employees'philosophies. Valero Energy, the Texas-based oil refiner and gas retailer, works hard to foster a sense of supervision satisfaction. When it comes to receiving bonuses, executives only get theirs when everyone else in the organization has received one? As a result, supervisors work harder to make sure that employees can get their jobs done.

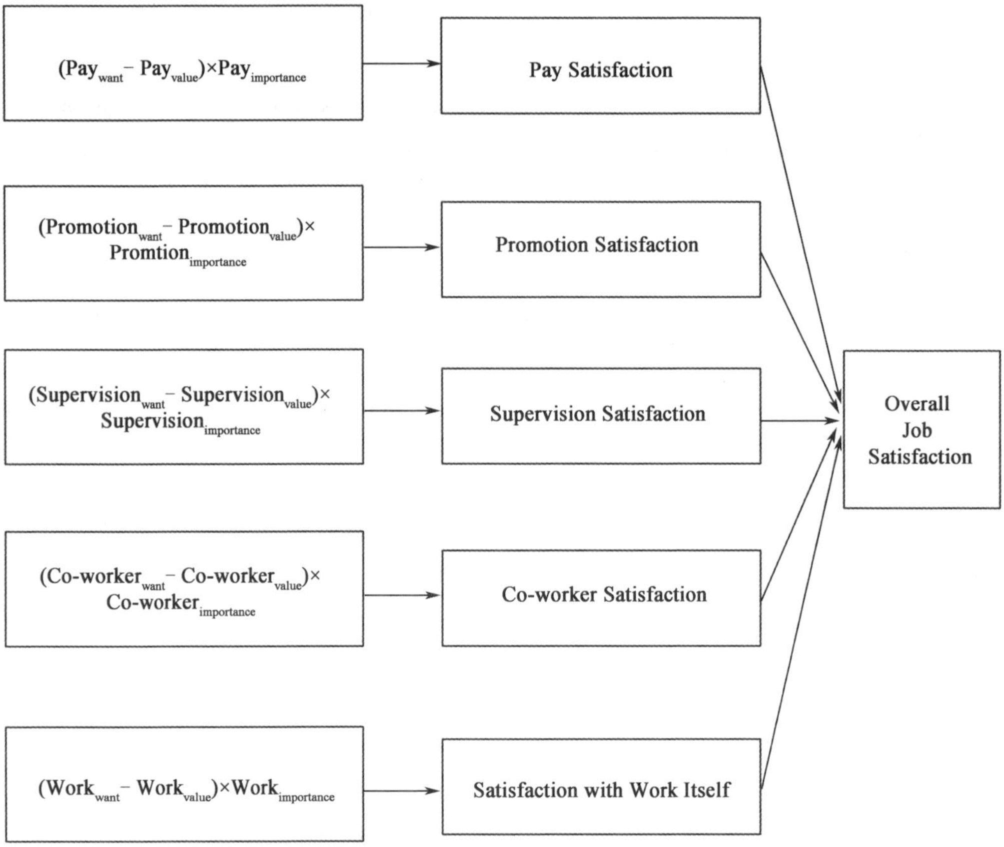

Figure 6 –1 The Value-Percept Theory of Job Satisfaction

Coworker satisfaction refers to employees' feelings about their fellow employees, including whether coworkers are smart, responsible, helpful, fun, and interesting as opposed to lazy, gossipy, unpleasant, and boring. Employees ask the same kinds of questions about their coworkers that they do about their supervisors: (1) "Can they help me do my job?" and(2) "Do I enjoy being around them?" The first question is critical because most of us rely, to some extent, on our coworkers when performing job tasks. The second question also is important because we spend just as much time with coworkers as we do members of our own family. Coworkers who are pleasant and fun can make the workweek go much faster, whereas coworkers who are disrespectful and annoying can make even one day seem like an eternity. Arbitron, the New York-based radio market research firm, takes an unusual step to increase coworker satisfaction. Employees can choose to recognize their coworkers'achievements with a \$100 American Express gift card, with no restrictions on how many they can give out. Last year, 300 of its 1,400-plus employees received rewards totaling \$50,000.

The last facet in Figure 6 – 1, satisfaction with the work itself, reflects employees' feelings about their actual work tasks, including whether those tasks are challenging, interesting, and respected, and make use of key skills rather than being dull, repetitive, and uncomfortable. Whereas the previous four facets described the outcomes that result from work (pay, promotions) and the people who surround work (supervisors, coworkers), this facet focuses on what employees actually do. After all, even the best boss or most interesting coworkers can't compensate for 40 or 50 hours of complete boredom each week! How can employers instill a sense of satisfaction with the work itself? Valassis, a Michigan-based publisher of newspaper inserts and coupons, gives employees annual skill assessments to get a better feel for what they're good at. It then provides employees with growth opportunities, sometimes even creating new positions to employ special talents.

In summary, value-percept theory suggests that employees will be satisfied when they perceive that their job offers the pay, promotions, supervision, coworkers, and work tasks that they value. Of course, this theory begs the question: which of those ingredients is most important? In other words, which of the five facets has the strongest influence on overall job satisfaction? Several research studies have examined these issues and come up with the results. It suggests that satisfaction with the work itself is the single strongest driver of overall job satisfaction. Supervision and coworker satisfaction are also strong drivers, and promotion and pay satisfaction have moderately strong effects. Why is satisfaction with the work itself so critical? Well, consider that a typical workweek contains around 2,400 minutes. How much of that time is spent thinking about how much money you make? 10 minutes? Maybe 20? The same is true for promotions—we may want them, but we don't necessarily spend hours a day thinking about them. We do spend a significant chunk of that time with other people though. Between lunches, meetings, hallway chats, and other conversations, we might easily spend 600 minutes a week with supervisors and coworkers. That leaves almost 1,800 minutes for just us and our work. As a result, it is difficult to be satisfied with your job if you don't like what you actually do. Of course, those of you who are full-time students might wonder what satisfaction means to you. See our OB for Students feature for some facets of student satisfaction.

Given how important enjoyable work tasks are to overall job satisfaction, it's worth spending more time describing the kinds of tasks that most people find enjoyable. Researchers began focusing on this question in the 1950s and 1960s, partly in reaction to practices based in the "scientific management" perspective. Scientific management focuses on increasing the efficiency of job tasks by making them more simplified and specialized and using time and motion studies to plan task movements and sequences carefully? The hope was that such steps would increase worker productivity and reduce the breadth of skills required to complete a job, ultimately improving organizational profitability. Instead, the simplified and routine jobs tended to lower job satisfaction while increasing absenteeism and turnover. Put simply: Boring jobs may be easier, but they're not necessarily better.

So what makes some work tasks particularly satisfying? To answer this question, there are three psychological states to be taken into account as suggested by research. The first psychological state is believing in the meaningfulness of work, which reflects the degree to which work tasks are viewed as something that "counts" in the employee's system of philosophies and beliefs. Trivial tasks tend to be less satisfying than tasks that make employees feel like they're aiding the organization or society in some meaningful way. The second psychological state is perceiving responsibility for outcomes, which captures the degree to which employees feel that they are key drivers of the quality of the unit's work. Sometimes employees feel like their efforts don't really matter because work outcomes are dictated by effective procedures, efficient technologies, or more influential colleagues. Finally, the third psychological state is knowledge of results, which reflects the extent to which employees know how well (or how poorly) they are doing. Many employees work in jobs in which they never find out about their mistakes or never fully realize that they've performed well.

6.4 Understand the job characteristics that can create a sense of satisfaction with the work itself

Did you feel especially proud of a job well done? At that moment, you were probably experiencing all three psychological states. You were aware of the result because some job had been done well. You felt you were somehow responsible for that result. Finally, you felt that the result of the work was somehow meaningful. The next obvious question is, "What kinds of tasks create these psychological states?"

Job characteristics theory, which describes the central characteristics of intrinsically satisfying jobs, attempts to answer this question. Highly satisfying jobs, as defined by this theory, have five major characteristics (variety, identity, significance, autonomy, and feedback, which you can remember with the acronym "VISAF"). Shown in Figure 6 – 2 is the relationships between job characteristics and the previously mentioned three psychological states, which eventually contributes to the overall satisfaction with the job.

Variety, identity and significance are three characteristics especially relevant to the perceived meaningfulness of work. Variety indicates the extent to how many different skills and talents are asked for by various activities enlisted in the job. When variety is high, almost every workday is different in some way, and job holders lack a feeling of tediousness and repetition. Of course, we could picture jobs that have a variety of boring tasks such as screwing different-sized nuts onto different-colored bolts, but such jobs do not involve a number of different skills and talents.

Identity is a characteristic of any jobs in which progression from start to finish is made visible via an accomplished, completed, distinct piece of work. It is what gives employees the opportunity for recognition of their own original work. They can easily point to a finished work with high identity and proclaim, "There, I did that." Such transformation from inputs to finished product is very identifiable for employees to sense. Finally, significance describes amount of substantial impact a piece of work may draw upon the lives of ordinary people in the world, especially beyond the office. Other than that, most job can be seen as significant as it provides breads for the employers' family, or it sustains their educational and recreational expenses. Sometimes, employees may feel particularly satisfied or proud, if they determine the meaning of their role in the wider world as a whole. Working in Patagonia, a company dedicated to producing the high quality garments in the most environmentally sustainable manner, is what makes employees feel their unique significance. As one puts it, "It's easy to go to work when you get paid to do what you love to do." That said, significance as a core job characteristic captures something beyond that—the belief that this job really matters.

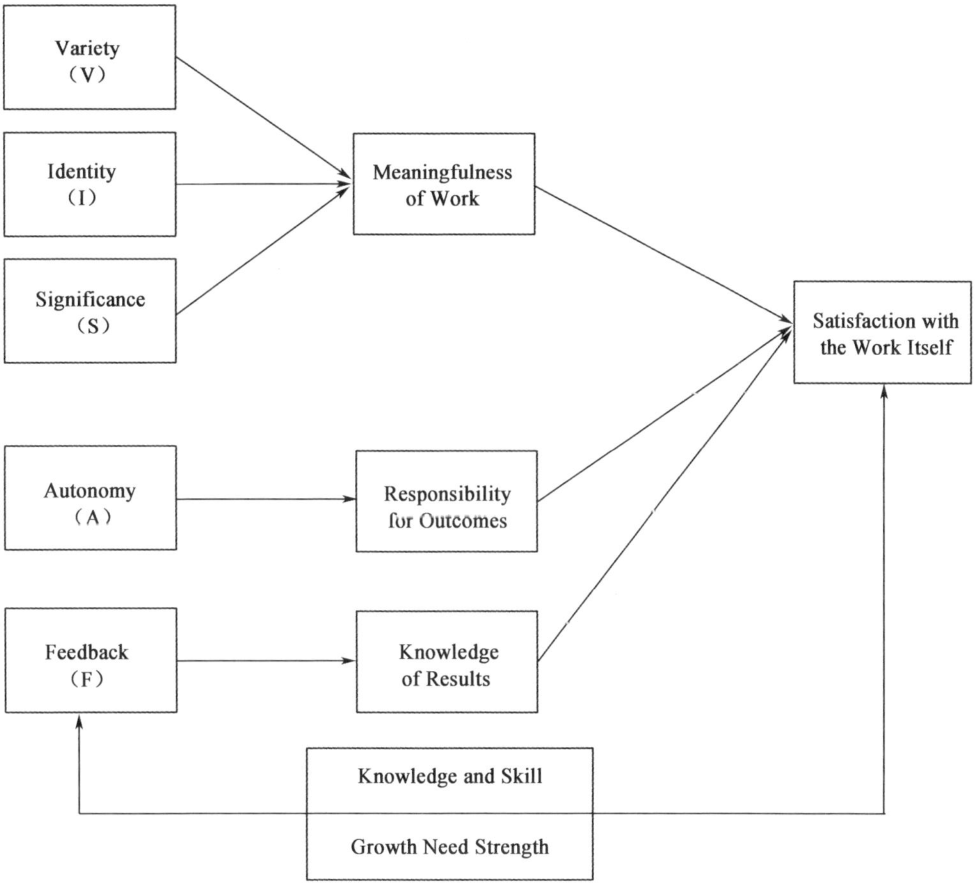

Figure 6 - 2 Job Characteristics Theory

There are two other characteristics captured by Figure 6 – 2 which contribute to employees' sense of responsibility and knowledge of work outcomes or results. Autonomy is the measure of how much freedom, independence and individual judgement or discretion may one possess in his/her work. For anyone who is satisfied with the amount of autonomy a job provides, surely the influence and careful instruction from his/her boss or strict procedural-manual is limited, so that the final outcome exhibits as the product of employee's own effort. Autonomy exists in various forms, including the freedom to of scheduling, sequencing of tasks, as well as methods implemented to complete work tasks. "Having a long leash", is what we might comment on a work of autonomy other than the phrase "micro-management", meaning the controlling of every part, however small, of activities.

Feedback is the degree to which carrying out the activities required by the job provides the worker withclear information about how well he or she is performing. A critical distinction must be noted: this core characteristic reflects feedback obtained directly from the job as opposed to feedback from coworkers or supervisors. Most employees receive formal performance appraisals from their bosses, but that feedback occurs once or maybe twice a year. When the job provides its own feedback, that feedback can be experienced almost every day.

Feedback is the degree to which carrying out the activities required by the job provides the worker with clear information about how well he or she is performing. However, it is important to notice one distinction: feedback comes as an intrinsic quality or the nature of tasks involved in the job itself, other thana feature of the social environment. Surely, many employees obtain feedbacks from colleagues or receive formal performance appraisals from their superiors. But they might receive them only occasionally. With the job itself providing feedback, information regarding performance can be attained daily for employees.

How important are the core characteristics to satisfaction with the work itself? A meta-analysis of 75 different research studies showed that the five core job characteristics are moderately to strongly related to work satisfaction. However, those results don't mean that every employee wants more variety, more autonomy, and so forth. There are two other variables to be considered: knowledge and skill and growth need strength (which captures whether employees have strong needs for personal accomplishment or developing themselves beyond their current status). In the jargon of theory diagrams, these variables are called "moderators". Rather than directly affecting other variables in the diagram, moderators influence the strength of the relationships between variables. If employees lack the required knowledge and skill or lack a desire for growth and development, more variety and autonomy should not increase their satisfaction very much. However, when employees are very talented and feel a strong need for growth, the core job characteristics become even more powerful. In conclusion, the relationship between the core job characteristics and satisfaction grows stronger when the moderators interplay well in between the previous two, sustaining as sturdy basis.

Many organizations recognize importance of the five core job characteristics to boosting job satisfaction. How might they employ this theory into practice for benefit among their workers? They can start this process by assessing the current level of the characteristics to arrive at a "satisfaction potential score". The organization, together with job design consultants, then attempts to redesign aspects of the job to increase the core job characteristic levels. Often this step results in job enrichment, such that the duties and responsibilities associated with a job are expanded to provide more variety, identity, autonomy, and so forth. Research suggests that such enrichment efforts can indeed boost job satisfaction levels. Moreover, enrichment efforts can heighten work accuracy and customer satisfaction, though training and labor costs tend to rise as a result of such changes.

We need to realize job satisfaction is sometimes influenced by irrational factors, beyond the well-grounded definitions about characteristics of the job. Let's say you're a satisfied employee, maybe because you get paid well and work for a good boss or because your work tasks provide you with variety and autonomy. Does this mean you'll definitely be satisfied at 11:00 a. m. next Tuesday? Or 2:30 p. m. the following Thursday? Obviously it doesn't. Each employee's satisfaction levels fluctuate over time, rising and falling like some sort of emotional stock market. This fluctuation might seem strange, given that people's pay, supervisors, coworkers, and work tasks don't change from one hour to the next. The key lies in remembering that job satisfaction reflects what you think and feel about your job. So part of it is rational, based on a careful appraisal of the job and the things it supplies. But another part of it is emotional, based on what you feel "in your gut" while you're at work or thinking about work. So a satisfied employee feels good about his or her job on average, but things happen during the course of the day to make him or her feel better at some times (and worse at others).

Next, we will take a look at how job satisfaction is affected by day-to-day events. Reading an annoying email from boss in the early morning might suddenly lead to decrease in satisfaction level, which may soon be boosted by a funny conversation with friends at work. Some employee may feel especially dissatisfied or reluctant, when they just left lunch to return to work. Realizing the demandingness of a new project might immediately grab some workers'interest for a couple of hours. In the end, they might describe their day as being relatively satisfied, despite of several ebbs and flows.

What's responsible for those ebbs and flows in satisfaction levels? Two related concepts: mood and emotions.

6.5 Define mood and emotions and describe the specific forms they take

Are you having a good mood or a bad one? Do you know why you are having that mood? Moods can easily fill up our minds and affect our attitudes. However, sometimes it is difficult for us to point out who deserves the credit or blame for our present mood. Also, moods come in many more categories other than just positive or negative. Both hostility and sadness make us feel negative. And you can pick out either enthusiasm or calmness, two distinct types, from the pool of positive moods if you would like to.

Moods are states of feelings that lasts for a period of time, long enough to impact our work, but maybe difficult enough for us to figure out their causation, let alone fixing them. Moods can be located on a scale of intensity. The most intense positive mood is characterized by feeling enthusiastic, excited, and elated. In contrast, the most intense negative mood is characterized by feeling hostile, nervous, and annoyed. This kind of mood often triggers you with the question, "Wow, what's gotten you in such a bad mood?" If we return to our discussion regarding satisfaction towards daily tasks, what kind of mood do you think the employee was in while answering the annoying emails from his boss? Probably a happy, cheerful, and pleased mood. And what kind of mood do you think the employee was in during the brainstorming meeting for the new project? Clearly, an enthusiastic, excited, and elated mood, which might lead to this employee reporting high job satisfaction at that moment.

Indeed, there are many types of moods. In the field of OB we tend to categorize them in two ways: pleasantness and engagement. Pleasantness reflects to whether you feel pleasant (in a good mood) or unpleasant (in a bad mood). Engagement illustrate a scale from a state of deactivated and unaroused to a state of engaged and aroused. Figure 6 – 3 summarizes how extent of pleasantness and engagement help define different types of moods.

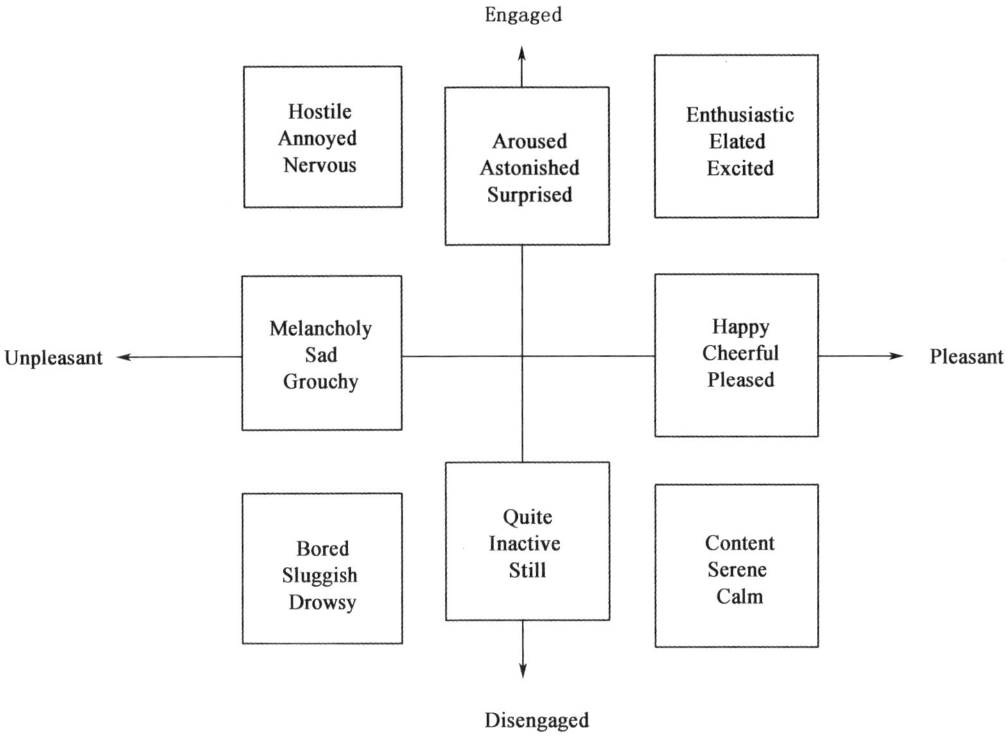

Figure 6 – 3 Different Kinds of Moods

Sometimes organizations strive to improve their employees' state of moods. Imagine working in an institution that has an on-site gym with a pool, volleyball courts, soccer fields, tennis courts, ping-pong tables, and billiards? This working environment dedicated to foster pleasant moods is attempted by the SAS Institute, the North Carolina-based maker of statistical software packages. What do you know, perhaps all it takes is a game with a colleague to erase the grumpiness from reading your boss's email! Griffin Hospital, based in Connecticut, offers its employees (and patients) family-style kitchens, strolling musicians, non-fluorescent lighting, and chair massages. Such perks may not rival the importance of pay, promotions, supervision, coworkers, and the work itself as far as job satisfaction is concerned, but they can help boost employees' moods during a particular workday.

Notice how moods can experience sudden changes within frame of a day. Why the dropping or the rising? Because negative or positive emotions, which are triggered by many specific events at work, lead our moods to the opposite directions. Compare emotions with moods. Emotions are feelings that are often intense, last for only a few minutes, and are clearly directed at (and caused by) someone or some circumstance. The difference between moods and emotions becomes clearer when we try to locate their origins. We describe moods by saying, "I'm feeling grouchy", but we describe emotions by saying, "I'm feeling angry at my boss". We fail at finding what our moods are about.

People experience a variety of different emotions during their daily lives. Positive emotions include joy, pride, relief, hope, love, and compassion. Negative emotions include anger, anxiety, fear, guilt, shame, sadness, envy, and disgust. What emotion do you think an employee may experience when reading a disrespectful e-mail from the boss? Probably anger. What emotion do you think when same employee enjoys during a funny conversation with a friend? Possibly joy. Leaving lunch to return to work might have triggered either anxiety (because the bad day might resume) or sadness (because the fun time with friends had ended). Luckily, the employee's sense of joy at taking on a new project that is interesting and challenging is right around the corner. The day might end on a down note, however, as the phone call signaling overdue paperwork is likely met with some mix of anger, fear, guilt, or even disgust (no one likes paperwork).

While some organizations aiming to foster positive moods, expression of emotion is limited in some workforce. Service jobs in particular, in which employees contact customers personally, requires the adage "never let them see you sweat" to be live up to. Employees are expected to conceal expression of any anxiety, annoyance, boredom or irritation. This demanding task of concealment is coined as emotional labor, or the need to manage emotions to complete job duties successfully. Flight attendants are trained to "put on a happy face" in front of passengers, retail salespeople trained to suppress any annoyance with customers, and restaurant servers are trained to act like they're having fun on their job even when they're not.

Should management actually require emotional labor? Discussions around this topic take two stands. Emotional labor is a relatively vital part of sound customer service. Research indicates that emotions are contagion; one person can "catch" or "be infected by" the emotions of another person. The annoyance of a shop assistant or an usher can be transferred to the customers. If that transfer occurs, it becomes less likely that customers will view the experience favorably and spend more money, which potentially harms the bottom line. Unfortunately, other evidence suggests that emotional labor places great strain on employees and that their "bottled up" emotions may end up bubbling over, sometimes resulting in angry outbursts against customers or emotional exhaustion and burnout on the part of employees.

We learned from pay to coworkers to job tasks to day-to-day moods and emotions, many factors influence employees' job satisfaction. This leads us to the question, "Why does job satisfaction matter?" Or more accurately, does job satisfaction have a significant impact on job performance and organizational commitment—the two primary outcomes in our integrative model of OB? Evidence from research indicates link job satisfaction to performance and commitment. This same sort of figure will appear in each of the remaining chapters of this book so that you can get a better feel for which of the concepts in our integrative model has the strongest impact on performance and commitment.

6.6 Understand how job satisfaction affects job performance and organizational commitment, as well as how it affects life satisfaction

Job satisfaction does influence job performance. Why? One reason is that job satisfaction is moderately correlated with task performance. Satisfied employees do a better job of fulfilling the duties described in their job descriptions, and evidence suggests that positive feelings improve creativity, problem solving, and decision making and enhance memory and recall of certain kinds of information. Positive feelings also improve general activity and energy levels. Apart from these sorts of findings, the benefits of job satisfaction for task performance might be explained on an hour-by-hour basis. At any given moment, employees wage a war between paying attention to a given work task and attending to "off-task" things such as stray thoughts, distractions, interruptions, and so forth. Positive feelings when working on job tasks can pull attention away from those distractions and channel people's attention to task accomplishment. When such concentration occurs, an employee is more focused on work at a given point in time. Of course, the relationship between satisfaction and task performance can work in reverse to some extent, such that people tend to enjoy jobs that they can perform more successfully.

Job satisfaction also is correlated moderately with citizenship behavior. Satisfied employees engage in more frequent "extra mile" behaviors to help their coworkers and their organization. Positive feelings increase their desire to interact with others and often result in spontaneous acts of helping because employees seek to behave in a manner that matches their current mood. In addition, job satisfaction has a moderate negative correlation with counterproductive behavior. Satisfied employees engage in fewer intentionally destructive actions that could harm their workplace. Intense dissatisfaction is often the trigger that prompts an employee to "lash out" by engaging in rule breaking, theft, sabotage, or other retaliatory behaviors. The more satisfied employees are, the less likely they will feel those sorts of temptations.

Job satisfaction influences organizational commitment. Why? Job satisfaction is strongly correlated with affective commitment, so satisfied employees are more likely to want to stay with the organization? After all, why would employees want to leave a place where they're happy? Another reason is that job satisfaction is strongly correlated with normative commitment. Satisfied employees are more likely to feel an obligation to remain with their firm and a need to "repay" the organization for whatever it is that makes them so satisfied, whether good pay, interesting job tasks, or effective supervision. However, job satisfaction is uncorrelated with continuance commitment because satisfaction does not create a cost-based need to remain with the organization. Still, when taken together, these commitment effects become more apparent when you consider the kinds of employees who withdraw from the organization. In many cases, dissatisfied employees are those who sit daydreaming at their desks, come in late, are frequently absent, and eventually decide to quit their jobs.

Of course, job satisfaction is important for other reasons as well—reasons that have little to do with job performance or organizational commitment. For example, job satisfaction is strongly related to life satisfaction, or the degree to which employees feel a sense of happiness with their lives. Research shows that job satisfaction is one of the strongest predictors of life satisfaction. Put simply, people feel better about their lives when they feel better about their jobs. This link makes sense when you realize how much of our identity is wrapped up in our jobs. What's the first question that people ask one another after being introduced? Often it is, "What do you do?" If you feel bad about your answer to that question, it's hard to feel good about your life.

As it turns out, increases in job satisfaction have a stronger impact on life satisfaction than do increases in salary or income. As the old adage goes, "money can't buy happiness." This finding may seem surprising, given that pay satisfaction is one facet of overall job satisfaction. However, you might recall that pay satisfaction is a weaker driver of overall job satisfaction than other facets, such as the work itself, supervision, or coworkers. We also should note that pay satisfaction depends less on absolute salary levels and more on relative salary levels (i. e., how your salary compares to your circle of peers). As the writer H. L. Mencken once remarked, "A wealthy man is one who earns $100 a year more than his wife's sister's husband." For more on the relationship between money and happiness, see our OB Internationally feature.

6.7 Takeaways

1. Job satisfaction is a pleasurable emotional state representing how you feel about your job and what you think about your job.

2. Values are things that people consciously or subconsciously want to seek or attain. According to value-percept theory, job satisfaction depends on whether you perceive that your job supplies those things that you value.

3. People often appraise their job satisfaction according to more specific facets of their job. These satisfaction facets include pay satisfaction, promotion satisfaction, supervision satisfaction, coworker satisfaction, and satisfaction with the work itself.

4. Job characteristics theory suggests that five "core characteristics"—variety, identity, significance, autonomy, and feedback—combine to result in particularly high levels of satisfaction with the work itself.

5. Apart from the influence of supervision, coworkers, pay, and the work itself, job satisfaction levels fluctuate during the day. Rises and falls in job satisfaction are triggered by experiences of positive and negative events. Those events trigger changes in emotions that eventually give way to changes in mood.

6. Moods are states of feeling that are often mild in intensity, last for an extended period of time, and are not explicitly directed at anything. Intense positive moods include being enthusiastic, excited, and elated, intense negative moods include being hostile, nervous, and annoyed. Emotions are states of feeling that are often intense, last only for a few minutes, and are clearly directed at someone or some circumstance. Positive emotions include joy, pride, relief, hope, love, and compassion. Negative emotions include anger, anxiety, fear, guilt, shame, sadness, envy, and disgust.

7. Job satisfaction has a moderately positive relationship with job performance and a strong positive relationship with organizational commitment. It also has a strong positive relationship with life satisfaction.

6.8 Discussion questions

1. Which of the values in Table 6 – 1 do you think are the most important to employees in general? Are there times when the values in the last three categories (altruism, status, and environment) become more important than the values in the first five categories (pay, promotions, supervision, coworkers, the work itself)?

2. What steps can organizations take to improve promotion satisfaction, supervision satisfaction, and coworker satisfaction?

3. Consider the five core job characteristics (variety, identity, significance, autonomy, and feedback). Do you think that any one of those characteristics is more important than the other four? Is it possible to have too much of some job characteristics?

4. We sometimes describe colleagues or friends as "moody". What do you think it means to be "moody" from the perspective of Figure 6 – 3?

Chapter 7 Stress

7.1 Define stress, stressors, and strains

Although you might want to believe that your stress will diminish after graduation, high stress on the job is more prevalent than it has ever been before. Table 7 – 1 enlists a series of job ranking from the least to the most stressful. Research indicates, in US, up to 40 percent of workers rate their jobs as "very stressful" or "extremely stressful". Of course, stress is also relevant from the organization's standpoint. Unfortunately, from a health care point of view, stress-related doctor visits are estimated to contribute a large section of between 60 and 90 percent to the total count. For those experience higher level of stress, they suffer around 50 percent more cost upon health care than their counterparts who experience less stress. Statistics from jobs in different industries indicate that the frequency of worker's compensation claims is dramatically higher when the level of stress on the job is high. As one example, the frequency of claims was more than 800 percent higher for a copy machine distributor when the level of stress at the job site was high. As you will learn in this chapter, stress has other implications for management of organizational behavior.

Table 7 – 1 Jobs Rated from Least Stressful (1) to Most Stressful (250)

Least Stressful Jobs	Stress Level	Most Stressful Jobs	Stress Level
1. Musical instrument repairer	18.77	212. Registered nurse	62.14
2. Florist	18.80	220. Attorney	64.33
4. Actuary	20.18	223. Newspaper reporter	65.26
6. Appliance repairer	21.12	226. Architect	66.92
8. Librarian	21.40	228. Lumberjack	67.60
10. File clerk	21.71	229. Fisherman	69.82
11. Piano tuner	22.29	230. Stockbroker	71.65
12. Janitor	22.44	231. U. S. congressperson	72.05
16. Vending machine repairer	23.47	233. Real estate agent	73.06
18. Barber	23.62	234. Advertising account exec	74.55
24. Mathematician	24.67	238. Public relations exec	78.52
29. Cashier	25.11	240. Air traffic controller	83.13
30. Dishwasher	25.32	241. Airline pilot	85.35
32. Pharmacist	25.87	243. Police officer	93.89

Table 7 – 1(continued)

Least Stressful Jobs	Stress Level	Most Stressful Jobs	Stress Level
40. Biologist	26.94	244. Astronaut	99.34
44. Computer programmer	27.00	245. Surgeon	99.46
50. Astronomer	28.06	246. Taxi driver	100.49
56. Historian	28.41	248. Senior corporate exec	108.62
67. Bank teller	30.12	249. Firefighter	110.93
78. Accountant	31.13	250. U. S. president	176.55

Source: Krantz L. Jobs Rated Almanac[M]. 6th ed. Fort Lee, NJ: Barricade Books, Inc., 2002.
The stress level score is calculated by summing points in 21 categories, including deadlines, competitiveness, environmental conditions, speed required, precision required, initiative required, physical demands, and hazards encountered.

When demands becomes something at stake for the individual, with which coping taxes or exceeds the individual's capacity or resources, the psychological response we termed as stress comes in. Stress involves both the demands or the stimulus triggering the response, termed as stressors, as well as the consequential undesirable psychological conditions, called strains. Henceforth, stress comes as an individual experience when it depends on both the nature of stressors and individual's coping mechanisms that leads to different levels of strains. We will first develop an understanding of the process of appraising or perceiving stressors.

Illustrated in Figure 7 – 1 the process of appraising stressors arrives in two stages. When people first encounter demands, the process of primary appraisal is triggered whereby people evaluate the significance and the meaning of the demands they are confronting. Here, individuals identify the stressors and consider the implications of the stressor in terms of their personal goals and overall wellbeing.

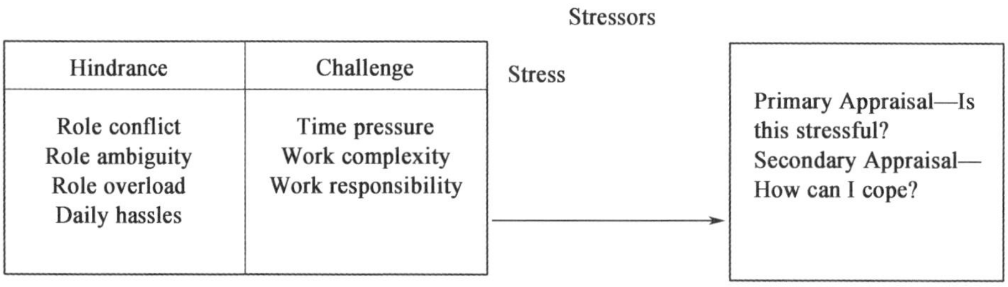

Figure 7 – 1 Stressors and their appraisal

As an example of a primary appraisal, consider the job of a cashier at a well-run convenience store. In this store, cashiers engage in routine sales transactions with customers. Under normal day-to-day circumstances at this store, a well-trained cashier would not likely feel that these transactions are overly taxing or exceeding his or her capacity. He/She encounters benign job demands under normal circumstances, since no particular stressors are identified.

If stressors do take place, how would cashiers perceive them and act accordingly? What would be the different scenarios that leads to stress response? Consider first how convenience store cashiers would react in a different store in which the cash register and credit card machine break down often and without warning. The cashiers who work at this store would likely view their job as more stressful because they would have to diagnose and fix problems with equipment while dealing with customers who are growing more and more impatient. Furthermore, the cashiers in this store might appraise the stressful situation as one that unnecessarily prevents them from achieving their goal of being viewed as an effective employee in the eyes of the customers and the store manager.

Finally, consider a third convenience store in which the cashier's workload is higher due to additional responsibilities that include receiving merchandise from vendors, taking physical inventor, and training new employees. In this store, the cashiers may appraise their jobs as stressful because of the higher workload and need to balance different priorities. However, in contrast to the cashiers in the previous example, cashiers in this store might appraise these demands as providing an opportunity to learn and demonstrate the type of competence that often is rewarded with satisfying promotions and pay raises.

7.2 Identify and describe the two main categories of stressors

In the previous two examples, the cashiers were confronted with demands that a primary appraisal would label as "stressful". However, research shows that the types of demands in the two examples have important differences. Dealing with equipment breakdowns or unhappy customers has little to no benefit to the employee in the long term. These kinds of stressors are called hindrance stressors—stressful demands that most people perceive as hindering progress toward personal accomplishments or goal attainment. Hindrance stressors tend to trigger negative emotions such as anger and anxiety. In contrast, managing additional responsibilities or higher workloads has a long-term benefit in that it helps build the employee's skills. These kinds of stressors are called challenge stressors—stressful demands that most people perceive as opportunities for learning, growth, and achievement. Although challenge stressors can be exhausting, they often trigger positive emotions and enhance motivation. As shown in Figure 7 – 1, there are several specific types of hindrance and challenge stressors.

7.2.1 Hindrance Stressors

Type one of the many hindrance stressors is role conflict, which refers to conflicting expectations that other people may have of us. For instance, call center operators are expected to contact people with efficiency to handle maximized number of calls, yet they should as well be responsive to any inquiries or concerns raised. Such dilemma creates the so-called roll conflict, resulting the operators to be put in an incompatible position where they are difficult to meet two distinct types of expectations.

Another case for role conflict to get into place is the discord between work role and family role. Role conflict may come about when demands of a work role hinder the fulfillment of the demands in a family role(or vice versa). When frustration at work overflows to family time, this "work to family conflict" interferes with successful switching between the two characters undertaken by the employee. "Family to work conflict" happens when perhaps marital conflicts cause someone to come to work harboring negative feelings that make it difficult to participate work effectively.

The second type of hindrance stressor, role ambiguity refers to the lack of information regarding what needs to be done in a role, as well as unpredictability regarding the consequences of performance in that role. With very few instructions or guidelines, employee may contemplate and hesitate with spending, duration, or the final desired outcomes of a project. This is especially frequent among new employees who lack experience of receiving comments from supervisors or observing role behaviors of senior colleagues, which might give them hard time before figuring out how to succeed. Role ambiguity is also the case for students, when lecturers stays vague about grading structures or learning outcomes.

Finally, hassles include having to deal with nuisances or penances such as unnecessary paperwork, office equipment malfunctions, conflict with abrasive coworkers, and useless communications. Although these examples of daily hassles may seem relatively minor, taken together, they can be extremely time consuming and stressful. According to survey, 40 percent of executives spend somewhere between a half day and a full day each week on communications that are not useful or necessary.

7.2.2 Challenge Stressors

One type of challenge stressor is time pressure—a strong sense that the amount of time you must do a task is just not quite enough. Although most people appraise situations with high time pressure as rather stressful, they also tend to appraise these situations as more challenging than hindering. People tend to strive to meet time pressure demands because success in meeting such demands can be rewarding and intrinsically satisfying. As an example of this positive effect of high time pressure, consider Michael Jones, an architect at a top New York firm. His job involves overseeing multiple projects with tight deadlines, and, as a result, he has to work at a hectic pace. Although Jones readily acknowledges that his job is stressful, he also believes that the outcome of having all the stress is satisfying. Jones can see the product of his labor over the Manhattan skyline, which makes him feel like he is a part of something.

Work complexity refers to the degree to which the requirements of the work, in terms of knowledge, skills, and abilities, tax or exceed the capabilities of the person who is responsible for performing the work. As an example of work complexity, consider the nature of employee development practices that organizations use to train future executives and organizational leaders. In many cases, these practices involve giving people jobs that require skills and knowledge that the people do not yet possess. A successful marketing manager who is being groomed for an executive-level position may, for example, be asked to manage a poorly performing production facility with poor labor relations in a country half-way around the world. Although these types of developmental experiences tend to be quite stressful, managers' report that being stretched beyond their capacity is well worth the associated discomfort.

Work responsibility refers to the nature of the obligations that a person has to others. Generally speaking, the level of responsibility in a job is higher when the number, scope, and importance of the obligations in that job are higher. As an example, consider the difference in responsibility levels of a grocery store manager compared with a grocery store bagger. Although the bagger is obligated to perform an important task—efficiently placing items in bags so as not to damage the items—the store manager is obligated to ensure that the store is profitable, the customers are satisfied, and the employees are happy and safe. As with people's reactions to time pressure and work complexity, people tend to evaluate demands associated with high responsibility as both stressful and potentially positive. For an example of exceptionally high work responsibility, see our OB on Screen feature.

7.2.3 Managing Stressors

One way that organizations try to manage stress is by managing the nature of the stressors that employees confront. The opening vignette illustrated how Best Buy accomplished this with the Results Only Work Environment. As another example of this approach to managing stress, 19 percent of organizations in one recent survey used job sharing to reduce role overload and foster work-life balance. Job sharing does not mean splitting one job into two, but, rather, two people sharing the responsibilities of a single job as if the two people were a single performing unit. The assumption underlying the practice is that "although businesses are becoming 24/7, people don't". You might be tempted to believe that job sharing would be most appropriate in lower-level jobs, where responsibilities and tasks are limited in number and relatively easy to divide. Job sharing is being used even at the highest levels in organizations. At Boston-based Fleet Bank, for example, two women shared the position of vice president for global markets and foreign exchange for six years until their department was dissolved when Fleet was acquired by Bank of America. During this time, they had one desk, one chair, one computer, one telephone, one voice-mail account, one set of goals, and one performance review. They each worked 20 ~ 25 hours a week and performed the role effectively and seamlessly.

7.3 Describe how individuals cope with stress

After people appraise a stressful demand, they ask themselves, "What should I do" and "What can I do" to deal with this situation? These questions, focusing on how people cope with the various stressors, reflect the secondary appraisal as depicted in Figure 7 – 1. Coping refers to the behaviors and thoughts that people use to manage both the stressful demands that they face, and the emotions associated with those stressful demands. Coping involves different types of activities that are grouped into four broad categories based on two dimensions. The first dimension refers to the method of coping(behavioral versus cognitive) ,and the second dimension refers to the focus of coping(problem solving versus regulation of emotions).

First, coping activities can be categorized on the basis of whether they involve behaviors or cognitions. Behavioral coping deal with stressful situation via a set of physical activities. In one example of behavioral coping, a person who is confronted with a lot of time pressure at work might chose to cope by working faster. In another example of behavioral coping, an employee who has several daily hassles might cope by avoiding work—coming in late, leaving early, or even staying home.

In contrast to behavioral coping, cognitive coping refers to the thoughts that are involved in trying to deal with a stressful situation. For example, the person who is confronted with an increase in time pressure might cope by strategizing alternative methods to approach work more efficiently. As another example, the employee who is confronted with daily hassles might try to convince him or herself that the hassles are not that bad after all.

Whereas the first dimension of coping involves defining the type of method, the second part refers to the focus of coping—that is, does the coping attempt to address the stressful demand itself or the emotions triggered by it? Problem-focused coping refers to behaviors and cognitions intended to manage the stressful situation itself. To understand problem-focused coping, consider how the people in the previous two paragraphs coped with time pressure. In the first example, the person attempted to address the time pressure by working harder, whereas in the second example, the person tried to identify a way to accomplish the work more efficiently. Although the specific coping methods differed, both people focused effort on meeting the demand rather than trying to avoid it.

In contrast to problem-focused coping, emotion-focused coping refers to the various ways in which people manage their own emotional reactions to stressful demands. The reactions to the daily hassles that we described previously illustrated two types of emotion-focused coping. In the first example, the employee used avoidance and distancing behaviors to reduce the emotional distress caused by the stressful situation. In the second example, the employee reappraised the demand to make it seem less stressful and threatening. Although people may be successful at changing the way different situations are construed to avoid feeling unpleasant emotions, the demand or problem that initially triggered the appraisal process remains.

It might be obvious to you by now that the choice of a coping strategy has important implications for how effectively people can meet or adapt to the different stressors they face. In the work context, for example, a manager would most likely want subordinates to cope with the stress of a heavy workload by using a problem-focused strategy—working harder—rather than an emotion-focused strategy—drinking two saki bombs at lunch to create distance from the stressor. Of course, there are some situations in which emotion-focused coping may be functional. As an example, consider a person who repeatedly fails to make it through the auditions for American Idol, despite years of voice lessons and countless hours of practice. If this person did not cope emotionally—perhaps by lowering her aspirations, or at least ignoring Simon Cowell's sarcastic barbs—this person's self-concept could be damaged, which could translate into reduced effectiveness in other roles that she fills. See our OB Internationally box to learn about the organizational implications of how expatriates cope with the stress of international assignments.

7.3.1 The Experience of Strain

Earlier in this chapter, we defined strains as the negative consequences associated with stress. How exactly does stress cause strain? Medical researchers who study stress have spent years examining the body's response to different sorts of stressful demands. Many of these findings have been summarized in a theory called the General Adaptation Syndrome(GAS). In a nutshell, GAS suggests that the body has a general set of responses that allow it to adapt and function effectively in the face of stressful demands. However, when stressful demands do not ramp down or demands occur too frequently, the body's adaptive responses become toxic, and this is what prompts strain.

Stages of the General Adaptation Syndrome. The first stage of the GAS is the alarm reaction. Upon being confronted with a stressor, there is a relatively brief period in which resistance to the stressor is temporarily lowered. At this point the body and mind haven't reacted yet—in essence, the stressor simply "sinks in" Immediately thereafter, the body activates defense mechanisms to resist the stressor. The body begins to secrete chemical compounds that cause increases in heart rate and blood pressure, and blood is redirected away from organs such as the spleen to the brain and skeletal muscles.

The changes that occur in the alarm stage prepare the mind and body for "fight or flight" After this point, the person is in the second stage of the GAS, the stage of resistance. Here, the increased arousal of his or her mind and body caused by the secretion of chemicals helps the person respond and adapt to the demand. Unfortunately, if the chemicals in the blood remain elevated because of prolonged or repeated exposure to the stressor, the body begins to break down, and exhaustion and even death may occur. This last stage is the stage of exhaustion. Although the GAS might sound like a theory that describes reactions to extreme types of stressors—being chased through a jungle by a hungry tiger, for example research suggests that most types of stressors evoke the same sequence of physiological events. As shown in Figure 7 - 2, those negative consequences of the stress process come in three varieties: physiological strains, psychological strains, and behavioral strains.

(1) Strains

Physiological strains that result from stressors occur in at least four systems of the human body. First, stressors can reduce the effectiveness of the body's immune system, which makes it more difficult for the body to ward off illness and infection. Second, stressors can harm the body's cardiovascular system, cause the heart to race, increase blood pressure, and create coronary artery disease. Third, stressors can cause problems in the body's musculoskeletal system. Tension headaches, tight shoulders, and back pain have all been linked to a variety of stressors. Fourth, stressors cause gastrointestinal system problems. Symptoms of this type of strain include stomachache, indigestion, diarrhea, and constipation.

Psychological strains that result from stressors include depression, anxiety, anger, hostility, reduced self-confidence, irritability, inability to think clearly, forgetfulness, lack of creativity, memory loss, and (not surprising, given the rest of this list) a loss of sense of humor.

These strains are likely to be a symptom of burnout, which refers to the emotional, mental, and physical exhaustion that results from having to cope with stressful demands on an ongoing basis. Our OB in Sports box describes how even the toughest people are susceptible to burnout.

Relative to physiological and psychological strains, behavioral strains are the least connected to GAS. In fact, unhealthy behaviors such as grinding one's teeth at night, being overly critical and bossy, excessive smoking, compulsive gum chewing, overuse of alcohol, and compulsive eating can be thought of as the behavioral symptoms of the other types of strains.

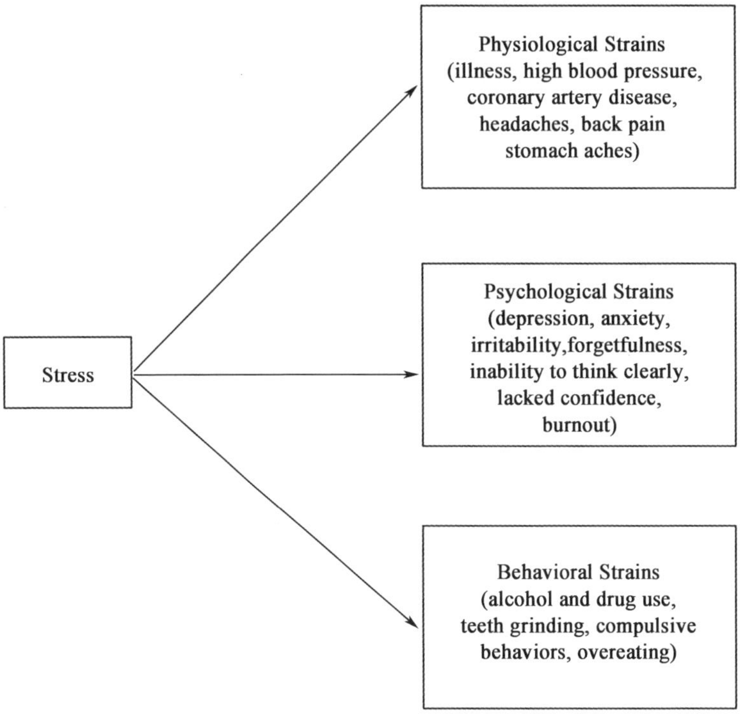

Figure 7 – 2 Examples of Strain

(2) Managing Employee Strain

Because strains are a natural consequence of jobs filled with stress, some organizations have instituted practices to help reduce them. One type of strain-reducing practice involves training in relaxation techniques such as progressive muscle relaxation, meditation, and miscellaneous calming activities like taking walks, writing in a journal, and deep breathing. Although these relaxation techniques differ, the basic idea is the same—they teach people how to counteract the effects of strain by engaging in activities that slow the heart rate, breathing rate, and blood pressure? As an example of a relatively simple relaxation technique, consider the recommendation of Herbert Benson, a physician and president of the Mind/Body Medical Institute in Boston. He suggests that people under stress should repeat a word, sound, prayer, phrase, or motion for 10 ~ 20 minutes once or twice a day and, during that time, try to completely ignore other thoughts that may come to mind.

A second category of strain-reducing practices involves training in cognitive-behavioral techniques. In general, these techniques attempt to help people appraise and cope with stressors in a more rational manner. To understand what these techniques involve, think of someone you know who not only exaggerates the level and importance of stressful demands but also predicts doom and disaster after quickly concluding that the demands simply cannot be met. If you know someone like this, you might recommend cognitive-behavioral training that involves "self-talk" a technique in which people learn to say things about stressful demands that reflect rationality and optimism. So, when confronted with a stressful demand, this person might be trained to say, "This demand isn't so tough; if I work hard I can accomplish it." In addition, cognitive-behavioral training typically involves instruction about tools that foster effective coping. So, in addition to the self-talk, the person might be trained on how to prioritize demands, manage time, communicate needs, and seek support.

A third category of strain-reducing practices involves health and wellness programs. For example, almost three-quarters of the organizations in one survey reported having employee assistance programs intended to help people with personal problems such as alcoholism and other addictions. More than 60 percent of organizations in this survey provided employees with wellness programs and resources. The nature of these programs and their resources vary a great deal from organization to organization, but, in general, they are comprehensive efforts that include health screening (blood pressure, cholesterol levels, pulmonary functioning) and health-related courses and information. Other examples of health and well-ness programs intended to reduce strain include smoking cessation programs, on-site fitness centers or fitness center memberships, and weight loss and nutrition programs.

7.4 Describe how the Type A Behavior Pattern influences the stress process

So far in this chapter, we've discussed how the typical or average person reacts to different sorts of stressors. Of course, people differ in terms of how they typically react to stressful demands. One way that people differ in their reaction to stress depends on whether they exhibit the Type A Behavior Pattern. "Type A" people have a strong sense of time urgency and tend to be impatient, hard-driving, competitive, controlling, aggressive, and even hostile. If you walk, talk, and eat at a quick pace, and if you find yourself constantly annoyed with people who do things too slowly, chances are that you're a Type A person.

The Type A Behavior Pattern is important because it can influence each variable in our general model of stress. First, the "Type A" Behavior Pattern may have a direct influence on the level of stressors that a person confronts. To understand why this connection might be true, consider that Type A persons tend to be hard-driving and have a strong desire to achieve. Because the behaviors that reflect these tendencies are valued by the organization, Type A individuals receive "rewards" in the form of increases in the amount and level of work required. Second, the Type A Behavior Pattern influences the appraisal process, in essence, Type A individuals are simply more likely to appraise demands as being stressful rather than being benign. Third, and perhaps most important, the Type A Behavior Pattern has been directly linked to coronary heart disease and other physiological, psychological, and behavioral strains. The size of the relationship between the Type A Behavior Pattern and these strains is not so strong as to suggest that if you're a Type A person, you should immediately dial 911. However, the linkage is strong enough to suggest that the risk of these problems is significantly higher for Type A people.

7.5 Describe how social support influences the stress process

Another individual factor that affects the way people manage stress is the degree of social support that they receive from supervisors, peers, friends, and family members. Social support refers to the help that people receive when they are confronted with stressful demands, and there are at least two major types. One type of social support is called instrumental support, which refers to the assistance people receive that can be used to address the stressful demand directly. For example, if a person is overloaded with work, a coworker could provide instrumental support by taking over some of the work or offering suggestions about how to do the work more efficiently. A second type of social support is called emotional support. This type of support refers to the help people receive in addressing the emotional distress that accompanies stressful demands. As an example, the supervisor of the individual who is overloaded with work might provide emotional support by showing interest in the employee's situation and appearing to be understanding and empathetic.

Most research on social support focuses on the ways that social support buffers the relationship between stressors and strains. According to this research, higher levels of social support provide a person with instrumental or emotional resources that are useful for coping with the stressor, which tends to reduce the harmful consequences of the stressor to that individual. With lower levels of social support, the person does not have extra coping resources available, so the stressor tends to have effects that are more harmful. Although not every research study has found support for the buffering effect of social support, the majority of research evidence has been supportive.

7.6 Describe the effects that stress has on job performance and organizational commitment?

At this point, you're probably curious about how stress impacts job performance and organizational commitment, the two outcomes in our integrative model of OB. However, describing the impact of stress is somewhat complicated because there are so many variables involved in the stress process. So, to simplify things a bit, we focus our discussion on effects that strains have. Strains have a moderately negative effect on job performance. A general explanation for this negative relationship between strains and job performance is that strains reduce the overall level of energy and attention that people could otherwise bring to their job duties. Certainly, it is easy to appreciate that physiological, psychological, and behavioral strains in the form of illnesses, exhaustion, and drunkenness detract from employee effectiveness in almost any job context.

Strains also have a strong negative effect on organizational commitment. Why might this be? Well, strains are generally dissatisfying to people, and, as we discussed in the previous chapter, satisfaction has a strong impact on the degree to which people feel committed to their organization. People who work at jobs that they know are causing them to feel constantly sick and exhausted will likely be dissatisfied with their jobs and feel less desire to stay with the organization and more desire to consider alternatives.

So in this discussion, we portray stress as something that has a negative impact on both job performance and organizational commitment. But this is not quite the whole story. In fact, though all types of stressors are positively associated with strains, certain types of stressors have positive relationships with performance and commitment. But how can that be? To understand this somewhat counterintuitive pattern of relationships, recall from our previous discussions that challenge stressors such as time pressure and responsibility tend to evoke positive emotions, and that when people are confronted with challenge stressors, they tend to deal with them using problem-focused coping strategies. The net benefits of those positive emotions and coping strategies tend to outweigh the costs of the added strain, and the result is that challenge stressors tend to have positive relationships with performance and commitment. These positive effects of challenge stressors on performance and commitment have been demonstrated for executives, employees in lower-level jobs, and, as our OB for students feature illustrates, students as well.

7.7 Takeaways

1. Stress refers to the psychological response to demands when there is something at stake for the individual and when coping with these demands would tax or exceed the individual's capacity or resources. Stressors are the demands that cause the stress response, and strains are the negative consequences of the stress response.

2. Stressors come in two general forms: challenge stressors, which are perceived as

opportunities for growth and achievement, and hindrance stressors, which are perceived as hurdles to goal achievement.

3. Coping with stress involves thoughts and behaviors that address one of two goals: addressing the stressful demand or decreasing the emotional discomfort associated with the demand.

4. Individual differences in the Type A Behavior Pattern affect the stress process in three ways. Type A people tend to experience more stressors, appraise more demands as stressful, and experience more strains.

5. Individual differences in social support influence the strength of the stress-strain relationship such that support acts as a buffer that prevents the onset of strain.

6. Although the body tries to adapt to different sorts of stressors along the lines of what is described by the General Adaptation Syndrome (GAS), overtime, this adaptive response wears out the body, and exhaustion and collapse may occur. The resulting strain has a moderate negative relationship with job performance and a strong negative relationship with organizational commitment.

7.8 Discussion questions

1. Prior to reading this chapter, how did you define stress? Did your definition of stress reflect stressors, the stress process, strains, or some combination?

2. Describe your dream job and then provide a list of the types of stressors that you would expect to be present. Is the list dominated by challenge stressors or hindrance stressors? Why do you think this is?

3. Think about the dream job that you described in the previous question. How much of your salary, if any at all, would you give up to eliminate the most important hindrance stressors? Why?

4. If you had several job offers after graduating, to what degree would the level of challenge stressors in the different jobs influence your choice of which job to take? Why?

5. How would you assess your ability to handle stress? Given the information provided in this chapter, what could you do to improve your effectiveness in this area?

6. If you managed people in an organization in which there were lots of hindrance stressors, what actions would you take to help ensure that your employees coped with the stressors using a problem-focused as opposed to an emotion-focused coping strategy?

Chapter 8 Trust, Justice and Ethics

8.1 Define trust and describe how it relates to justice and ethics

Trust is defined as the willingness to be vulnerable to an authority based on positive expectations about the authority's actions and intentions. When we trust, we become willing to "put ourselves out there", even though that choice could be met with disappointment. This definition can be used to highlight the important distinction between "trust" and "risk", Actually making oneself vulnerable to an authority is a risk; trust reflects the willingness to take that risk. This definition also illustrates where trust comes from, as it is based on an assessment of how a given authority is likely to behave in a particular situation.

Who is the authority referenced in the trust definition? Sometimes that authority is person-based, as when a specific soft drink company CEO is trusted to be honest about a product's ingredients. Sometimes that authority is organization-based, as when you trust that the soft-drink company as a whole will treat your cousin fairly if he accepts a job. Because we don't usually have direct knowledge about the company as a whole, an organization-based version of trust depends largely on a company's reputation.

Issues of trust are intertwined with two related concepts. Justice reflects the perceived fairness of an authority's decision making. When employees perceive high levels of justice, they believe that decision outcomes are fair and that decision-making processes are designed and implemented in a fair manner. Justice concepts can be used to explain why employees judge some authorities as more trustworthy than others. Ethics reflects the degree to which the behaviors of an authority are in accordance with generally accepted moral norms. When employees perceive high levels of ethics, they believe that things are being done the way they "should be" or "ought to be" done. Ethics concepts can be used to explain why authorities decide to act in a trustworthy or untrustworthy manner.

Think about a particular boss or instructor—one whom you've spent a significant amount of time around. Do you trust that person? Would you be willing to let that person have significant influence over your professional or educational future? For example, would you be willing to let that person serve as a reference for you or write you a letter of recommendation, even though you'd have no way of monitoring what he or she said about you? When you think about the level of trust you feel for that particular authority, what exactly makes you feel that way? This question speaks to the factors that drive trust—the factors that help inspire a willingness to be vulnerable.

8.2 Understand the three sources in which trust can be rooted

As shown in Figure 8 - 1, trust is rooted in different kinds of factors. Sometimes trust is disposition-based, meaning that your personality traits include a general propensity to trust others. Sometimes trust is cognition-based, meaning that it is rooted in a rational assessment of the authority's trustworthiness. Sometimes trust is affect-based, meaning that it depends on feelings toward the authority that go beyond any rational assessment. The sections that follow describe each of these trust forms in more detail.

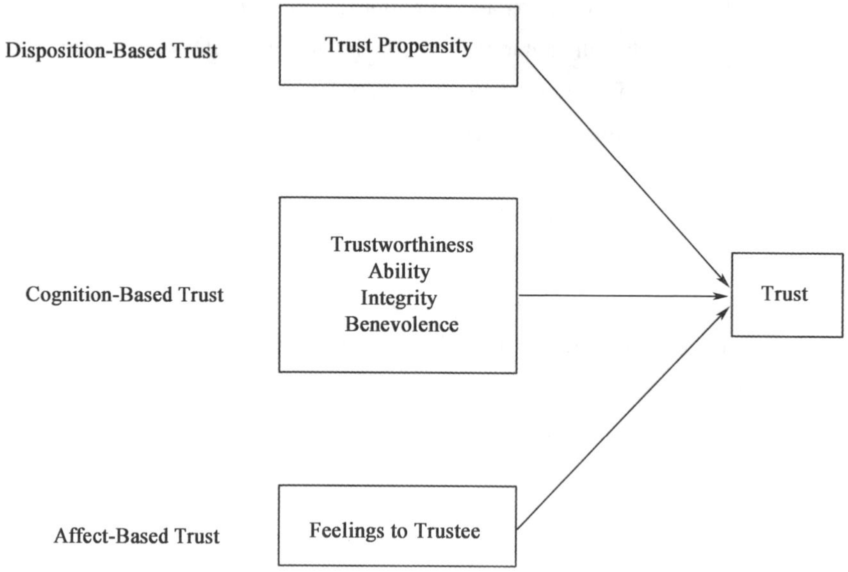

Figure 8 - 1 Factors Than Influence Trust Levels

Disposition-based Trust has less to do with the authority and more to do with the trustor. Some trustors are high in trust propensity—a general expectation that the words, promises, and statements of individuals and groups can be relied upon. Some have argued that trust propensity represents a sort of "faith in human nature", in that trusting people view others in more favorable terms than do suspicious people. The importance of trust propensity is most obvious in interactions with strangers, in which any acceptance of vulnerability would amount to "blind trust". On the one hand, people who are high in trust propensity may be fooled into trusting others who are not worthy of it. On the other hand, those who are low in trust propensity may be fooled by not trusting someone who is actually deserving of it. Both situations can be damaging. As one scholar noted, "We are doomed if we trust all and equally doomed if we trust none."

Where does our trust propensity come from? As with all traits, trust propensity is a product of both nature and nurture. If our parents are dispositionally suspicious, we may either inherit that tendency genetically or model it as we watch them exhibit distrust in their day-to-day lives. Research also suggests that trust propensity is shaped by early childhood experiences. In fact, trust propensity may be one of the first personality traits to develop because infants must immediately learn to trust their parents to meet their needs. The more our needs are met as children, the more trusting we may become; the more we are disappointed as children, the less trusting we may become. Our propensities continue to be shaped later in life as we gain experiences with friends, schools, churches, local government authorities, and other relevant groups.

The nation in which we live also affects our trust propensity. Research by the World Values Study Group examines differences between nations on various attitudes and perceptions. The study group collects interview data from 45 different societies with a total sample size of more than 90, 000 participants. One of the questions asked by the study group measures trust propensity. Specifically, participants are asked, "Generally speaking, would you say that most people can be trusted or that you can't be too careful in dealing with people?" The results reveal that trust propensity levels are relatively high in the United States, especially in relation to countries in Europe and South America. In fact, the nation with lowest percentage of people agreeing that "most people can be trusted" is Brazil.

8.3 Describe the dimensions that can be used to describe how trust-worthy an authority is

8.3.1 Cognition-Based Trust

Disposition-based trust guides us in cases when we don't yet have data about a particular authority. However, eventually we gain enough knowledge to gauge the authority's trustworthiness, defined as the characteristics or attributes of a trustee that inspire trust. At that point, our trust begins to be based on cognitions we've developed about the authority, as opposed to our own personality or disposition. In this way, cognition-based trust is driven by the authority's "track record". If that track record has shown the authority to be trustworthy, then vulnerability to the authority can be accepted. If that track record is spotty, however, then trust may not be warranted. Research suggests that we gauge the track record of an authority along three dimensions: ability, integrity, and benevolence.

The first dimension of trustworthiness is ability, defined as the skills, competencies, and areas of expertise that enable an authority to be successful in some specific area (see Chapter 3 on Personality, Cultural Values, and Ability for ore discussion of ability). Think about the decision-making process that you go through when choosing a doctor, lawyer, or mechanic. Clearly one of the first things you consider is ability because you're not going to trust them if they don't know a scalpel from a retractor, a tort from a writ, or a camshaft from a crankshaft. Of course, listing a specific area is a key component of the ability definition; you wouldn't trust a mechanic to perform surgery, nor would you trust a doctor to fix your car! The ability of business authorities may be considered on a number of levels. For example, a manager may be judged according to the functional expertise of a particular industry or vocation but also according to his or her leadership skills and general business sense.

The second dimension of trustworthiness is integrity, defined as the perception that the authority adheres to a set of values and principles that the trustor finds acceptable. When authorities are perceived to have integrity, it means that they have good character—that they have honest motives and intentions. Integrity also conveys an alignment between words and deeds—a sense that authorities keep their promises, "walk the talk" and "do what they say they will do". Unfortunately, a recent survey indicated that only around 20 percent of American workers view senior managers as acting in accordance with their words. The series of high-profile scandals at companies like Enron, World Com, and Tyco can be viewed as examples of the costs of low integrity. In those cases, top management hid debt, misstated earnings, and used profits for personal gain—all of which constituted dishonest actions that went against the espoused values and principles of those companies.

The third dimension of trustworthiness is benevolence, defined as the belief that the authority wants to do good for the trustor, apart from any selfish or profit-centered motives. When authorities are perceived as benevolent, it means that they care for employees, are concerned about their well-being, and feel a sense of loyalty to them. The mentor-protege relationship provides a good example of benevolence at work. The best mentors would never do anything to hurt their proteges. They go out of their way to be helpful, even at the cost of their own personal productivity and in the absence of any financial reward. Clearly benevolence, along with ability and integrity, provides a set of good reasons to trust a particular authority.

8.3.2 Affect-Based Trust

Although ability, integrity, and benevolence provide three good reasons to trust an authority, the third form of trust isn't really rooted in reason at all. Affect-based trust is more emotional than rational. With affect-based trust, we trust because we have feelings for the person in question; we really like them and have a fondness for them. Those feelings are what prompt us to accept vulnerability to another person. Put simply, we trust them because we like them.

Affect-based trust acts as a supplement to the types of trust discussed previously—the various forms of trust can build on one another over time. In new relationships, trust depends solely on our own trust propensity. In most relationships, that propensity eventually gets supplemented by knowledge about ability, integrity, or benevolence, at which point cognition-based trust develops. In a select few of those relationships, an emotional bond develops, and our feelings for the trustee further increase our willingness to accept vulnerability. These relationships are characterized by a mutual investment of time and energy, a sense of deep attachment, and the realization that both parties would feel a sense of loss if the relationship were dissolved.

8.3.3 Summary

Taken together, disposition-based trust, cognition-based trust, and affect-based trust provide three completely different sources of trust in a particular authority. In the case of disposition-based trust, our willingness to be vulnerable has little to do with the authority and more to do with our genes and our early life experiences. In the case of affect-based trust, our willingness to be vulnerable has little to do with a rational assessment of the authority's merits and more to do with our emotional fondness for the authority. Only in the case of cognition-based trust do we rationally evaluate the pluses and minuses of an authority, in terms of ability, integrity, and benevolence. But how exactly do we gauge those trustworthiness forms? One way is to consider whether authorities adhere to rules of justice.

8.4 Understand the four dimensions that can be used to evaluate the fairness of an authority's decision making

8.4.1 Justice

It's often difficult to assess the ability, integrity, and benevolence of authorities accurately, particularly early in a working relation ship. What employees need in such circumstances is some sort of observable behavioral evidence that an authority might be trust-worthy. Justice provides that sort of behavioral evidence because authorities who treat employees more fairly are usually judged to be more trustworthy. As shown in Table 8 – 1, employees can judge the fairness of an authority's decision making along four dimensions: distributive justice, procedural justice, interpersonal justice, and informational justice.

Table 8 – 1 The Four Dimensions of Justice

Distributive Justice Rules	Description
Equity vs. equality vs. need	Are rewards allocated to the proper forms?
Procedural Justice Rules	
Voice	Do employees get to provide input into procedures?
Correctability	Do procedures build in mechanisms for appeals?
Consistency	Are procedures consistent across people and time?
Bias suppression	Are procedures neutral and unbiased?

Table 8 – 1(continued)

Distributive Justice Rules	Description
Representativeness	Do procedures consider the needs of all groups?
Accuracy	Are procedures based on accurate information?
Interpersonal Justice Rules	
Respect	Do authorities treat employees with sincerity?
Propriety	Do authorities refrain from improper remarks?
Informational Justice Rules	
Justification	Do authorities explain procedures thoroughly?
Truthfulness	Are those explanations honest?

(1) Distributive Justice

Distributive justice reflects the perceived fairness of decision-making outcomes. Employees gauge distributive justice by asking whether decision outcomes such as pay, rewards, evaluations, promotions, and work assignments are allocated using proper norms. In most business situations, the proper norm is equity, with more outcomes allocated to those who contribute more inputs (see Chapter 4 on Motivation for more discussion of equity). The equity norm is typically judged to be the fairest choice in situations in which the goal is to maximize the productivity of individual employees.

However, other allocation norms become appropriate in situations in which other goals are critical. In team-based work, building harmony and solidarity in work groups can become just as important as individual productivity. In such cases, an equality norm may be judged fairer, such that all team members receive the same amount of relevant rewards. The equality norm is typically used in student project groups, in which all group members receive the same grade on a project, regardless of their individual productivity levels. In cases in which the welfare of a particular employee is the critical concern, a need norm may be judged fairer. For example, PricewaterhouseCoopers, the New York-based accounting firm, wired $4,000 to 43 employees who were affected by Hurricane Katrina. The company also gave those employees food, lodging, and transportation for a three-month period.

(2) Procedural Justice

In addition to judging the fairness of a decision outcome, employees may consider the process that led to that outcome. Procedural justice reflects the perceived fairness of decision-making processes. Procedural justice is fostered when authorities adhere to rules of fair process. One of those rules is voice, which concerns giving employees a chance to express their opinions and views during decision making. A related rule is correctability, which provides employees with a chance to request an appeal when a procedure seems to have worked ineffectively. Research suggests that voice improves employees' reactions to decisions, largely because it gives employees a sense of ownership over the decisions that occur at work. In fact, employees value voice even when it doesn't always result in the outcomes they want or when their appeals don't always reverse the decisions that were made. Why? Because employees like to be heard—the expression of opinions is a valued end, in and of itself, if employees feel those opinions were truly considered.

Aside from voice and correctability, procedural justice is fostered when authorities adhere to four rules that serve to create equal employment opportunity. The consistency, bias suppression, representativeness, and accuracy rules help ensure that procedures are neutral and objective, as opposed to biased and discriminatory. These sorts of procedural rules are relevant in many areas of working life. As one example, the rules can be used to make hiring practices fairer by ensuring that interview questions are unbiased and asked in the same manner across applications. As another example, the rules can be used to make compensation practices fairer by ensuring that accurate measures of job performance are used to provide input for merit raises.

You might be wondering, "Does procedural justice really matter—don't people just care about the outcomes that they receive?" If an employee receives favorable pay, rewards, evaluations, promotions, and work assignments, does he or she really care about the process? Research suggests that distributive justice and procedural justice combine to influence employee reactions. It's true that when outcomes are good, people don't spend as much it me worrying about how fair the process was. In other words, procedural justice has little impact on reactions when distributive justice is high. However, when outcomes are bad, procedural justice becomes enormously important. Research shows that negative or unexpected events trigger a thorough examination of process issues, making adherence to rules like consistency, bias suppression, and accuracy much more vital.

In fact, research shows that procedural justice tends to be a stronger driver of reactions to authorities than distributive justice. For example, a meta-analysis of 183 studies showed that procedural justice was a stronger predictor of satisfaction with supervision, overall job satisfaction, and organizational commitment than distributive justice. Why does the decision-making process sometimes matter more than the decision-making outcome? Likely because employees understand that outcomes come and go—some may be in your favor while others may be a bit disappointing. Procedures, however, are more long-lasting and stay in place until the organization redesigns them or a new leader arrives to revise them.

(3) Interpersonal Justice

In addition to judging the fairness of decision outcomes and processes, employees might consider how authorities treat them as the procedures are implemented. Interpersonal justice reflects the perceived fairness of the treatment received by employees from authorities. Interpersonal justice is fostered when authorities adhere to two rules. The respect rule pertains to whether authorities treat employees in a dignified and sincere manner, and the propriety rule reflects whether authorities refrain from making improper or offensive remarks. From this perspective, interpersonal injustice occurs when authorities bad-mouth employees; criticize, berate, embarrass, or humiliate them in public; or refer to them with racist or sexist labels.

How common are instances of interpersonal injustice? A survey of nearly 5,000 employees found that 36 percent reported persistent hostility from authorities and coworkers, when persistent hostility was defined as experiencing one abusive act at least weekly for a period of one year. How damaging are such acts? One study asked 41 employees to complete a survey on interactions with authorities and coworkers four times a day for 2 to 3 weeks using a palmtop computer. Two kinds of interactions were coded—positive experiences and negative experiences—and participants also reported on their current mood(e. g., happy, pleased, sad, blue, unhappy). The results of the study showed that positive interactions were more common than negative interactions, but the effects of negative interactions on mood were five times stronger than the effects of positive interactions. Such findings suggest that violations of the respect and propriety rules loom much larger than adherence to such rules. Indeed, research indicates that violations of interpersonal justice rules reduce employees' job satisfaction, life satisfaction, and organizational commitment while increasing feelings of depression, anxiety, and burnout.

(4) Informational Justice

Finally, employees may consider the kind of information that authorities provide during the course of organizational decision making. Informational justice reflects the perceived fairness of the communications provided to employees from authorities. Informational justice is fostered when authorities adhere to two rules. The justification rule mandates that authorities explain decision-making procedures and outcomes in a comprehensive and reasonable manner, and the truthfulness rule requires that those communications be honest and candid. Although it seems like common sense that organizations would explain decisions in a comprehensive and adequate manner, that's often not the case. For example, RadioShack, the Texas-based home electronics retailer, was recently criticized for firing 400 employees via e-mail. Employees at the Fort Worth headquarters received messages on a Tuesday morning saying: "The work force reduction notification is currently in progress. Unfortunately, your position is one that has been eliminated." After receiving the 18-word message, employees had 30 minutes to make phone calls and say goodbye to fellow employees before packing up their belongings in boxes and plastic bags.

These sorts of informational injustices are all too common, for a variety of reasons. One reason is that sharing bad news is the worst part of the job for many managers, leading them to distance themselves when it's time to play messenger. Another reason is that managers worry about triggering a lawsuit if they comprehensively and honestly explain the real reasons for a layoff, a poor evaluation, or a missed promotion. Ironically, that defense mechanism is typically counterproductive because research suggests that honest and adequate explanations are a powerful strategy for reducing retaliation responses against the organization. In fact, low levels of informational justice can come back to haunt the organization if a wrongful termination claim is filed. How? Because the organization typically needs to provide performance evaluations for the terminated employee over the past few years to show that the employee was fired for poor performance, if managers refrained from offering candid and honest explanations on those evaluations, then the organization can't offer anything to justify the termination.

One study provides a particularly effective demonstration of the power of informational justice (and interpersonal justice). The study occurred in three plants of a Midwestern manufacturing company that specialized in small mechanical parts for the aerospace and automotive industries, the company had recently lost two of its largest contracts and was forced to cut wages by 15 percent in two of the three plants. The company was planning to offer a short, impersonal explanation for the pay cut to both affected plants. However, as part of a research study, the company was convinced to offer a longer, more sincere explanation at one of the plants. Theft levels were then tracked before, during, and after the 10-week pay cut using the company's standard accounting formulas for inventory "shrinkage".

The informational (and interpersonal) justice articulated through the company's two types of explanation of pay cut, draw different impacts on employee theft rate. In the plant without the pay cut, no change in theft levels occurred over the 10-week period. In the plant with the short, impersonal explanation, theft rose dramatically during the pay cut, likely as a means of retaliating for perceived inequity, before falling to previous levels once the cut had passed. Importantly, in the plant with the long, sincere explanation, the rise in theft was much less significant during the pay cut, with theft levels again falling back to normal levels once the cut had ended. Clearly, the higher levels of informational and interpersonal justice were worth it from a cost-savings perspective. The difference in theft across the two plants is remarkable, given that the long, sincere explanation was only 143 words longer than the short, impersonal explanation. What's an extra 45 seconds if it can save a few thousand dollars?

(5) Summary

Taken together, distributive, procedural, interpersonal, and informational justice can be used to describe how fairly employees are treated by authorities. When an authority adheres to the justice rules in Table 6 – 1, it provides behavioral data that the authority might be trustworthy. Studies show that all four justice forms have strong correlations with trust levels. All else being equal, employees trust authorities who allocate outcomes fairly; make decisions in a consistent, unbiased, and accurate way; and communicate decision-making details in a respectful, comprehensive, and honest manner. Which authorities are most likely to adhere to these sorts of rules? Research on ethics can provide some answers.

8.4.2 Ethics

Research on ethics seeks to explain why people behave in a manner consistent with generally accepted norms of morality, and why they sometimes violate those norms? Some ethics studies focus on behaviors that exceed minimum standards of morality, such as charitable giving or whistle blowing, which occurs when employees expose illegal actions by their employer. Other studies focus on behaviors that fall below minimum standards of morality, such as lying and cheating. Still other studies focus on behaviors that merely reach minimum standards of morality, such as obeying the law. Regardless of the area of focus, such research continues to be a critical area of OB because unethical acts are so common in organizations. For example, recent surveys suggest that 76 percent of employees have observed illegal or unethical conduct on the job within the past 12 months in the US.

How can we explain exactly why an authority would choose to act in an unethical manner? One set of answers can be derived from research in social psychology. As shown in Figure 8 - 2, the four-component model of ethical decision making argues that ethical behaviors result from a multistage sequence beginning with moral awareness, continuing on to moral judgment, and then moral intent and ethical behavior. The sections that follow review the components of this model in more detail.

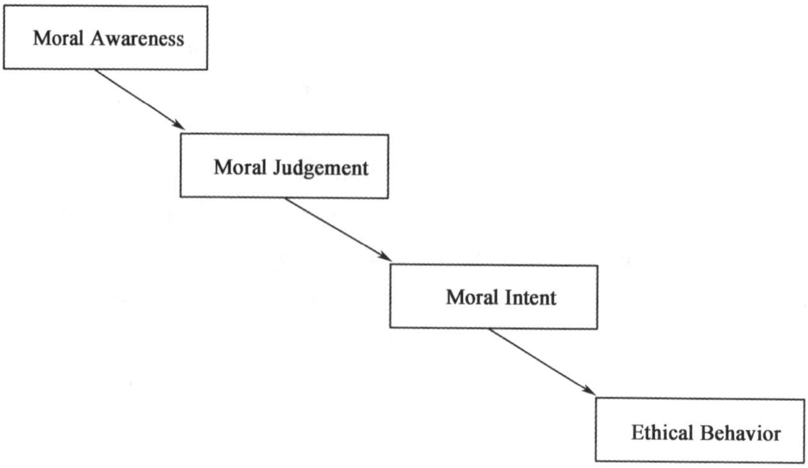

Figure 8 - 2 The Four-Component Model of Ethical Decision Making

8.5 Understand the four-component model of ethical decision making

8.5.1 Moral Awareness

The first step needed to explain why an authority acts ethically is moral awareness, which occurs when an authority recognizes that a moral issue exists in a situation or that an ethical standard or principle is relevant to the circumstance. Ethical issues rarely come equipped with "red flags" that mark them as morally sensitive—something is needed to make moral standards salient. As an example, assume you worked for a videogame company whose most popular game involves assuming the role of a criminal in a big city and taking part in multiple story lines involving a variety of illegal activities, such as car jacking, bank robbery, assassination, and the killing of law enforcement personnel and innocent bystanders. A member of this game's development team has suggested embedding hidden sex scenes into the game, which is currently rated "mature" by the Entertainment Software Rating Board.

Is there an ethical issue at play here? On the one hand, you might be tempted to say that the game is already rated "mature" and that such hidden scenes are only extending the already less-than-wholesome nature of the game. Besides, "Easter eggs"—hidden objects in movies, DVDs, or computer and video games—have a long history in the entertainment industry. On the other hand, the hidden scenes constitute deception of the rating board, the customer, and potentially the customer's parents. And that deception issue stands apart from any moral issues raised by the actual content of the hidden scenes. If this story sounds familiar to you, it's because it actually happened with Grand Theft Auto: San Andreas, a game manufactured by a division of Take Two Interactive Software. The hidden scenes, which began with the invitation, "How about some coffee?" could be accessed using software available on the Internet. Take Two contends that the code for the scenes was put into early drafts of the game but was supposed to be removed before the game went to market.

Moral awareness depends in part on the characteristics of the authority involved. An authority's ethical sensitivity reflects the ability to recognize that a particular decision has ethical content. Ethical sensitivity can be measured by giving people a business case to read that includes a few somewhat subtle ethical issues, along with a number of other sorts of issues (work sequencing challenges, organizing challenges, specific technical issues). Participants describe the issues that are raised in the case in an open-ended fashion, with ethical sensitivity captured by the number of ethical issues spotted within the case. In the Take Two example, it may be that the employees in charge of the Grand Theft Auto game weren't sensitive enough to recognize that the hidden scenes represented an ethical issue. That premise makes some sense, given that Take Two has had other ethical struggles, including having to settle charges of fraudulent accounting with the Securities and Exchange Commission.

Moral awareness also depends on the characteristics of the issue itself. Moral intensity captures the degree to which the issue has ethical urgency. Moral intensity is driven by six facets, summarized in Table 8 – 2. A particular issue is high in moral intensity if the magnitude of its consequences are high, there is strong social consensus about the act, the probability of the act occurring and having the predicted consequences is high, those consequences will occur soon, the decision makers are close to those who will be affected, and the consequences are not concentrated on a select few. In the case of the Grand Theft Auto hidden scenes, it may be that Take Two felt that the consequences of the act would be minor, the scenes might not be discovered, or the people who would be adversely affected are very different in a psychological sense.

Table 8 – 2 The Six Facets of Moral Intensity

Facet	Description
Magnitude of consequences	How much harm (or benefit) would be done to other people
Social consensus	How much agreement is there that the proposed act would be evil (or good)?
Probability of effect	How likely is that the act will actually occur and that the assumed consequences will match the predictors?

Table 8 – 2(续)

Facet	Description
Temporal immediacy	How much in time will pass between the act and the onset of its consequences?
Proximity	How near(in a psychological or physical sense) is the authority to those who will be affected?
Concentration of effect	Will the consequences be concentrated on a limited set of people, or will they be more far reaching?

8.5.2 Moral Judgment

Assuming an authority recognizes that a moral issue exists in a situation, the next step is moral judgment, which is when the authority accurately identifies the morally "right" course of action. What factors affect moral judgment? One factor is moral development, as described by Kohlberg's theory of cognitive moral development. This theory argues that as people age and mature, they move through several stages of moral development—each more mature and sophisticated than the prior one. These stages are shown in Figure 8 – 3. Research suggests that most children are at the preconventional level, so their actions are motivated by the avoidance of punishment (Stage 1) and the maintenance of "You scratch my back, I'll scratch yours" sorts of relationships (Stage 2). Most adults, in contrast, are at the conventional level, with their ethical thinking influenced by the opinions of relevant authorities (Stage 3), along with more formal rules and standards (Stage 4). That positioning is relevant for organizations because it suggests that the ethical decisions of employees can be influenced by organizational norms, practices, and reward systems.

Research suggests that fewer than 20 percent of Americans reach the principled (sometimes called "post-conventional") level. The principles those individuals utilize during ethical decision making are called ethical ideologies. Those in Stage 5 may be more likely to adopt a relativism ideology and reject the notion of universal moral rules. Relativists agree with statements like, "Whether a lie is judged to be moral or immoral depends upon the circumstances surrounding the decision." Such people also may be more likely to adopt a utilitarianism ideology in which ethical actions are defined as those that achieve the most valuable ends. When asked to describe the character traits that are most important to them, utilitarians prioritize traits such as "resourceful", "effective" "productive" and "winner". In contrast, those in Stage 6 should be more likely to adopt an idealism ideology and embrace the notion of universal moral rules. Idealists agree with statements like, "The existence of potential harm to others is always wrong, irrespective of the benefits to be gained." Such people also maybe more likely to adopt a formalism ideology that defines ethical actions using a set of guiding principles. When asked to describe the character traits that are most important to them, formalists prioritize traits like "trustworthy" "honest" "principled" and "dependable".

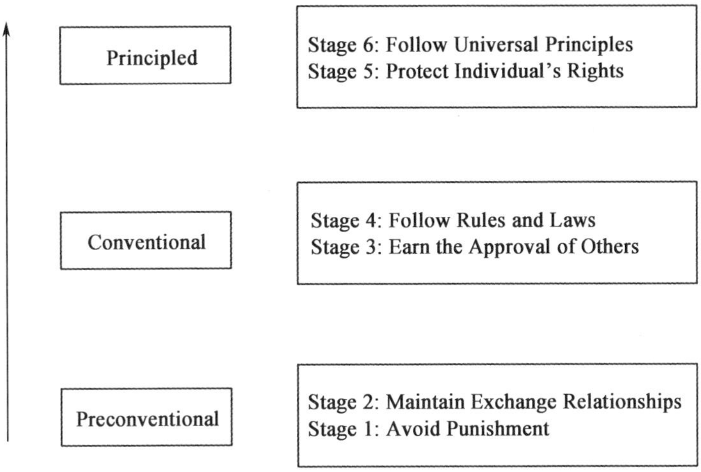

Figure 8 – 3 Stages of Cognitive Moral Development

Moral Intent

If an authority recognizes that a moral issue exists in a situation and possesses the cognitive moral development to choose the right course of action, one step remains: the authority has to want to act ethically. Moral intent reflects an authority's degree of commitment to the moral course of action. The distinction among awareness, judgment, and intent is important because many unethical people know and understand that what they do is wrong—they just don't really care. One driver of moral intent is moral identity—the degree to which a person sees himself or herself as a "moral person". Having a strong moral identity increases ethical behaviors because failing to act morally will trigger a strong sense of guilt or shamc. However, moral intent also is driven by a number of situational factors, including the existence of on-the-job pressures, role conflict, and rewards and incentives that can be more easily attained by unethical means.

8.6 Understand how trust affects job performance and organizational commitment

Does trust have a significant impact on the two primary outcomes in our integrative model of OB—does it correlate with job performance and organizational commitment? Yes, trust does influence job performance. Why? One reason is that trust is moderately correlated with task performance. A study of employees in eight plants of a tool manufacturing company sheds some light on why trust benefits task performance. The study gave employees survey measures of their trust in two different authorities: their plant's manager and the company's top management team. Both trust measures were significant predictors of employees' ability to focus, which reflects the degree to which employees can devote their attention to work, as opposed to "covering their backside" "playing politics" and "keeping an eye on the boss". The ability to focus is clearly vital to task performance in many jobs, particularly when job duties become more complex. Trust also influences citizenship behavior and counterproductive behavior Why? One reason is that the willingness to accept vulnerability changes the nature of the employee-employer relationship. Employees become more likely to do "extra things" to help out the organization because they trust that relevant authorities will have their best interests in mind and repay their efforts over the long term.

Trust also affects organizational commitment. Why? One reason is that trusting an authority increases the likelihood that an emotional bond will develop, particularly if that trust is rooted in positive feelings for the authority. Trusting an authority also makes it more likely that a sense of obligation will develop because employees feel more confident that the authority deserves that obligation. When negative events occur, employees who trust the authority are willing to accept the vulnerability that comes with continued employment, remaining confident in their belief that the situation will eventually improve.

8.7 Takeaways

1. Trust is the willingness to be vulnerable to an authority based on positive expectations about the authority's actions and intentions. Justice reflects the perceived fairness of an authority's decision making and can be used to explain why employees judge some authorities as more trustworthy than others. Ethics reflects the degree to which the behaviors of an authority are in accordance with generally accepted moral norms and can be used to explain why authorities choose to act in a trustworthy manner.

2. Trust can be disposition-based, meaning that one's personality includes a general propensity to trust others. Trust also can be cognition-based, meaning that it's rooted in a rational assessment of the authority's trustworthiness. Finally, trust can be affect-based, meaning that it is rooted in feelings toward the authority that go beyond any rational assessment of trustworthiness.

3. Trustworthiness is judged along three dimensions: ability, integrity, and benevolence. Ability reflects the skills and competencies of an authority. Integrity reflects whether the authority adheres to a set of acceptable values and principles. Benevolence reflects the belief that the authority wants to "do good" for the trustor.

4. The fairness of an authority's decision making can be judged along four dimensions. Distributive justice reflects the perceived fairness of decision-making outcomes. Procedural justice reflects the perceived fairness of decision-making processes. Interpersonal justice reflects the perceived fairness of the treatment received by employees from authorities. Informational justice reflects the perceived fairness of the communications provided to employees from authorities.

5. The four-component model of ethical decision making argues that ethical behavior depends on three concepts. Moral awareness reflects whether an authority recognizes that a moral issue exists in a situation. Moral judgment reflects whether the authority can accurately identify the

"right" course of action. Moral intent reflects an authority's degree of commitment to the moral course of action.

6. Trust has a moderate positive relationship with job performance and a strong positive relationship with organizational commitment.

8.8 Discussion questions

1. Consider the three dimensions of trustworthiness (ability, integrity, and benevolence). Which of those dimensions would be most important when deciding whether to trust your boss? What about when deciding whether to trust a friend? If your two answers differ, why do they?

2. Putting yourself in the shoes of a manager, which of the four justice dimensions (distributive, procedural, interpersonal, informational) would you find most difficult to maximize? Which would be the easiest to maximize?

3. Which component of ethical decision making do you believe best explains student cheating: moral awareness, moral judgment, or moral intent? Why do you feel that way?

4. Assume you were applying for a job at a company known for its fair and ethical practices. How important would that information be to you when deciding whether to accept a job offer?

Section V Group Mechanisms

Chapter 9 Teams

When is your last time using a mouse or keyboard, a streaming webcam, or a controller or racing wheel for your PS4? Chances are good that it was designed and manufactured by Logitech, the Swiss company known for innovative "personal peripherals". Logitech uses teams of highly specialized members who are dispersed throughout the globe, practicing the mode of "follow the sun". Specifically, work was accomplished continuously because members of a team who finished their workday in one country handed off the work to team members of another country who had just started their workday. Such practice made product development and launching much more efficiently.

Granted, you probably have not been a member of a team such as Logitech in opening vignette; however, it is likely that you have had first-hand experiences that will help you relate to the material in this chapter. For example, most of you have participated in a team sport at some point in your life. As another example, many of you have worked in a team with classmates to complete assignments. Finally, some of you may have been a member of an organizational team responsible for making a product, providing a service, or generating recommendations for solving company problems. These teams are obviously different from one another; however, there are some striking similarities as well. In fact, teams are simply groups that possess a set of defining characteristics. Specifically, a team is a group of two or more people who work interdependently over some time period to accomplish common goals related to some task-oriented purpose.

9.1 Define teams and identify their characteristics

Today, teams are used in the majority of organizations in the United States, regardless of whether the organization is large or small. In fact, some researchers have suggested that almost all major U.S. companies are currently using teams or planning to implement them and that up to 50 percent of all employees in the United States work in a team as part of their job. Thus, whereas the use of teams was limited to pioneers such as Procter & Gamble in the 1960s, teams are currently used in all types of industries to accomplish all the types of work necessary to make organizations run effectively. Why have teams become widespread? The most obvious reason is that the nature of the work today requires them. As work has become more complex, interaction among individuals has become more vital because it facilitates the pooling and synthesis of complementary knowledge and skill.

The concepts and theories we will be discussing in this chapter can be grouped into two broad categories, as shown in Figure 9 – 1. We will begin by discussing team characteristics, or the various qualities of teams and team members. Team characteristics can be taken into account when designing teams, and this is very important because team characteristics impact team processes and team performance. We then overview team processes, which can be defined as the characteristic behaviors and attitudes that emerge in a team after members work with one another for some time.

Understanding the various categories of team processes is important because effective processes can result in synergies that translate into improved team performance.

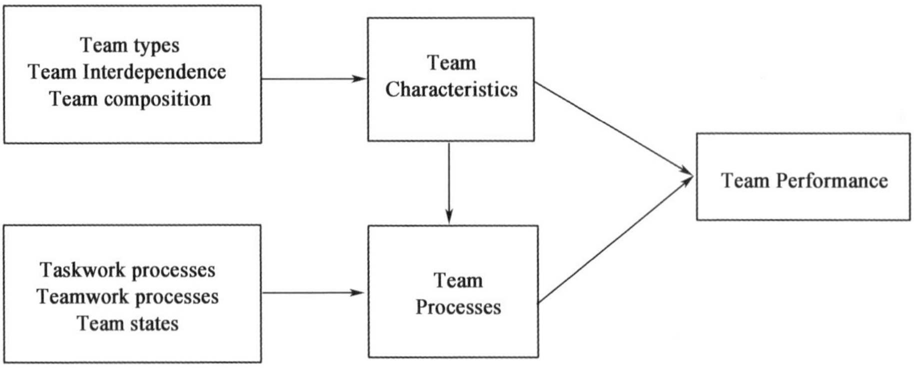

Figure 9 – 1　Team Characteristics and Processes

9.1.1　Team Characteristics

Although teams can be described by referring to many different characteristics, it is helpful to organize them into three general categories: team types, team interdependence, and team composition.

9.1.2　Team Types

One way to describe teams is to refer to taxonomies that organize teams into various types. One such taxonomy is illustrated in Table 9 – 1. This table shows that there are five general types of teams, and that each is associated with a number of defining characteristics, including the team's purpose, the life span of a team's existence, and the amount of time involvement required of its individual members.

Table 9 – 1　Types of Teams

Types of Team	Purpose and Activities	Life Span	Member Involvement	Specific Examples
Work team	Produce goods or provide services	Long	High	Self-managed work team
Management team	Integrate activities of subunits across business functions	Long	Moderate	Top management team
Parallel team	Provide recommendations and resolve issues	Varies	Low	Quality circle Advisory council Committee

Table 9 – 1(continued)

Types of Team	Purpose and Activities	Life Span	Member Involvement	Specific Examples
Project team	Produce a one-time output (product, service, plan, design, etc.)	Varies	Varies	Product design team Research group Planning team
Action team	Perform complex tasks that vary in duration and take place in highly visible or challenging circumstances.	Varies	Varies	Surgical team Musical team Expedition team Sports team

9.1.3 Team Interdependence

In addition to taxonomies of team types, we can describe teams by talking about the interdependence that governs connections among team members. In a general sense, you can think of interdependence as the way in which the members of a team are linked to one another.

9.1.4 Team Composition

You probably already agree that team effectiveness hinges on team composition—or the mix of people who make up the team in terms of the five characteristics shown in Figure 9 – 2. Team composition is important in determining team effectiveness. For example, if you've been a member of a particularly effective team, you may have noticed that the team members were not only capable of performing their role responsibilities effectively, but they also were reliable and cooperative.

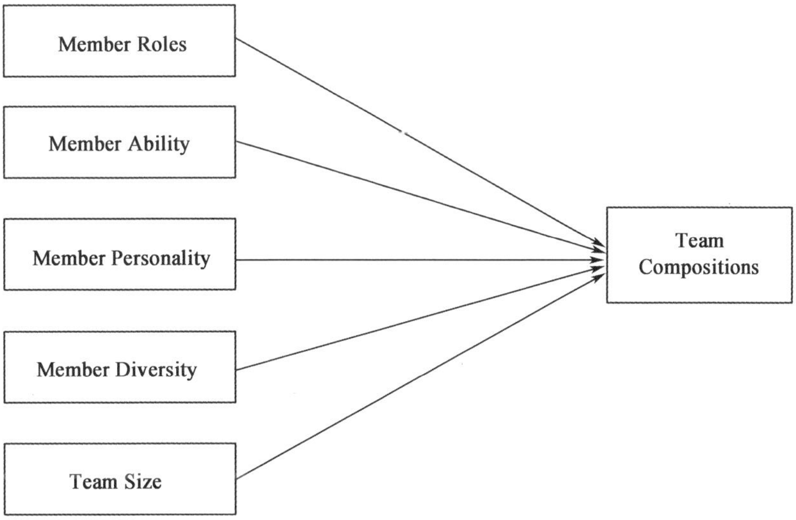

Figure 9 – 2 Five Aspects of Team Composition

9.2 Identify and describe the five general team types

9.2.1 Work Teams

Work teams are designed to be relatively permanent. Their purpose is to produce goods or provide services, and they generally require a full-time commitment from their members. Although all work teams have these defining characteristics, they can vary a great deal across organizations in other important ways. One way that work teams vary is in the degree to which members have autonomy in defining their roles and decision making. In traditional work teams, members have very specific sets of job duties, and their decision making is confined to the activities required by those duties. Members of self-managed work teams, in contrast, are not locked into specific jobs. Instead, they jointly decide how to organize themselves and carry out the team's work.

9.2.2 Management Teams

Management teams are similar to work teams in that they are designed to be relatively permanent; however, they are also distinct in a number of important ways. Whereas work teams focus on the accomplishment of core operational-level production and service tasks, management teams participate in managerial tasks that affect the entire organization. Specifically, management teams are responsible for coordinating the activities of organizational subunits—typically departments or functional areas—to help the organization achieve its long-term goals. Top management teams, for example, consist of senior-level executives who meet to make decisions about the strategic direction of the organization. It also may be worth mentioning that because members of management teams are typically heads of departments, their commitment to the management team is offset somewhat by the responsibilities they have in leading their own unit.

9.2.3 Parallel Teams

Parallel teams are composed of members from various jobs who provide recommendations to managers about important issues that run "parallel" to the organization's production process. Parallel teams require only part-time commitment from members, and they can be permanent or temporary, depending on their aim. Quality circles, for example, consist of individuals who perform their own jobs but also meet as a team regularly to identify problems and opportunities for improvements in production. As an example of a more temporary parallel team, a committee might form to deal with an issue that arises only periodically.

9.2.4 Project Teams

Project teams are formed to take on "one-time" tasks that are generally complex and require a lot of input from members with different types of training and expertise. Although project teams only exist as long as it takes to finish a project, some projects are quite complex and can take years to complete. Some project teams require full-time commitment, whereas others demand only part-time commitment. A planning team comprised of engineers, architects, designers, and builders, charged with designing a suburban town center, might work together full-time for a year or more. In contrast, the engineers and artists who constitute a team responsible for designing a toothbrush might work together for a month on the project while also serving on other project teams.

9.2.5 Action Teams

Action teams perform tasks that are normally limited in duration. However, those tasks are quite complex and take place in contexts that are either highly visible to an audience or of a highly challenging nature. Some types of action teams work together for an extended period of time. For example, sport teams typically remain together for a season, and musical groups like the Rolling Stones may stick together for decades. Other types of action teams stay together only as long as the task takes to complete. A surgical team or an aircraft flight crew may only work together as a unit for a single two-hour surgery or flight.

9.2.6 Variations within Teams: Virtuality

Even knowing whether a team is a project team, an action team, or some other type of team doesn't tell you the whole story. Often there are important variations within those categories that determine a team's functioning. For example, virtual teams are teams in which the members are geographically dispersed, and interdependent activity occurs through electronic communications such as email, instant messaging, and Web conferencing. Although communications and group networking software is far from perfect, it has advanced to the point that it is possible for almost all types of teams to function virtually. In other words, there are examples of teams in every category of Table 9 – 1 that could function either face-to-face or virtually with the right technology. As we mentioned for Logitech, virtual teams are not just an efficient way to accomplish work when members are geographically separated. They also may be used to make continuous progress on word tasks without members having to work 24/7.

9.2.7 Variations within Teams: Phase of Team Development

In addition to varying in their "virtuality", teams of any type can differ in the amount of experience they have working together. One way to understand this point is to consider what occurs in teams as they progress from a newly formed group of individuals to a well-established team. According to the Four Stage Theory of team development, teams go through a progression of four stages shown in the top panel of Figure 9 –3. In the first stage, called forming, members orient themselves by trying to understand the boundaries the team. Members try to get a feel for what is expected of them, what types of behaviors are out of bounds, and who's in charge. In the next stage, called storming, members remain committed to ideas they bring with them to the team. This initial unwillingness to accommodate others' ideas triggers conflict that negatively affects some interpersonal relationships and harms the team's progress. During the next stage, norming, members realize that they need to work together to accomplish team goals, and, consequently, they begin to cooperate with one another. Feelings of solidarity develop as members work toward team goals. Over time, norms and expectations develop regarding what different members are responsible for doing. In the final stage of team development, which is called performing, members are comfortable working within their roles, and the team makes progress toward goals.

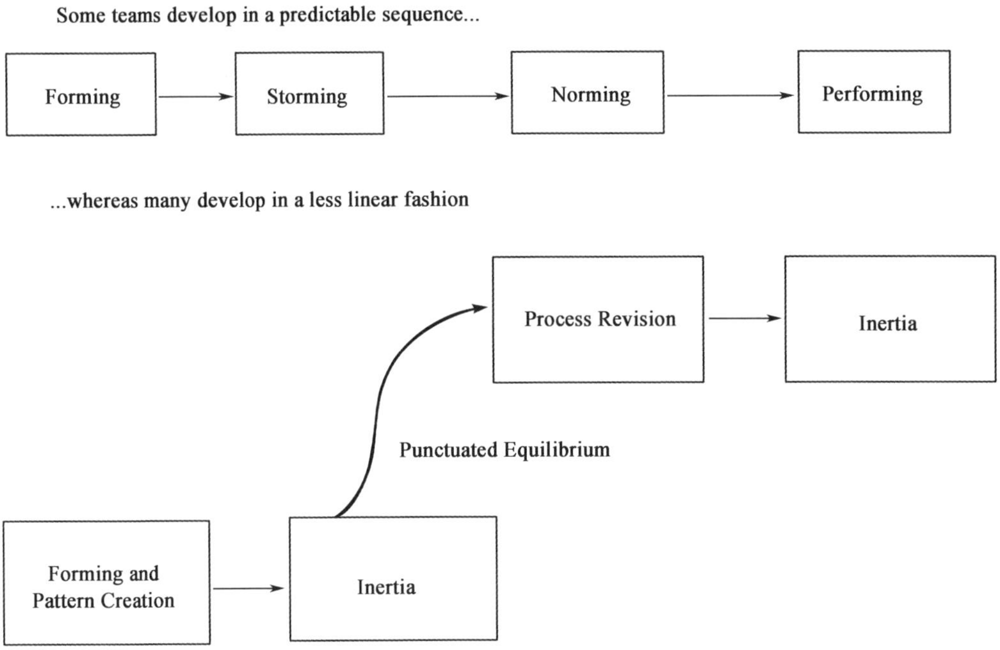

Figure 9 –3　Two Models of Team Development

A theory of team development that may be more applicable to certain types of project teams is called punctuated equilibrium. The sequence of team development described by this theory appears in the bottom panel of Figure 9 – 3. At the initial team meeting, members make assumptions and establish a pattern of behavior that for the first half of its life. That pattern of behavior continues to dominate the team's behavior as it settles into a sort of inertia. At the midway point of the project—and this is true regardless of the length of the project—something remarkable happens. Members realize that they have to change their task paradigm fundamentally to complete it on time. Teams that take this opportunity to plan a new approach during this transition tend to do well, and the new framework dominates their behavior until task completion. However, teams that do not take the opportunity to change their approach tend to persist with their original pattern and may "go down with a sinking ship".

9.3 Describe the three general types of team interdependence

9.3.1 Task Interdependence

Task interdependence refers to the degree to which team members interact with and rely on other team members for the information, materials, and resources needed to accomplish work for the team. As Figure 9 – 4 illustrates, there are four primary types of task interdependence, and each requires a different degree of interaction and each requires a different degree of interaction and coordination.

The type of task interdependence with the lowest degree of required coordination is pooled interdependence. With this type of interdependence, group members complete their work independently, and then this work is "piled up" to represent the group's output. Consider what pooled interdependence would be like on a fishing boat. Each fisherman would bait his or her own pole, drop the baited line into the water, reel the fish in, remove the fish from the hook, and, finally, throw the fish into a tank filled with ice and other fish. At the end of the day, the boat's production would be the weight of the total fish that were caught.

The next type of task interdependence is called sequential interdependence. With this type of interdependence, different tasks are done in a prescribed order, and the group is structured such that the members specialize in these tasks. Although members in groups with sequential interdependence interact to carry out their work, the interaction only occurs between members who perform tasks that are next to each other in the sequence. Moreover, the member performing the task in the latter part of the sequence depends on the member performing the task in the earlier part of the sequence, but not the other way around. The classic assembly line in manufacturing contexts provides an excellent example of this type of interdependence. In this context, an employee attaches a part to the unit being built, and once this is accomplished, the unit moves on to another employee who adds another part. The process typically ends with the unit being inspected and then packaged for shipping.

Reciprocal interdependence is the next type of task interdependence. Similar to sequential interdependence, members are specialized to perform specific tasks. However, instead of a strict sequence of activities, members interact with a subset of other members to complete the team's work. To understand reciprocal interdependence, consider a team of people who are involved in a business that designs custom homes for wealthy clients. After meeting with a client, the salesperson would provide general criteria, structural and aesthetic details, and some rough sketches to an architect who would work up some initial plans and elevations. The architect then would submit the initial plans to the salesperson, who would review the plans with the customer. Typically, the plans need to be revised by the architect several times, and during this process, customers have questions and requests that require the architect to consult with other members of the team. For example, the architect and structural engineer may have to interact to decide where to locate support beams and load-bearing walls. The architect and construction supervisor also might have to meet to discuss revisions to a design feature that turns out to be too costly. As a final example, the salesperson might have to interact with the designers to assist the customer in the selection of additional features, materials, and colors, which would then need to be included in a revision of the plan by the architect.

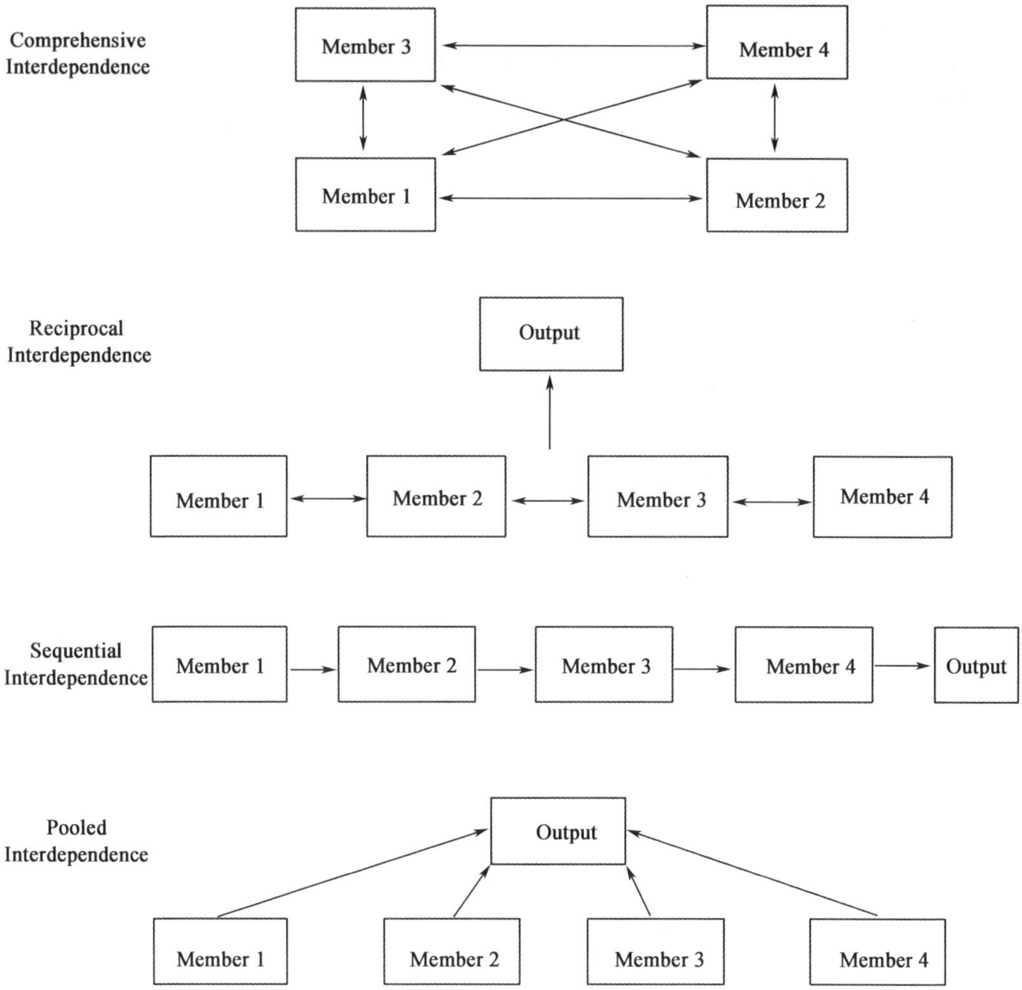

Figure 9 – 4　Task Interdependence and Coordination Requirement

Finally, comprehensive interdependence requires the highest level of interaction and coordination among members as they try to accomplish work. With comprehensive interdependence, each member has a great deal of discretion in terms of what he or she does and with whom he or she interacts in the course of the collaboration involved in accomplishing the team's word. Teams at IDEO, arguably the world's most successful product design firm, function with comprehensive interdependence. These teams are composed of individuals from very diverse backgrounds, and they meet as a team quite often to share knowledge and ideas to solve problems related to their design projects.

There is no one right way to design teams with respect to task interdependence. However, it is important to recognize the trade-offs associated with the different types. On the one hand, as the level of task interdependence increases, members must spend increasing amounts of time communicating and coordinating with other members to complete tasks. These additional demands decrease productivity. Which is the ratio of work completed per the amount of time worked. On the other hand, increases in task interdependence increase the ability of the team to adapt to new situations. The more members interact and communicate with one another, the more likely it is that the team will be able to devise solutions to novel problems it faces.

9.3.2 Goal Interdependence

In addition to being linked to one another by task activities, members may be linked by their goals. A high degree of goal interdependence exists when team members have a shared vision of the team's goal and align their individual goals with that vision as a result. To understand the power of goal interdependence, visualize a rowboat with several people on board, each with a paddle. If each person on the boat wants to go the exact same place on the other side of a lake, they will all row in the same direction, and the boat will arrive at the desired location. If, however, each person believes the boat should go someplace different, each person will row in a different direction, and the boat will have major problems getting anywhere.

So how do you create high levels of goal interdependence? One thing to do would be to ensure that the team has a formalized mission statement. Mission statements can take a variety of forms, but good ones clearly describe what the team is trying to accomplish in a way that creates a sense of commitment and urgency among team members. Mission statements can come directly from the organization or team leaders, but in many circumstances, it makes sense for teams to go through the process of developing their own mission statements. This process helps members better understand what the team needs to do, and it increases feelings of ownership toward the mission itself.

9.3.3 Outcome Interdependence

The final type of interdependence relates to how members are linked to one another in terms of the feedback and outcomes they receive as a consequence of working in the team. A high degree of outcome interdependence exists when team members share in the rewards that the team earns, with reward examples including pay, bonuses, formal feedback and recognition, pats on the back, extra time off, and continued team survival. Of course, because team achievement depends on the performance of each team member, high outcome interdependence also implies that team members depend on the performance of other team members for the rewards that they receive. In contrast, low outcome interdependence exists in teams in which individual members receive rewards and punishments on the basis of their own performance, without regard to the performance of the team.

Outcome interdependence presents managers with a tough dilemma when it's considered in team design. High outcome interdependence promotes higher levels of cooperation because members understand that they share the same fate—if the team wins, everyone wins, and if the team fails, everyone fails. However, at the same time, high outcome interdependence may result in reduced motivation, especially among higher performing members. The reason is that high performers may perceive that they are not paid in proportion to what they contributed to the team and that their teammates are taking advantage of this inequity for their own benefit.

One solution to this dilemma has been to implement a level of outcome interdependence that matches the level of task interdependence. Members tend to be more productive in high task interdependence situations when there is also high outcome interdependence. Similarly, members prefer low task interdependent situations when there is low outcome interdependence. To understand the power of aligning task and outcome interdependence, consider scenarios in which there is not g good match. For example, how would you react if you worked very closely with your teammates on a project in one of your classes, and though your professor said the team's project was outstanding, she awarded an A to one of your team members, a B to another, and a C to you? Similarly, consider how you would react if you scored enough points for an A on your final exam, but your professor averaged everyone's grades together and gave all students a C. Chances are you wouldn't be happy with either scenario.

9.4 Describe factors involved in team composition

9.4.1 The mix of member roles

The first aspect of team composition is the mix of member roles, where a role refers to the set of behaviors a person is expected to display in a given context. In a team setting, there are three broad categories of roles that members can take or develop, and depending on the specific situation, the presence or absence of members who possess these roles may have a strong impact on team effectiveness.

Team task roles refer to behaviors that directly facilitate the accomplishment of team tasks. Examples include the orienter who establishes the direction for the team, the devil's advocate who offers constructive challenges to the team's status quo, and the energizer who motivates team members who motivates team members to work harder toward team goals. As you may have realized, the importance of specific task-oriented roles depends on the nature of the work in which the team is involved. The orienter role may be particularly important in teams involved in work for which the team has autonomy about how to accomplish the work. The devil's advocate role may be particularly important in team contexts in which decisions are "high stakes" in nature and in situations where teams reach consensus on decisions before considering a reasonable range of alternatives. Finally, the energizer role may be most important in team contexts in which the work is important but not intrinsically motivating.

In contrast to task-oriented roles, team-building roles refer to behaviors that influence the quality of the team's social climate. Examples of team-building roles include the harmonizer who steps in to resolve differences among teammates, the encourager who praises the work of teammates, and the compromiser who helps the team see alternative solutions that teammates can accept. As you might have gathered, the presence of members who take on team-building roles helps teams manage conflicts that could hinder team effectiveness.

Finally, whereas task roles and team-building roles focus on activities that benefit the team, individualistic roles reflect behaviors that benefit the individual members at the expense of the team. For example, the aggressor "puts down" or deflates fellow teammates. The recognition seeker takes credit for team successes. The dominator manipulates teammates to acquire control and power. If you've ever been on a team in which members took on individualistic roles, you realize just how damaging they can be. Having teammates who take on individualistic roles is not only dissatisfying—trying to cope with the associated problems also requires a great deal of time and effort.

8.4.2 Abilities

A second aspect of team composition refers of member abilities, and in the context of managerial work, cognitive abilities may be particularly important to consider when designing teams (see Chapter 3 for a discussion of cognitive ability). In general, teams with members who possess higher levels of cognitive ability perform better because teamwork tends to be quite complex. Team members not only have to be involved in several different aspects of the team's task, but they also have to learn how best to combine their individual efforts to accomplish team goals. In fact, the more that this type of learning is required, the more important team member cognitive ability becomes. Research has shown that cognitive ability is more important to teams when team members have to learn from one another to adapt to changes, compared with contexts in which team members perform their assigned tasks in a routine fashion.

9.4.3 Personality

A third aspect of team composition refers to member personality traits (see Chapter 3 for a discussion of personality), which affect how teams function and perform. For example, team composition in terms of members' conscientiousness is important to teams. After all, almost any team would benefit from having members who tend to be dependable and work hard to achieve team goals. What might be less obvious to you is the strong negative effect on the team of having even one member who is particularly low on conscientiousness. To understand why this is true, consider how you would react to a team member who was not dependable and did not appear to be motivated to work hard toward team goals. If you're like most people, you would find the situation dissatisfying, and you would consider different ways of dealing with it. Some people might try to motivate the person to be more responsible and work harder; others might try to get the person ejected from the team. The problem is that these natural reactions to a low-conscientiousness team member not only divert attention away from accomplishing work responsibilities, but they also can result in some very uncomfortable and time-consuming interpersonal conflicts. Moreover, even if you and the other members of the team work harder to compensate for this person, it would be difficult for your team to perform as effectively as other teams in which all members are more interpersonally responsible and engaged in the team's work.

The agreeableness of team members is also an important consideration. In general, research has shown that in team settings, the overall level of members' agreeableness may be even more important than conscientiousness. Why? Because agreeable people tend to be more cooperative and trusting, tendencies that promote positive attitudes about the team and smooth interpersonal interactions. Moreover, because agreeable people may be more concerned about their team's interests than their own, they should work hard on behalf of the team. There is a caveat regarding agreeableness in teams, however. Because agreeable people tend to prefer harmony and cooperation over conflict and competition, they may be less apt to speak up and offer constructive criticisms that might help the team improve. Thus, when composed of highly agreeable members, there is a chance that the team will behave in a way that enhances harmony at the expense of task accomplishment.

People who are extraverted tend to perform more effectively in interpersonal contexts and are more positive and optimistic in general. Therefore, it shouldn't surprise you to hear that having extraverted team members is generally beneficial to the social climate of the group, as well as to team effectiveness in the eyes of supervisors. At the same time, however, research has shown that having too many members who are very high on extraversion can hurt the team. The reason for this can be attributed to extraverts' tendency to be assertive and dominant. As you would expect when there are too many members with these types of tendencies, power struggles and unproductive conflict occur with greater frequency.

9.4.4 Diversity

Another aspect of team composition refers to the degree to which members are different from one another in terms of any attribute that might be used by someone as a basis of categorizing people. We refer to those differences as team diversity. Trying to understand the effects of team diversity is somewhat difficult because there are so many different characteristics that may be used to categorize people. There are also several reasons diversity might influence team functioning and effectiveness, and some of these reasons seem contradictory.

The predominant theory that has been used to explain why diversity has positive effects is called the value in diversity problem-solving approach. From this perspective, diversity in teams is beneficial because it provides for a larger pool of knowledge and perspectives from which a team can draw as it carries out its work. Teams that engage in work that is relative complex and requires creativity benefit most from diversity, and research on teams that are diverse in terms of many different characteristics related to knowledge and perspectives—ethnicity, expertise, personality, attitudes—supports this idea.

A theory that has been used widely to explain why diversity may have detrimental effects on teams is called the similarity-attraction approach. According to this perspective, people tend to be more attracted to others who are perceived as more similar. People also tend to avoid interacting with those who are perceived to be dissimilar to reduce the likelihood of having uncomfortable disagreements. Consistent with this perspective, research has shown that diversity on attributes such as cultural background, race, and attitudes is associated with communication problems and ultimately poor team effectiveness.

So it appears that there are two different theories about diversity effects that are relevant to teams, and each has been supported in research. Which perspective is correct? As it turns out, one key to understanding the impact of team diversity requires that you consider both the general type of diversity and the length of time the team has been in existence. Surface-level diversity refers to diversity regarding observable attributes such as race, ethnicity, sex, and age. Although this type of diversity may have a negative impact on teams early in their existence because of similarity-attraction issues, those negative effects tend to disappear as members become more knowledgeable about one another. In essence, the stereotypes that members have about one another based on surface differences are replaced with knowledge regarding underlying characteristics that are more relevant to social and task interactions.

Deep-level diversity, in contrast, refers to diversity with respect to attributes that are less easy to observe initially but that can be inferred after more direct experience. Differences in attitudes, values, and personality are good examples of deep-level diversity. In contrast to the effects of surface-level diversity, time appears to increase the negative effects of deep-level diversity on team functioning and effectiveness. Over time, as team members learn about one another, differences that relate to underlying values and goals become increasingly apparent. Those differences can therefore create problems among team members that ultimately result in reduced effectiveness.

9.4.5 Team Size

In addressing team size, two adages are relevant: "the more the merrier" and "too many cooks spoil the broth". But which statement do you believe is true in terms of how many members to include on a team? The answer, according to research, is that having a greater number of members is beneficial for management and project teams but not for teams engaged in production tasks. Management and project teams engage in work that is complex and knowledge intensive, and these teams therefore benefit from the additional resources and expertise contributed by additional members. In contrast, production teams tend to engage in routine tasks that are less complex. Having additional members beyond what is necessary to accomplish the work tends to result in unnecessary coordination and communication problems. Additional members may therefore be less productive because there is more socializing and they feel less accountable for team outcomes. Although making a claim about the absolute best team size is impossible, research with student teams concluded that team members tend to be most satisfied with their team when the number of members is between 4 and 5 (4.6 to be exact). Of course, there are other rules of thumb you can use to keep team size optimal. Jeff Bezos, the CEO of Amazon. Com, uses the two-pizza rule: "If a team can't be fed by two pizzas, it's too large".

9.4.6 Team Processes

Team process is a term that refers to the different types of activities and interactions that occur within teams that contribute to their ultimate end goals. Some of the team processes we describe in this chapter are observable by the naked eye. For example, it would be possible to see team members gathering information, building on one another's ideas, and collaborating to solve some problem. Other team processes, in contrast, are less visible. As an example, an outside observer wouldn't be able to directly see the emotional bonds between members of a highly cohesive team. Thus, team processes include interactions among members that occur behaviorally, as well as the hard-to-see feelings and thoughts that coalesce as a consequence of member interactions.

9.5 Define team process and discuss how team process can result in process gain process loss

Why are processes important to learn about? One reason is that effective team processes allow teams to benefit fromprocess gain, or getting more from the team than you would expect according to the capabilities of its individual members. Process gain is synonymous with synergy and is most critical in situations in which the complexity of the work is high or tasks require combinations of members' knowledge, skills, and efforts to solve problems. In essence, process gain is important because it results in useful resources and capabilities that did not exist before the team created them. A team that achieves process gain develops capabilities that help it achieve much more than what most people would rationally expect.

Of course, process loss, or getting less from the team than you would expect based on the capabilities of its individual members, is also possible. What factors conspire to create process loss? One factor is that in teams, members have to work to not only accomplish their own tasks but also coordinate their activities with the activities of their teammates. Although this extra effort focused on integrating work is a necessary aspect of the team experience, it is called coordination loss because it consumes time and energy that could otherwise be devoted to task activity. Such coordination losses are often driven by production blocking, which occurs when members have to wait on one another before they can do their part of the team task. If you've ever worked in a team in which you felt like you couldn't get any of your own work done because of all the time spent in meetings, following up requests for information from other team members, and waiting on team members to do their part of the team task, you already understand how frustrating production blocking (and coordination loss) can be.

The second force that fosters process loss in team contexts is motivational loss, or the loss in team productivity that occurs when team members do not work as hard as they could. Why does motivation loss occur in team contexts? One explanation is that it's often quite difficult to gauge exactly how much each team member contributes to the team. Members of teams can work together on projects over an extended period of time, and, therefore, it's difficult to keep an accurate accounting of who does what. Similarly, members contribute to their team in many different ways, and contributions of some members may be less obvious than others. Finally, members of teams do not always work together at the same time as a unit. Regardless of the reasons for it, uncertainty regarding "who contributes what" results in team members feeling less accountable for team outcomes. Those feelings of reduced accountability, in turn, cause members to exert less effort when working on team tasks than they would if they worked alone on those same tasks. This phenomenon is called social loafing, and it can significantly hinder a team's effectiveness.

Having described process gains and process losses, it's time to describe the particular team processes that can help teams increase their synergy while reducing their inefficiency. One relevant category of team processes is taskwork processes, which are the activities of team members that relate directly to the accomplishment of team tasks. In a general sense, taskwork occurs any time that team members interact with the tools or technologies that are used to complete their work. In this regard, taskwork is similar to the concept of task performance described in Chapter 2. However, in the context of teams, especially those that engage in knowledge work, the two types of taskwork shown in Figure 9 – 5 are crucially important: creative behavior and decision making.

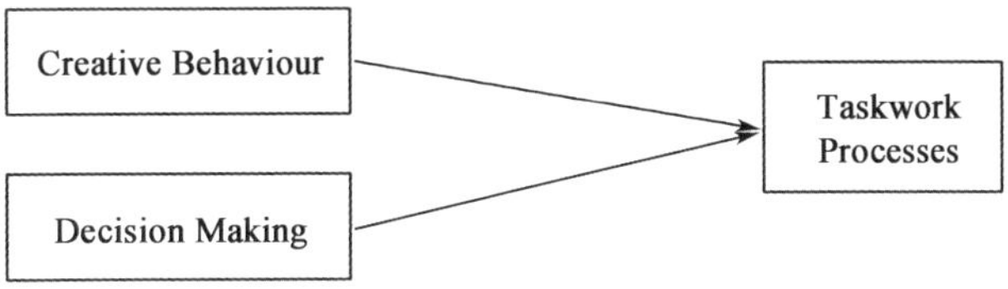

Figure 9 – 5 Taskwork Processes

9.6 Define taskwork and describe examples of team activities that fit into this process category

9.6.1 Creative Behavior

Creative behavior involves team members engaging in activities focused on generating novel and useful ideas and solutions. In Chapter 3 on Personality, Cultural Values, and Ability, we noted that creative behavior is driven in part by the creativity of individual employees because some employees are simply more original and imaginative than others. However, the team environment is also uniquely suited to fostering creative outcomes because with teams, the unique knowledge and skills of members can be combined in a manner that results in novel and useful ideas. However, achieving such outcomes depends on much more than just putting a diverse mix of people together and letting them go at it. In fact, creative behavior in teams can be fostered when members participate in a specific set of taskwork activities.

Perhaps the best-known activity that teams use to foster creative behavior is brainstorming. Brainstorming involves a face-to-face meeting of team members in which each offers as many ideas as possible about some focal problem or issue. Most brainstorming sessions center around the following rules:

(1) Express all ideas that come to mind (no matter how strange);

(2) Go for quantity of ideas rather than quality;

(3) Don't criticize or evaluate the ideas of others;

(4) Build on the ideas of others. The theory is that if a team follows these rules, it will develop a large pool of ideas that it can use to address the issue at hand. This concept sounds good in theory, so it may surprise you to learn then that traditional brainstorming sessions rarely work as well as intended. In fact, research suggests that team members would be better off coming up with ideas on their own, as individuals, before pooling those ideas and evaluating them to arrive at a solution.

Why doesn't brainstorming work as well as individual idea generation? There appear to be at least three reasons. First, there may be a tendency for people to social loaf in group brainstorming contexts. That is, members may not work as hard to think up ideas as they would have if they had to turn in an individually generated list with their name on it. Second, though the brainstorming rules explicitly forbid criticizing others' ideas, members may be hesitant to express ideas that seem silly or not well thought-out. Third, brainstorming results in production blocking because members have to wait their turn to express their ideas. This waiting around consumes time that could otherwise be used by individuals to generate new ideas.

Given the problems associated with brainstorming, why do organizations continue to use it? One reason is that the general idea of brainstorming is well-known, and common-sense leads people to believe that it works as advertised. Another reason is that there are benefits of brainstorming beyond just generating ideas. For example, brainstorming builds morale and results in the sharing of knowledge that might otherwise be locked inside the minds of the individual team members. Although this knowledge may not be useful for the particular problem that's being debated, it might be useful for issues that arise in the future.

One offshoot of brainstorming that addresses some of its limitations is the nominal group technique. Similar to a traditional brainstorming session, this process starts off by bringing the team together and outlining the purpose of the meeting. The next step takes place on an individual level, however, as members have a set period of time to write down their own ideas on a piece of paper. The subsequent step goes back into the team setting, as members share their ideas with the team in a round-robin fashion. After the ideas are recorded, members have a discussion intended to clarify the ideas and build on the ideas of others. After this, it's back to an individual environment; members rank order ideas on a card that they submit to a facilitator. A facilitator then tabulates the scores to determine the winning idea. From this description, you probably can guess how the nominal group technique addresses the problems with brainstorming. By making people write down ideas on their own, it decreases social loafing and production blocking. In addition, ranking items as individuals makes people less apprehensive about voicing support for an unpopular idea.

9.6.2 Decision Making

In Chapter 5 on Learning and Decision Making, we described how people use information and intuition to make specific decisions. In team contexts, however, decision making is somewhat more complex because it involves multiple members gathering and considering information that is relevant to their area of specialization, and then making recommendations to a team leader who is ultimately responsible for the final decision. If you ever watched the TV show The Apprentice, you should be able to understand this process quite clearly. The show typically begins with Donald Trump assigning two teams a fairly complex task. A member from each team then volunteers to be project leader, and this person assigns to the other team members roles like marketing, logistics, and sales. Throughout the project, members make suggestions and recommendations to the leader, who ultimately is responsible for making the decisions that determine the success of the project. Of course, project success is important because someone from the losing team—most often the project leader—gets to hear Trump say those famous words: "You're fired".

What factors account for a team's ability to make effective decisions in this type of context? At least three factors appear to be involved. The first factor is decision informity, which reflects whether members possess adequate information about their own task responsibilities. Project teams on The Apprentice often fail, for example, because the team member in charge of marketing does not gather information necessary to help the team understand the desires and needs of the client. The second factor is staff validity, which is the degree to which members make good recommendations to the leader. Team members can possess all the information needed to make a valid recommendation but then fail to do so because of a lack of ability, insight, or good judgment. The third factor is hierarchical sensitivity, which is the degree to which the leader effectively weighs the members' recommendations. Whom does the leader listen to, and whom does the leader ignore? Teams that make good decisions tend to have leaders that do a good job giving recommendations the weight they deserve. So how can knowledge of these three factors be used to improve team decision making?

Research shows that more experienced teams tend to make better decisions. Over time members develop an understanding of the information that's needed and how to use it, and leaders develop an understanding of which members provide the best recommendations. Thus, because experience is so important, it may be important to give decision-making teams a chance to work together before they are assigned to critical team responsibilities. As another example, team decision making may be improved by giving members feedback about the three variables involved in the decision-making process. For example, a team can improve its decision making if the members are told that they have to share and consider additional pieces of information before making recommendations to the leader. Although this recommendation may seem obvious, all too often teams only receive feedback about their final decision. There also may be a benefit to separating the process of sharing information from the process of making recommendations and final decisions, at least in terms of how information is communicated among members. Whereas teams tend to share more information when they meet face to face, leaders do a better job considering recommendations and making final decisions when they're away from the members. Once they're separated, they don't have to deal with pressure from members who may be more assertive or better at articulating and defending their positions. Teams composed of members from different countries have unique challenges in decision making; however, there are some things they can do to manage these issues.

9.6.3 Teamwork Processes

The second major category of team processes is teamwork processes, which refer to the interpersonal activities that facilitate the accomplishment of the teams work but do not directly involve task accomplishment itself. You can think of teamwork processes as the behaviors that create the setting or context in which taskwork processes can be carried out. So what types of behaviors do teamwork processes involve? Figure 9 – 6 summarizes research that has identified several teamwork processes, and we describe these in detail below.

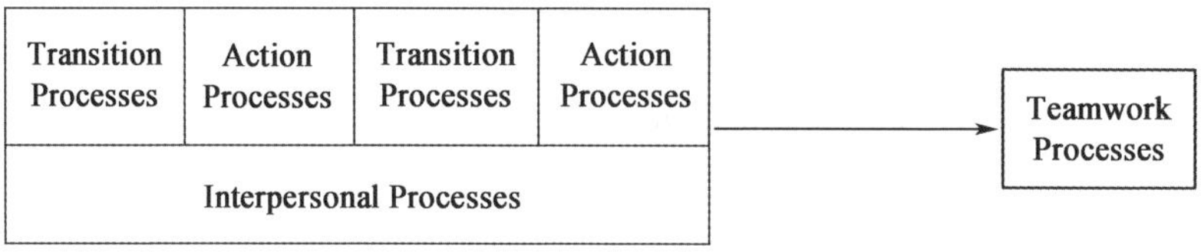

Figure 9 – 6 Teamwork Processes

9.7 Define team states and describe concepts that fit into this process category

9.7.1 Cohesion

For a number of different reasons, members of teams can develop strong emotional bonds to other members of their team and to the team itself. This emotional attachment, which is called cohesion, tends to foster high levels of motivation and commitment to the team, and, as a consequence, cohesiveness tends to promote higher levels of team performance. But is a cohesive team necessarily a good team? According to researchers, the answer to this question is no. In highly cohesive teams, members may try to maintain harmony by striving toward consensus on issues without ever offering, seeking, or seriously considering alternative viewpoints and perspectives. This drive toward conformity at the expense of other team priorities is called groupthink and is thought to be associated with feelings of overconfidence about the team's capabilities. In the end, groupthink has been blamed for decision-making fiascos in politics as well as in business. Some famous examples include John F. Kennedy's decision to go forward with the Bay of Pigs invasion of Cuba, NASA's decision to launch the space shuttle Challenger in unusually cold weather, and Enron's board of directors'decisions to ignore illegal accounting practices.

So how do you leverage the benefits of cohesion without taking on the potential costs? One way is to acknowledge that cohesion can potentially have detrimental consequences. A good first step in this regard would be to measure the team's cohesion using an assessment such as the one included at the end of this chapter. A high score on cohesion may indicate potential vulnerability to groupthink. A second step in preventing problems associated with cohesion would be to formally institute the role of devil's advocate. The person filling this role would be responsible for evaluating and challenging prevailing points of view in a constructive manner and bringing in fresh perspectives and ideas to the team. Although the devil's advocate role could be filled by an existing team member, it's also possible that the team could bring in an outsider to fill that role.

9.7.2 Potency

The second team state, potency, refers to the degree to which members believe that the team can be effective across a variety of situations and tasks. When a team has high potency, members are confident that their team can perform well, and, as a consequence, they focus more of their energy on achieving team goals. When a team has low potency, members are not as confident about their team, and so they begin to question the team's goals and one another. Ultimately, this reaction can result in members focusing their energies on activities that don't benefit the team. As a result, research studies have shown that potency has a strong positive impact on team performance. So how does high potency develop in teams? Team members' confidence in their own capabilities, their trust in other members' capabilities, and feedback about past performance are all likely to play a role. Specifically, team potency is promoted in teams in which members are confident in themselves and their teammates and when the team has found success in the past.

9.7.3 Mental Models

Mental models refer to the level of common understanding among team members regarding important aspects of the team and its task. A team may have shared mental models with respect to the capabilities that members bring to the team as well as the processes the team needs to use to be effective. How can these two types of mental models foster team effectiveness? When team members share in their understanding of one another's capabilities, they're more likely to know where to go for the help they might need to complete their work. In addition, they should be able to anticipate when another member needs help to do his or her work. When members have a shared understanding of which processes are necessary to help the team be effective, they can carry out these processes efficiently and smoothly. To help you understand why this is true, consider what would happen in a team of students who had different understandings about how the team should manage conflict. Few disagreements would get resolved if some of the members believed that direct confrontation was best, whereas others believed that avoidance was best.

9.7.4 How Important are Team Processes?

How much do team processes affect performance and commitment? Answering this question is somewhat complicated because when we say "performance and commitment", we are not referring to the performance of individuals or their attachment to the organization. Instead, we are referring to the performance of teams and the degree to which team members are collectively committed to the team. In the jargon of research on teams, are concerned with team performance and cohesion. Additionally, as have we described throughout this chapter, there are several different types of team processes that we could consider in our summary.

9.8 Describe how team processes affect team performance and team commitment

Research conducted in a wide variety of team settings has shown that teamwork processes have a moderate positive relationship with team performance. This same moderate positive relationship appears to hold true, regardless of whether the research examines transition processes, action processes, or interpersonal processes. Apparently, effectiveness with respect to a wide variety of teamwork processes is needed to help teams achieve process gain and, in turn, perform effectively. Activities that prepare teams for work appear to be just as important as those that help members integrate their work and those that build team confidence and a positive team climate.

Research also indicates that teamwork processes have a strong positive relationship with team commitment. In other words, teams that engage in effective teamwork processes tend to have members who are psychologically connected to one another and a desire for the team to remain intact. Why should teamwork and team commitment be so strongly related? One reason is that people tend to be satisfied in teams in which there are effective interpersonal interactions, and, as a consequence, they go out of their way to do things that they believe will help the team stick together. Think about a team situation that you've been in when everyone shared the same goals for the team, work was coordinated smoothly, and everyone was positive, pleasant to be around, and willing to do their fair share of the work. If you've ever actually been in a situation like this—and we hope that you have—chances are that you did your best to make sure the team could continue together. It's likely that you worked extra hard to make sure that the team achieved its goals. It's also likely that you expressed positive sentiments about the team and your desire for the team to remain together.

9.9 Takeaways

1. Teams are groups comprised of two or more people who work interdependently over some time period to accomplish common goals related to some task-oriented purpose.

2. There are several different types of teams: work teams, management teams, parallel teams, project teams, and parallel teams.

3. Teams can be interdependent in terms of the team task, goals, and outcomes. Each type of interdependence has important implications for team functioning and effectiveness.

4. Team composition refers to the characteristics of the members who work in the team. These characteristics include roles, ability, personality, and member diversity, as well as the number of team members.

5. Team process reflects the different types of activities and interactions that occur within teams that contribute to their ultimate end goals.

6. Taskwork processes are the activities of team members that relate directly to the accomplishment of team tasks. Taskwork processes include creative behavior and decision making.

7. Teamwork processes refer to the interpersonal activities that facilitate the accomplishment of the team's work but do not directly involve task accomplishment itself. Teamwork processes include transition processes, action processes, and interpersonal processes.

8. Team states refer to specific types of feelings and thoughts that coalesce in the minds of team members as a consequence of their experience working together. Team states include cohesion, potency, and mental models.

9 Teamwork processes have a moderate positive relationship with team performance and a strong positive relationship with team commitment.

9.10 Discussion questions

1. In which types of teams have you worked? Were these teams consistent with the team types discussed in this chapter, or were they a combination of types?

2. Think about your student teams. Which aspects of both models of team development apply the most and least to teams in this context?

3. Think about a highly successful team with which you are familiar. What types of task, goal, and outcome interdependence does this team have? Describe how changes in task, goal, and outcome interdependence might have a negative impact on this team.

4. What type of roles do you normally take on in a team setting? Are there task or social roles that you simply don't perform well? If so, why do you think this is?

5. What is the most important team composition factor in your student teams? If a student team has limitations in its composition, what can it do to improve?

6. Think of a team in which you worked that performed poorly. Were any of the causes of the poor performance related to the forces that tend to create process loss? If so, which force was most particularly problematic? What steps, if any, did your team take to deal with the problem?

7. Think of a team in which you worked that performed exceptionally well. What type of taskwork process did the team engage in? Which teamwork processes did the team seem to depend on most to produce the exceptional results?

8. Which types of teamwork training would your student team benefit most from? What exactly would this training cover? What specific benefits would you expect? What would prevent a team from training itself on this material?

Chapter 10 Leadership

10.1 Define leadership, power, and explain what role power plays in leadership

10.1.1 Leadership

There is perhaps no subject written more in the business circle than the topic of leadership. Given all the interest in this topic, a natural question becomes, "What exactly is a leader?" We define leadership as the use of power to direct the activities of followers toward goal achievement. That direction can affect follower's interpretation of events, the organization of their work activities, their commitment to key goals, their relationships with other followers, and their access to cooperation and support from other work units. This chapter focuses on how leaders get the power and influence they use to direct others and how they actually use their power and influence to help followers achieve their goals.

10.1.2 Power and Influence

What exactly comes to mind when you think of the term "power"? Does it raise a positive or negative image for you? Certainly, it's easy to think of leaders who have used power for what we would consider good purposes, but it's just as easy to think of leaders who have used power for unethical or immoral purposes. For now, try not to focus on how leaders use power but instead on how they acquire that power. Power can be defined as the ability to influence the behavior of others and resist unwanted influence in return. Note that this definition gives us a couple of key points to think about. First, just because a person has the ability to influence others does not mean he or she will actually choose to do so. In fact, many times in organizations, the most powerful employees don't even realize how influential they could be! Second, in addition to influencing others, power can be seen as the ability to resist the influence attempts of others. This resistance could come in the form of the simple voicing of a dissenting opinion, the refusal to perform a specific behavior, or the organization of an opposing group of coworkers. Sometimes leaders need to resist the influence of other leaders or higher-ups to do what's best for their own unit. Other times leaders need to resist the influence of their own employees to avoid being a "push-over" when employees try to go their own way.

10.1.3 Acquiring Power

Think about the people you currently work with or have worked with in the past, or think of students that are involved in many of the same activities you are. Do any of those people seem to have especially high levels of power, meaning that they had the ability to influence your behavior? What is it that gives them that power? In some cases, their power may come from some formal position (e. g., supervisor, team leader, teaching assistant, resident advisor). However, sometimes the most powerful people we know lack any sort of formal authority. It turns out that power in organizations can come from a number of different sources. Specifically, there are five major types of power that can be grouped along two dimensions: organizational power and personal power. These types of power are illustrated in Figure 10 - 1.

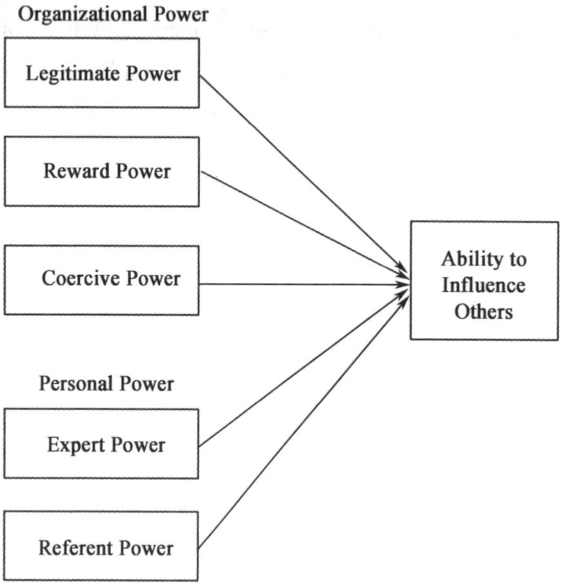

Figure 10 - 1 Types of Power

10.2 Describe the different types of power that leaders possess and when they can use those types most effectively

10.2.1 Organizational Power

The three types of organizational power derive primarily from a person's position within the organization. These types of power are considered to be more formal in nature. Legitimate power is derived from a position of authority inside the organization and is sometimes referred to as "formal authority". People with legitimate power have some title—some term on an organizational chart or on their door that says, "Look, I'm supposed to have influence over you." Those with legitimate power have the understood right to ask others to do things that are considered within the scope of their authority. When a manager asks an employee to stay late to work on a project, work on one task instead of another, or work faster, he or she is exercising legitimate power. The higher up in an organization a person is, the more legitimate power he or she generally possesses.

Legitimate power does have its limits, however. It doesn't generally give a person the right to ask employees to do something outside the scope of their jobs or roles within the organization. For example, if a manager asked an employee to wash her car or mow his lawn, it would likely be seen as an inappropriate request. As we'll see later in this chapter, there is a big difference between having legitimate power and using it effectively.

The next two forms of organizational power are somewhat intertwined with legitimate power. Reward power exists when someone has control over the resources or rewards another person wants. For example, managers generally have control over raises, performance evaluations, awards, more desirable job assignments, and the resources an employee might require to perform a job effectively. Those with reward power have the ability to influence others if those being influenced believe they will get the rewards by behaving in a certain way. Coercive power exists when a person has control over punishments in an organization. Coercive power operates primarily on the principle of fear. It exists when one person believes that another has the ability to punish him or her and is willing to use that power. For example, a manager might have the right to fire, demote, suspend, or lower the pay of an employee. Sometimes the limitations of a manager to impose punishments are formally spelled out in an organization. However, in many instances, managers have a considerable amount of leeway in this regard. Coercive power is generally regarded as a poor form of power to use regularly because it tends to result in negative feelings toward those who wield it.

10.2.2 Personal Power

Of course, leader don't just have some formal title that affords them the ability to reward and punish others. There's something else about them as people that provides them additional capabilities to influence others. Personal forms of power capture that "something else". Expert power is derived from a person's expertise, skill, or knowledge on which others depend. When people have a track record of high performance, the ability to solve problems, or specific knowledge that is necessary to accomplish tasks, they are more likely to be able to influence other people who need that expertise. Consider a lone programmer who knows how to operate a piece of antiquated software, a machinist who was recently trained to operate a new piece of equipment, or the only engineer who has experience working on a specific type of project. All of these individuals will have a degree of expert power because of what they individually bring to the organization. Pat Woertz, the CEO of Archer Daniels Midland (ADM), the Illinois-based agricultural firm, emerges as one of the yearly Fortune's 10 Most Powerful Women in business largely because of her expert power. ADM hired Woertz as CEO because it felt that her time at Chevron would provide energy expertise that could help the firm in its push for renewable fuels. There is perhaps no place where expert power comes into play more than in Silicon Valley, where it is widely perceived that the best leaders are those with significant technological experience and expertise. Jerry Yang, one of the cofounders of Yahoo!, returned as CEO in the summer of 2007, only to step down in November of 2008. During his brief tenure, Yang's expert power gave him immediate levels of authority that the prior CEO never had.

Referent power exists when others have a desire to identify and be associated with a person. This desire is generally derived from an affection, admiration, or loyalty toward a specific individual. Although our focus is on individuals within organizations, there are many examples of political leaders, celebrities, and sports figures who seem to possess high levels of referent power. Bill Clinton, Angelina Jolie, and Peyton Manning all possess referent power to some degree because others want to emulate them. The same could be said of leaders in organizations who possess a good reputation, attractive personal qualities, or a certain level of charisma. Oprah Winfrey, the chairperson of Harpo, Inc., clearly wields an incredible amount of referent power. The people who watch Oprah on TV or listen to her on satellite radio admire her views and often seek to emulate her actions.

Of course, it's possible for a person to possess all of the forms of power at the same time. In fact, the most powerful leaders have bases of power that include all five dimensions. From an employee's perspective, it's sometimes difficult to gauge what form of power is most important. Why exactly do you do what your boss asks you to do? Is it because the boss has the formal right to provide direction, because the boss controls your evaluations, or because you admire and like the boss? Many times, we don't know exactly what type of power leaders possess until they attempt to use it. Generally speaking, the personal forms of power are more strongly related to organizational commitment and job performance than are the organizational forms. If you think about the authorities for whom you worked the hardest, they probably possessed some form of expertise and charisma, rather than just an ability to reward and punish.

10.2.3 Contingency Factors

Power contingency factors are certain situations in organizations that are likely to increase or decrease the degree to which leaders can use their power to influence others. Most of these situations revolve around the idea that the more other employees depend on a person, the more powerful that person becomes. A person can have high levels of expert and referent power, but if he or she works alone and performs tasks that nobody sees, the ability to influence others is greatly reduced. That being said, there are four factors that have an effect on the strength of a person's ability to use power to influence others. These factors are summarized in Table 10 – 1.

Table 10 - 1 The Contingencies of Power

Contingencies	Leader's ability to influence others increases when...
Substitutability	There are no substitutes for the rewards or resources the leader controls
Centrality	The leader's role is important and interdependent with others in the organization
Discretion	The leader has the freedom to make his or her own decisions without being restrained by organizational rules
Visibility	Others know about the leader and the resources he or she can provide

Substitutability is the degree to which people have alternatives in accessing resources. Leaders that control resources to which no one else has access can use their power to gain greater influence. Discretion is the degree to which managers have the right to make decisions on their own. If managers are forced to follow organizational policies and rules, their ability to influence others is reduced. Centrality represents how important a person's job is and how many people depend on that person to accomplish their tasks. Leaders who perform critical tasks and interact with others regularly have a greater ability to use their power to influence others. Visibility is how aware others are of a leader's power and position. If everyone knows that a leader has a certain level of power, the ability to use that power to influence others is likely to be high.

Ken Loughridge, an information technology manager working for MWH Global—an environmental and engineering consulting firm based in England—took these ideas to heart when he changed jobs within the organization. He used a survey the company had done to map out the "social network" within his organization. He used the network map to tell where his employees went for information, who possessed certain types of expertise, and who offered the most help to his employees. He then went to each of the most well-connected individuals so that he can meet them face to face. In a sense, he was seeking out and networking with the individuals in his organization who were likely to have the most power. Companies are increasingly using such networking maps to understand the power structures in their organizations.

10.2.4 Using Influence

Until now, we have discussed the types of power leaders possess and when their opportunities to use that power will grow or diminish. Now we turn to the specific strategies that leaders use to translate that power into actual influence. Recall that having power increases our ability to influence behavior. It does not mean that we will use or exert that power. Influence is the use of an actual behavior that causes behavioral or attitudinal changes in others. There are two important aspects of influence to keep in mind. First, influence can be seen as directional. It most frequently occurs downward (managers influencing employees) but can also be lateral (peers influencing peers) or upward (employees influencing others). Second, influence is all relative. The absolute power of the "influencer" and "influence" is not as important as the disparity between them.

10.3 Explain what behaviors leaders exhibit when trying to influence others. Understand which of these behaviors is most effective

10.3.1 Influence Tactics

Leaders depend on a number of tactics to cause behavioral or attitudinal changes in others. In fact, there are 10 types of tactics that leaders can use to try to influence others. These tactics and their general levels of effectiveness are illustrated in Figure 10 – 2. The four most effective tactics have been shown to be rational persuasion, inspirational appeals, consultation, and collaboration. Rational persuasion is the use of logical arguments and hard facts to show the target that the request is a worthwhile one. Research shows that rational persuasion is most effective when it helps show that the proposal is important and feasible. Rational persuasion is particularly important because it's the only tactic that is consistently successful in the case of upward influence. An inspirational appeal is a tactic designed to appeal to the targets' values and ideals, thereby creating an emotional or attitudinal reaction. To use this tactic effectively, leaders must have insight into what kinds of things are important to the target. Consultation occurs when the target is allowed to participate in deciding how to carry out or implement a request. This tactic increases commitment from the target, who now has a stake in seeing that his or her opinions were right. A leader uses collaboration by attempting to make it easier for the target to complete the request. Collaboration could involve the leader helping complete the task, providing required resources, or removing obstacles that make task completion difficult.

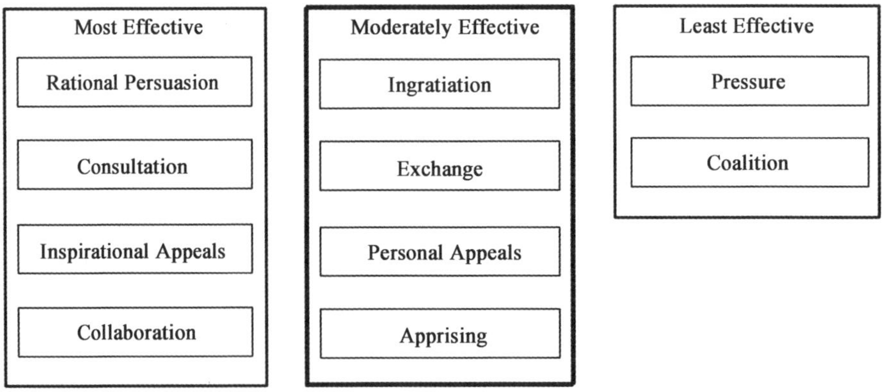

Figure 10 – 2 Influence Tactics and Their Effectiveness

Four other influence tactics are sometimes effective and sometimes not. Ingratiation is the use of favors, compliments, or friendly behavior to make the target feel better about the influencer. You might more commonly hear this referred to this as "sucking up", especially when used in an upward-influence sense. Ingratiation has been shown to be more effective when used as a long-term strategy and not nearly as effective when used immediately prior to making an influence attempt. Personal appeals are when the requestor asks for something based on personal friendship or loyalty. The stronger the friendship, the more successful the attempt is likely to be. An exchange tactic is used when the requestor offers a reward or resource to the target in return for performing a request. This type of request requires that the requestor have something of value to offer. Finally, apprising occurs when the requestor clearly explains why performing the request will benefit the target personally. It differs from rational persuasion in that it focuses solely on the benefit to the target as opposed to simple logic or benefits to the group or organization. It differs from exchange in that the benefit is not necessarily something that the requestor gives to the target but rather something that results from the action.

The two tactics that have been shown to be least effective and could result in resistance from the target are pressure and coalitions. Of course, this does not mean that they aren't used or can't be effective at times. Pressure is the use of coercive power through threats and demands. As we have discussed previously, coercion is a poor way to influence others and may only bring benefits over the short term. The last tactic is the formation of coalitions. Coalitions occur when the influencer enlists other people to help influence the target. These people could be peers, subordinates, or one of the targets' superiors. Coalitions are generally used in combination with one of the other tactics. For instance, if rational persuasion is not strong enough, the influencer might bring in another person to show that that person agrees with the logic of the argument.

Two points should be noted about leaders' use of influence tactics. First, influence tactics tend to be most successful when used in combination. Many tactics have some limitations or weaknesses that can be overcome using other tactics. Second, the influence tactics that tend to be most successful are those that are "softer" in nature. Rational persuasion, consultation, inspirational appeals, and collaboration take advantage of personal rather than organizational forms of power. Leaders that are the most effective at influencing others will generally rely on the softer tactics, make appropriate requests, and ensure the tactics they use match the types of power they have.

10.3.2 Responses to Influence Tactics

As illustrated in Figure 10 - 3, there are three possible responses people have to influence tactics. Engagement occurs when the target of influence agrees with and becomes committed to the influence request. For a leader, this is the best outcome because it results in employees putting forth the greatest level of effort in accomplishing what they are asked to do. Engagement reflects a shift in both the behaviors and the attitudes of employees. Compliance occurs when targets of influence are willing to do what the leader asks, but they do it with a degree of ambivalence. Compliance reflects a shift in the behaviors of employees but not their attitudes. This behavior is the most common response to influence attempts in organizations because anyone with some degree of power who makes a reasonable request is likely to achieve compliance. That response allows leaders to accomplish their purpose, but it doesn't bring about the highest levels of employee effort and dedication. Still, it's clearly preferable to resistance, which occurs when the target refuses to perform the influence request and puts forth an effort to avoid having to do it. Employee resistance could come in the form of making excuses, trying to influence the requestor in return, or simply refusing to carry out the request. Resistance is most likely when the influencer's power is low relative to the target or when the request itself is inappropriate or unreasonable.

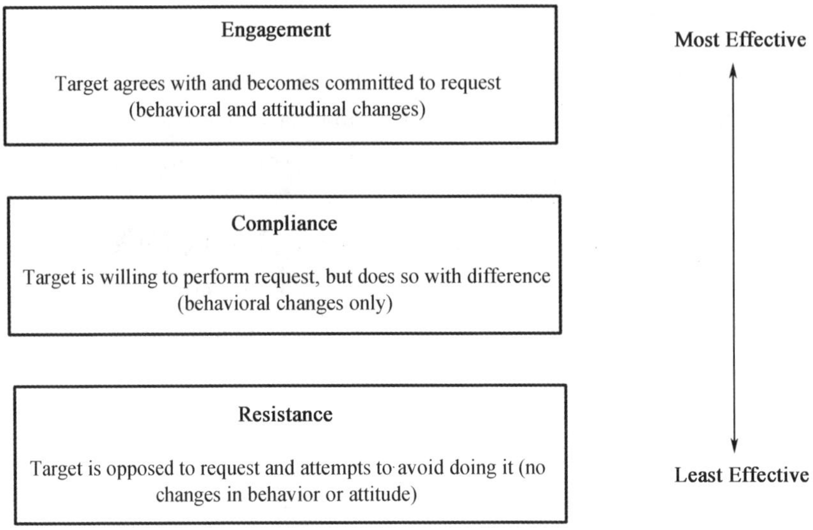

Figure 10 – 3 Responses to Influence Attempts

10.4 Explain how leaders use their power and influence to resolve conflicts in the workplace

One highly important area in which leaders can use their influence is in the context of conflict resolution. Conflict arises when two or more individuals perceive that their goals are in opposition. When conflict arises in organizations, leaders have the ability to use their power and influence to resolve it. As illustrated in Figure 10 – 4, there are five different styles a leader can use when handling conflict, each of which is appropriate in different circumstances. The five styles can be viewed as combinations of two separate factors: how assertive leaders want to be in pursuing their own goals and how cooperative they are with regard to the concerns of others.

Competing (high assertiveness, low cooperation) occurs when one party attempts to get his or her own goals met without concern for the other party's results. It could be considered a win – lose approach to conflict management. Competing occurs most often when one party has high levels of organizational power and can use legitimate or coercive power to settle the conflict. It also generally involves the hard forms of influence such as pressure or coalitions. Although this strategy for resolving conflict might get the result initially, it won't win a leader many friends, given the negative reactions that tend to accompany such tactics. Its best used in situations in which the leader knows he or she is right and a quick decision needs to be made.

Avoiding(low assertiveness, low cooperation) occurs when one party wants to remain neutral, stay away from conflict, or postpone the conflict to gather information or let things cool down. Avoiding usually results in an unfavorable result for everyone, including the organization, and may result in negative feelings toward the leader. Most important, avoiding never really resolves the conflict. Accommodating(low assertiveness, high cooperation) occurs when one party gives in to the other and acts in a completely unselfish way. Leaders will typically use an accommodating strategy when the issue is really not that important to them but is very important to the other party. It's also an important strategy to think about when the leader has less power than the other party. If leaders know they are going to lose the conflict due to their lack of power anyway, it might be a better long-term strategy to give in to the demands from the other party.

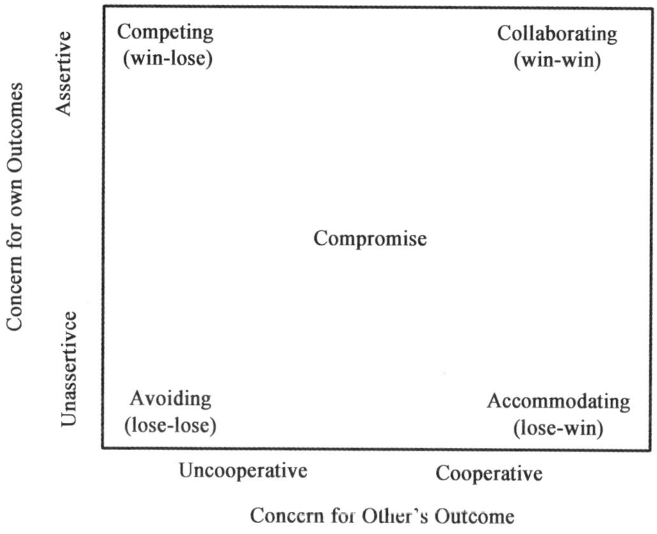

Figure 10 – 4 Styles of Conflict Resolution

Collaboration(high assertiveness, high cooperation) occurs when both parties work together to maximize outcomes. Collaboration is seen as a win-win form of conflict resolution. Collaboration is generally regarded as the most effective form of conflict resolution, especially in reference to task-oriented rather than personal conflicts. However, it's also the most difficult to come by because it requires full sharing of information by both parties, a full discussion of concerns, relatively equal power between parties, and a lot of time investment to arrive at a resolution. However, this style also results in the best outcomes and reactions from both parties. Compromise (moderate assertiveness, moderate cooperation) occurs when conflict is resolved through give-and-take concessions. Compromise is perhaps the most common form of conflict resolution, whereby each party's losses are offset by gains and vice versa. It is seen as an easy form of resolution, maintains relations between parties, and generally results in favorable evaluations for the leader.

One recent and unique example of conflict resolution is occurring through the One Laptop per Child project. Nicolas Negroponte is the founder and chairperson of this nonprofit organization whose mission is to make millions of $100 laptops for undereducated children in the world's poorest nations. Needless to say, manufacturing a $100 laptop (named the XO) is no small feat. Negroponte is leading a network of vastly different individuals, all working on their own time or on loan from other organizations, through a painstaking collaboration process of design and manufacturing. The process hasn't always been easy. There have been times when Negroponte has had to adopt a competing style of conflict resolution to make a custom wireless system for the laptop function. This competitive response upset a faction of volunteers who subsequently quit the project. However, other times Negroponte has facilitated collaboration among very disparate groups. As a leader with varying degrees of power, Negroponte constantly has to balance the needs of the project with the needs of individuals and attempt to resolve conflict effectively.

There is perhaps no better place for leaders to use their power, influence, and conflict resolution skills than when conducting negotiations. Negotiation is a process in which two or more interdependent individuals discuss and attempt to come to an agreement about their different preferences. Negotiations can take place inside the organization or when dealing with organizational outsiders. Negotiations can involve settling a contract dispute between labor and management, determining a purchasing price for products, haggling over a performance review rating, or determining the starting salary for a new employee. Clearly, negotiations are a critical part of organizational life, for both leaders and employees.

10.5 Describe what it means for a leader to be "effective"

The first half of this chapter described how leaders get the power and the types of influence needed to direct others. The rest of the chapter describes how leaders actually use their power and influence in an effective way. Of course, most leaders can't judge their performance by pointing to changes in stock price. Although organizations gauge leader effectiveness in a number of ways, for our purposes, leader effectiveness will be defined as the degree to which the leader's actions result in the achievement of the units goals, the continued commitment of the units employees, and the development of mutual trust, respect, and obligation with followers.

One of the most important things leaders do is make decisions. Think about the job you currently hold or the last job you had. Now picture your boss. How many decisions did he or she have to make in a given week? How did he or she go about making those decisions? A leaders decision-making style reflects the process the leader uses to generate and choose from a set of alternatives to solve a problem (see Chapter 5 on Learning and Decision Making for more on such issues). Decision-making styles capture how a leader decides as opposed to what a leader decides.

The most important element of a leader's decision-making style is this: Does the leader decide most things for him or herself, or does the leader involve others in the process? We've probably all had bosses (or professors, or even parents) who made virtually all decisions by themselves, stopping by to announce what had happened once the call had been made. We've probably also had other bosses (or professors, or parents) who tended to do the opposite—involving us, asking our opinions, or seeking our vote even when we didn't even care about what was being discussed. It turns out that this issue of leader versus follower control can be used to define some specific decision-making styles. Figure 10 – 5 shows those styles, arranged on a continuum from high follower control to high leader control.

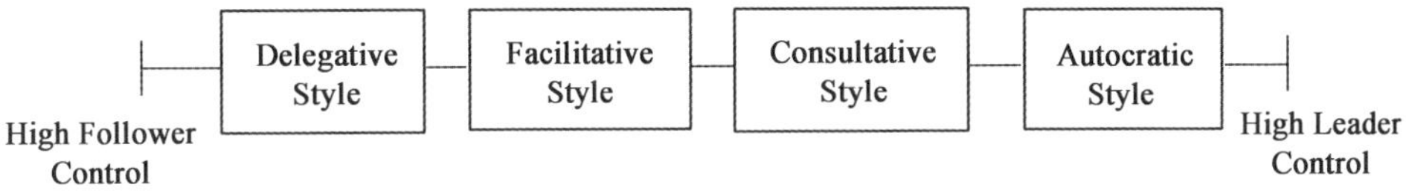

Figure 10 – 5 Leader Decision-Making Styles

10.6 Explain the four styles leaders can use to make decisions

With an autocratic style, the leader makes the decision alone without asking for the opinions or suggestions of the employees in the work unit. The employees may provide information that the leader needs but are not asked to generate or evaluate potential solutions. In fact, they may not even be told about the decision that needs to be made, knowing only that the leader wants information for some reason. This decision-making style seems to be a favorite of Mike Jeffries, the quirky CEO of Abercrombie & Fitch, the Ohio-based clothing retailer best known for its racy catalog and preppy but edgy styles. Even as CEO, Jeffries interviews every model used in the company's catalog, approves all merchandise in the stores, and describes how clothes should be folded on store tables.

The next two styles in Figure 10 – 5 offer more employee involvement. With a consultative style, the leader presents the problem to individual employees or a group of employees, asking for their opinions and suggestions before ultimately making the decision him or herself. With this style, employees do "have a say" in the process, but the ultimate authority still rests with the leader. That ultimate authority changes with a facilitative style, in which the leader presents the problem to a group of employees and seeks consensus on a solution, making sure that his or her own opinion receives no more weight than anyone else's. With this style, the leader is more facilitator than decision maker. Disney CEO Bob Iger seems to embrace a combination of consultative and facilitative styles. Since taking over for Michael Eisner, Iger has made meetings with his division heads less autocratic. Whereas Eisner held court, Iger encourages a conversation. Iger describes his style this way: "You put good people in jobs and give them room to run. . . . You involve yourself in a responsible way, but not to the point where you are usurping their authority. I don't have the time or concentration—and you could argue maybe even the talent—to do that."

With a delegative style, the leader gives an individual employee or a group of employees the responsibility for making the decision within some set of specified boundary conditions. The leader plays no role in the deliberations unless asked, though he or she may offer encouragement and provide necessary resources behind the scenes. Phil Knight, the chairman of Nike, the Oregon-based athletic apparel company, often embraces a delegative style. A quiet and enigmatic figure, Knight has been described as the ultimate delegator, with executives interpreting his silences and nods as the freedom to make their own decisions, even when those decisions take the company in different directions. The management style that has defined Knight's approach over the past 40 years is straightforward: find people who care about the product and let them handle the details. Given his delegative style, it's ironic that Knight has had trouble ceding the CEO position to others during his tenure at Nike.

When Are the Styles Most Effective? Which decision-making style is best? As you may have guessed, there is no one decision-making style that's effective across all situations, and all styles have their pluses and minuses. There are many factors to consider when leaders choose a decision-making style. The most obvious consideration is the quality of the resulting decision because making the correct decision is the ultimate means of judging the leader. However, leaders also have to consider whether employees will accept and commit to their decision. Research studies have repeatedly shown that allowing employees to participate in decision making increases their job satisfaction. Such participation also helps develop employees'own decision-making skills.

Of course, such participation has a downside for employees because it takes up time. Many employees view meetings as an interruption of their work. One recent study found that employees spend, on average, six hours a week in scheduled meetings, and that time spent in meetings was negatively related to job satisfaction when employees didn't depend on others in their jobs, were focused on their own task accomplishment, and felt that meetings were run ineffectively. Consider the case of Paul Pressler, whose five-year term as CEO of The Gap Inc., the California-based apparel company, ended in 2007. Pressler had been hired from Disney to use his expertise to bring discipline to the struggling company. His tenure was criticized for its increase in meetings, with employees asked to explain incredibly specific details to the Gap Inc.'s new chief financial officer. One former employee describes the demands as "the antithesis of being creative and nimble. It was talking about the work vs. doing the work." Criticisms about decision-making style were also leveled at Cynthia Harriss, whom Pressler had hired to lead the Gap brand, "She made no decisions," says one employee, "She defaulted to Paul, who made no decisions."

How can leaders effectively manage their choice of decision-making styles? The time-driven model of leadership offers one potential guide. The model suggests that the focus should shift away from autocratic, consultative, facilitative, and delegative leaders to autocratic, consultative, facilitative, and delegative situations. More specifically, the model suggests that seven factors combine to make some decision-making styles more effective in a given situation and other styles less effective. Those seven factors include

· Decision significance: Is the decision significant to the success of the project or the organization?

· Importance of commitment: Is it important that employees "buy in" to the decision?

· Leader expertise: Does the leader have significant knowledge or expertise regarding the problem?

· Likelihood of commitment: How likely is it that employees will trust the leader's decision and commit to it?

· Shared objectives: Do employees share and support the same objectives, or do they have an agenda of their own?

· Employee expertise: Do the employees have significant knowledge or expertise regarding the problem?

· Teamwork skills: Do the employees have the ability to work together to solve the problem, or will they struggle with conflicts or inefficiencies?

Figure 10 – 6 illustrates how these seven factors can be used to illustrate the most effective decision-making style in a given situation. The figure asks whether levels of each of the seven factors are "high" (H) or "low" (L). The figure functions like a funnel moving from left to right, with each answer bringing you closer to the eventual recommended style (dashes mean that a given factor can be skipped with that combination). Although the model seems complex on first look, the principles within it are straightforward. Autocratic styles are reserved for decisions that are insignificant or decisions for which employee commitment is unimportant. The only exception is when the leader's expertise is high and the leader is trusted. Going with the autocratic style in these situations should result in an accurate decision that makes the most efficient use of employees'time. Delegative styles are reserved for circumstances in which employees have strong teamwork skills and aren't likely to just commit to whatever decision the leader provides. Deciding between the remaining two styles—consultative and facilitative—is more nuanced and requires a more complete consideration of all seven factors.

Research has tended to support many of the time-driven model's propositions, particularly when the research uses practicing managers as participants. For example, one study asked managers to recall past decisions, the context surrounding those decisions, and the eventual successes (or failures) of their decisions. When managers used the decision-making styles recommended by the model, those decisions were rated as successful 68 percent of the time. When managers went against the models' prescriptions, their decisions were only rated as successful 22 percent of the time. It's also interesting to note that studies suggest that managers tend to choose the style recommended by the model only around 40 percent of the time and exhibit less variation in styles than the model suggests they should. In particular, managers seem to overuse the consultative style and underutilize autocratic and facilitative styles.

	Decision Significance	Importance of Commitment	Leader Expertise	Shared Objectives	Likelihood of Commitment	Employee Expertise	Teamwork Skills		
START HERE	H	H	H	H	—	—	—	Autocratic	END HERE
				L	H	H	H	Delegative	
							L	Consultative	
						L	—		
					L	—	—		
			L	H	H	H	H	Facilitative	
							L	Consultative	
						L	—		
					L	—	—		
				L	H	H	H	Facilitative	
							L	Consultative	
						L	—		
					L	—	—		
		L	H	—	—	—	—	Autocratic	
			L	—	H	H	H	Facilitative	
							L	Consultative	
						L	—		
					L	—	—		
	L	H	—	H	—	—	—	Autocratic	
				L	—	—	H	Delegative	
							L	Facilitative	
		L	—	—	—	—	—	Autocratic	

Figure 10 – 6　The Time-Driven Model of Leadership

10.7 Describe the two dimensions that capture most of the day-to-day leadership behaviors that leaders engage in

10.7.1 Day-to-day Leadership Behaviors

Leaving aside how they go about making decisions, what do leaders do on a day-to-day basis? When you think about bosses that you've had, what behaviors do they tend to perform as part of their daily leadership responsibilities? A series of studies at Ohio State in the 1950 s attempted to answer that question. Working under grants from the Office of Naval Research and the International Harvester Company, the studies began by generating a list of all the behaviors leaders engage in—around 1,800 in all. Those behaviors were trimmed down to 150 specific examples, then grouped into several categories, as shown in Table 10 – 2. The table reveals that many leaders spend their time engaging in a mix of initiating, organizing, producing, socializing, integrating, communicating, recognizing, and representing behaviors. Although eight categories are easier to remember than 1,800 behaviors, further analyses suggested that the categories in Table 10 – 2 really boil down to just two dimensions: initiating structure and consideration.

Table 10 – 2 Day-to-day Behaviors Performed by Leaders

Behavior	Description
	Initiating Structure
Initiation	Originating, facilitating, and sometimes resisting new ideas and practices
Organization	Defining and structuring work, clarifying leader versus member roles, coordinating employee tasks
Production	Setting goals and providing incentives for the effort and productivity of employees
	Consideration
Membership	Mixing with employees, stressing informal interactions, and exchanging personal services
Integration	Encouraging a pleasant atmosphere, reducing conflict, promoting individual adjustment to the group
Communication	Providing information to employees, seeking information from them, showing an awareness of matters that affect them
Recognition	Expressing approval or disapproval of the behaviors of employees
Representation	Acting on behalf of the group, defending the group, and advancing the interests of the group

Initiating structure reflects the extent to which the leader defines and structures the roles of employees in pursuit of goal attainment. Leaders who are high on initiating structure play a more active role in directing group activities and prioritize planning, scheduling, and trying out new ideas. They might emphasize the importance of meeting deadlines, describe explicit standards of performance, ask employees to follow formalized procedures, and criticize poor work when necessary. Consideration reflects the extent to which leaders create job relationships characterized by mutual trust, respect for employee ideas, and consideration of employee feelings. Leaders who are high on consideration create a climate of good rapport and strong, two-way communication and exhibit a deep concern for the welfare of employees. They might do personal favors for employees, take time to listen to their problems, "go to bat" for them when needed, and treat them as equals.

The Ohio State studies argued that initiating structure and consideration were (more or less) independent concepts, meaning that leaders could be high on both, low on both, or high on one and low on the other. That view differed from a series of studies conducted at the University of Michigan during the same time period. Those studies identified concepts similar to initiating structure and consideration, calling them production-centered (or task-oriented) and employee-centered (or relations-oriented) behaviors. However, the Michigan studies framed their task-oriented and relations – oriented concepts as two ends of one continuum, implying that leaders couldn't be high on both dimensions. In fact, a recent meta-analysis of 78 studies showed that initiating structure and consideration are only weakly related—knowing whether a leader engages in one brand of behavior says little about whether he or she engages in the other brand. To see how much initiating structure and consideration you engage in during leadership roles, see the assessment at the end of the chapter.

After an initial wave of research on initiating structure and consideration, leadership experts began to doubt the usefulness of the two dimensions for predicting leadership effectiveness. More recent research has painted a more encouraging picture, however. A meta-analysis of 103 studies showed that initiating structure and consideration both had beneficial relationships with a number of outcomes. For example, consideration had a strong positive relationship with perceived leader effectiveness, employee motivation, and employee job satisfaction. It also had a moderate positive relationship with overall unit performance. For its part, initiating structure had a strong positive relationship with employee motivation and moderate positive relationships with perceived leader effectiveness, employee job satisfaction, and overall unit performance.

10.7.2 Transformational Leadership Behaviors

By describing decision-making styles and day-to-day leader behaviors, we've covered a broad spectrum of what it is that leaders do. Still, something is missing. Take a small piece of scrap paper and jot down five people who are famous for their effective leadership. They can come from inside or outside the business world and can be either living people or historical figures. All that's important is that their name be practically synonymous with great leadership. Once you've compiled your list, take a look at the names. Do they appear on your list because they tend to use the right decision-making styles in the right situations and engage in effective levels of consideration and initiating structure? What about the case of Anne Mulcahy? Do decision-making styles and day-to-day leadership behaviors explain her importance to the fortunes of Xerox?

The missing piece of this leadership puzzle is what leaders do to motivate their employees to perform beyond expectations. Transformational leadership involves inspiring followers to commit to a shared vision that provides meaning to their work while also serving as role models who help followers develop their own potential and view problems from new perspectives. Transformational leaders heighten followers' awareness of the importance of certain outcomes while increasing their confidence that those outcomes can be achieved. What gets "transformed" is the way followers view their work, causing them to focus on the collective good more than just their own short-term self-interests and to perform beyond expectations as a result. Former President Dwight D. Eisenhower once noted, "Leadership is the ability to decide what is to be done, and then to get others to want to do it." Former President Harry S. Truman similarly observed, "A leader is a man who has the ability to get other people to do what they don't want to do, and like it." Both quotes capture a transformation in the way followers view their work and what motivates them on the job.

Transformational leadership is viewed as a more motivational approach to leadership than other managerial approaches. Figure 10 – 7 contrasts various approaches to leadership according to how active or passive they are and, ultimately, how effective they prove to be. The five cubes in the figure represent five distinct approaches to motivating employees, and the depth of the cubes represents how much a leader prioritizes each of the approaches. The figure therefore represents an optimal leadership approach that prioritizes more effective and more active behaviors. That optimal approach includes low levels of laissez-faire (i. e., hands-off) leadership, represented by the first cube (counting from the left), which is the avoidance of leadership altogether. Important actions are delayed, responsibility is ignored, and power and influence go unutilized. One common measure of leadership reflects laissez-faire styles with this statement: "The leader avoids getting involved when important issues arise."

The three cubes in the middle represent transactional leadership, which occurs when the leader rewards or disciplines the follower depending on the adequacy of the follower's performance. With passive management-by-exception, the leader waits around for mistakes and errors, then takes corrective action as necessary. After all, "if it isn't broke, don't fix it!" This approach is represented by statements like: "The leader takes no action until complaints are received." With active management-by-exception, the leader arranges to monitor mistakes and errors actively and again takes corrective action when required. This approach is represented by statements like: "The leader directs attention toward failures to meet standards." Contingent reward represents a more active and effective brand of transactional leadership, in which the leader attains follower agreement on what needs to be done using promised or actual rewards in exchange for adequate performance. Statements like "The leader makes clear what one can expect to receive when performance goals are achieved" exemplify contingent reward leadership.

Transactional leadershiprepresents the "carrot-and-stick" approach to leadership, with management-by-exception providing the "sticks" and contingent reward supplying the "carrots". Of course, transactional leadership represents the dominant approach to motivating employees in most organizations, and research suggests that it can be effective. A meta-analysis of 87 studies showed that contingent reward was strongly related to follower motivation and perceived leader effectiveness (see Chapter 4 on Motivation for more discussion of contingent reward issues). Active management-by-exception was only weakly related to follower motivation and perceived leader effectiveness, however, and passive management-by-exception seems to actually harm those outcomes. Such results support the progression shown in Figure 10 – 7, with contingent reward standing as the most effective approach under the transactional leadership umbrella.

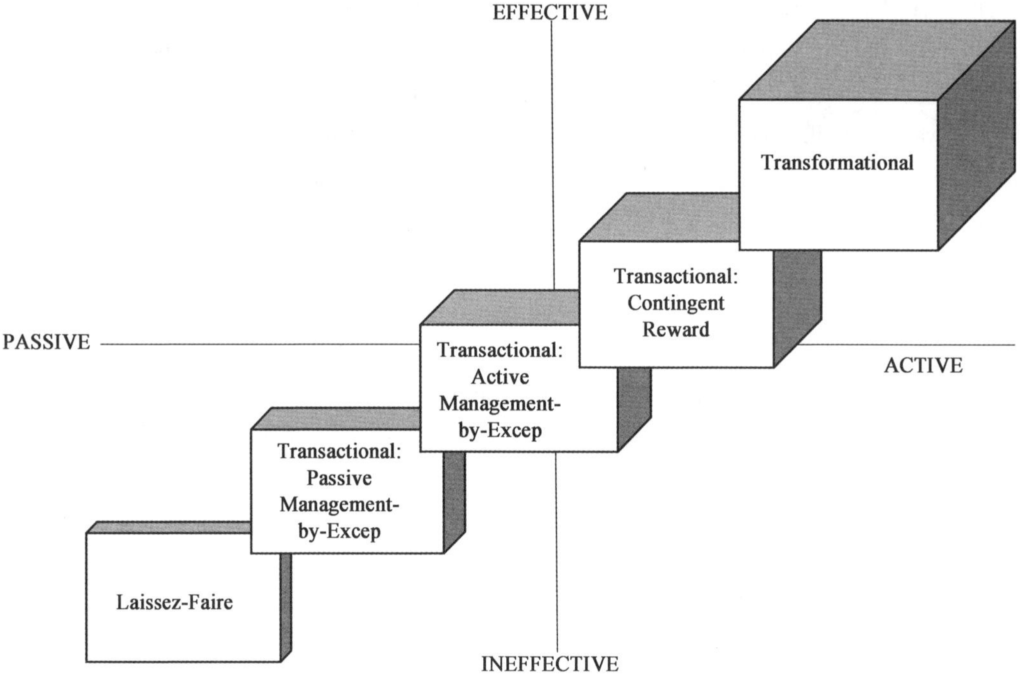

Figure 10 – 7 Laissez-Faire, Transactional, and Transformational Leadership

10.8 Understand how transformational leadership differs from transactional leadership

Finally, the last cube on the right represents transformational leadership—the most active and effective approach in Figure 10 – 7. How effective is transformational leadership? Well, we'll save that discussion for the "How Important Is Leadership" section that concludes this chapter, but suffice it to say that transformational leadership has the strongest and most beneficial effects of any of the leadership variables described in this chapter. It's also the leadership approach that is most universally endorsed across cultures, as described in our OB Internationally feature. In addition, it probably captures the key qualities of the famous leaders we asked you to list a few paragraphs back. To understand why it's so powerful, we need to dig deeper into the specific kinds of actions and behaviors that leaders can utilize to become more transformational. We'll also take a look at the transformational behaviors of a well-known transformational leader: Steve Jobs, the CEO of Apple. It turns out that the full spectrum of transformational leadership can be summarized using four dimensions: idealized influence, inspirational motivation, intellectual stimulation, and individualized consideration.

Idealized influence involves behaving in ways that earn the admiration, trust, and respect of followers, causing followers to want to identify with and emulate the leader. Idealized influence is represented by statements like "The leader instills pride in me for being associated with him/her". Idealized influence is synonymous with charisma—a Greek word that means "divinely inspired gift"—which reflects a sense among followers that the leader possesses extraordinary qualities. Charisma is a word often associated with Steve Jobs. One observer noted that even though Jobs could be very difficult to work with, his remarkable charisma created a mysterious attraction that drew people to him, keeping them loyal to his collective sense of mission.

Inspirational motivation involves behaving in ways that foster an enthusiasm for and commitment to a shared vision of the future. That vision is transmitted through a sort of "meaning-making" process in which the negative features of the status quo are emphasized while highlighting the positive features of the potential future. Inspirational motivation is represented by statements like "The leader articulates a compelling vision of the future." At Apple, Steve Jobs is renowned for spinning a "reality distortion field" that reshapes employees' views of the current work environment. One Apple employee explained, "Steve has this power of vision that is almost frightening. When Steve believes in something, the power of that vision can literally sweep aside any objections, problems, or whatever. They just cease to exist."

Intellectual stimulation involves behaving in ways that challenge followers to be innovative and creative by questioning assumptions and reframing old situations in new ways. Intellectual stimulation is represented by statements like "the leader gets others to look at problems from many different angles." Intellectual stimulation has been a staple of Jobs' tenure at Apple. He pushed for a different power supply on the Apple Ⅱ so that the fan could be removed, preventing it from humming and churning like other computers of the time. Years later, he insisted on removing the floppy drive from the iMac because it seemed silly to transfer data one megabyte at a time, a decision that drew merciless criticism when the iMac debuted.

Individualized consideration involves behaving in ways that help followers achieve their potential through coaching, development, and mentoring. Not to be confused with the consideration behavior derived from the Ohio State studies, individualized consideration represents treating employees as unique individuals with specific needs, abilities, and aspirations that need to be tied into the unit's mission. Individualized consideration is represented by statements like "The leader spends time teaching and coaching". Of the four facets of transformational leadership, Steve Jobs seems lowest on individualized consideration. Employees who are not regarded as his equals are given a relatively short leash and sometimes face an uncertain future in the company. In fact, some Apple employees resist riding the elevator for fear of ending up trapped with Jobs for the ride between floors. As one observer describes it, by the time the doors open, you might have had your confidence undermined for weeks.

10.9 Explain how leadership affects job performance and organizational commitment

How important is leadership? As with some other topics in organizational behavior, that's a complicated question because "leadership" isn't just one thing. Instead, all of the leadership styles and behaviors have their own unique importance. However, transformational leadership stands apart from the rest to some extent, with particularly strong effects in organizations. Groups led by a transformational leader tend to be more financially successful and bring higher-quality products and services to market at a faster rate. Transformational leaders also tend to foster relationships with their followers that are of higher quality, marked by especially strong levels of mutual respect and obligation.

What if we focus specifically on the two outcomes in our integrative model of OB: performance and commitment? Indeed, transformational leadership affects the job performance of the employees who report to the leader. Employees with transformational leaders tend to have higher levels of task performance and engage in higher levels of citizenship behaviors. Why? One reason is that employees with transformational leaders have higher levels of motivation than other employees. They feel a stronger sense of psychological empowerment, feel more self-confident, and set more demanding work goals for themselves. They also trust the leader more, making them willing to exert extra effort even when that effort might not be immediately rewarded.

Employees with transformational leaders tend to be more committed to their organization. They feel a stronger emotional bond with their organization and a stronger sense of obligation to remain present and engaged in their work. Why? One reason is that employees with transformational leaders have higher levels of job satisfaction than other employees. One study showed that transformational leaders can make employees feel that their jobs have more variety and significance, enhancing intrinsic satisfaction with the work itself. Other studies have shown that charismatic leaders express positive emotions more frequently and that those emotions are "caught" by employees through a sort of "emotional contagion" process. For example, followers of transformational leaders tend to feel more optimism and less frustration during their workday, which makes it a bit easier to stay committed to work.

Although leadership is very important to unit effectiveness and the performance and commitment of employees, there is evidence that there are contexts in which the importance of the leader can be reduced. The substitutes for leadership model suggest that certain characteristics of the situation can constrain the influence of the leader, making it more difficult for the leader to influence employee performance. Those situational characteristics come in two varieties, as shown in Table 10 – 3. Substitutes reduce the importance of the leader while simultaneously providing a direct benefit to employee performance. For example, a cohesive work group can provide its own sort of governing behaviors, making the leader less relevant, while providing its own source of motivation and job satisfaction. Neutralizers, in contrast, only reduce the importance of the leader—they themselves have no beneficial impact on performance. For example, spatial distance lessens the impact of a leader's behaviors and styles, but distance itself has no direct benefit for employee job performance.

Table 10 – 3 Leader Substitutes and Neutralizers

Substitutes	Description
Task feedback	Receiving feedback on performance from the task itself
Training and experience	Gaining the knowledge to act independently of the leader
Professionalism	Having a professional specialty that offers guidance
Staff support	Receiving information and assistance from outside staff
Group cohesion	Working in a close-knit and interdependent work group
Intrinsic satisfaction	Deriving personal satisfaction from one's work
Neutralizers	—
Task stability	Having tasks with a clear, unchanging sequence of steps
Formalization	Having written policies and procedures that govern one's job
Inflexibility	Working in an organization that prioritizes rule adherence
Spatial distance	Being separated from one's leader by physical distance

10.10 Takeaways

1. Leadership is the use of power and influence to direct the activities of followers toward goal achievement. Power is the ability to influence the behavior of others and resist unwanted influence in return. Power is necessary, in that it gives leaders the ability to influence others.

2. Leaders have five major types of power. There are three organizational forms of power: Legitimate power is based on authority or position, reward power is based on the distribution of resources or benefits, and coercive power is based on the handing out of punishments. There are two personal forms of power: expert power is derived from expertise and knowledge, whereas referent power is based on the attractiveness and charisma of the leader. These types of power can be used most effectively when leaders are central to the work process, are highly visible, have discretion, and are the sole controllers of resources and information.

3. Leaders can use 10 different influence tactics to achieve their objectives. The most effective are rational persuasion, consultation, inspirational appeals, and collaboration. The least effective

are pressure and the forming of coalitions. Tactics with moderate levels of effectiveness are ingratiation, exchange, personal appeals, and apprising.

4. Leaders use power and influence to resolve conflicts through five conflict resolution styles: avoidance, competing, accommodating, collaborating, and compromising. The most effective and also most difficult tactic is collaboration.

5. A leader is "effective" to the degree to which the leader's actions result in the achievement of the unit's goals, the continued commitment of the unit's employees, and the development of mutual trust, respect, and obligation with followers.

6. Leaders can use a number of styles to make decisions. Beginning with high leader control and moving to high follower control, they include autocratic, consultative, facilitative, and delegative styles. According to the time-driven model of leadership, the appropriateness of these styles depends on decision significance, the importance of commitment, leader expertise, the likelihood of commitment, shared objectives, employee expertise, and teamwork skills.

7. Most of the day-to-day leadership behaviors that leaders engage in are examples of either initiating structure or consideration. Initiating structure behaviors include initiation, organization, and production sorts of duties. Consideration behaviors include membership, integration, communication, recognition, and representation sorts of duties.

8. Transactional leadership emphasizes "carrot-and-stick" approaches to motivating employees, whereas transformational leadership fundamentally changes the way employees view their work. More specifically, transformational leadership inspires them to commit to a shared vision or goal that provides meaning and challenge to their work. The specific behaviors that underlie transformational leadership include the "Four I's": idealized influence, inspirational motivation, intellectual stimulation, and individualized consideration.

9. Transformational leadership has a moderate positive relationship with job performance and a strong positive relationship with organizational commitment. It has stronger effects on these outcomes than other leadership behaviors

10.11 Discussion question

1. Can a leader influence others without power? How exactly would that influence take place?

2. Which forms of power do you consider to be the strongest? Which types of power do you currently have? How could you go about obtaining higher levels of the forms that you're lacking?

3. Who is the most influential leader you have come in contact with personally? What forms of power did he or she have, and which types of influence did he or she use to accomplish objectives?

4. The time-sensitive model of leadership argues that leaders aren't just concerned about the accuracy of their decisions when deciding among autocratic, consultative, facilitative, and delegative styles; they're also concerned about the efficient use of time. What other considerations could influence a leader's use of the four decisionmaking styles?

5. Consider the four dimensions of transformational leadership: idealized influence, inspirational motivation, intellectual stimulation, and individualized consideration. Which of those dimensions would you respond to most favorably? Why?

6. Can you think of any potential "dark sides" to transformational leadership? What would they be?

Section Ⅵ
Organization Mechanisms

Chapter 11 Organizational Structure

Think about some of the jobs you've held in the past(or perhaps the job you hope to have after graduation). What types of employees did you interact with on a daily basis? Were they employees who performed the same tasks that you performed? Or maybe they didn't do exactly what you did, but did they serve the same customer? How many employees did your manager supervise? Was every decision you made scrutinized by your supervisor, or were you given a "long leash"? Those questions all lead to answers that are influenced by organizational structure. An organizational structure formally dictates how jobs and tasks are divided and coordinated between individuals and groups within the company. Organizational structures can be relatively simple when the company only has 5 to 20 employees, but can also grow incredibly complex. One of the world's largest employers, the New York multinational technology company IBM, hosts 375,000 employees who provide hundreds of products and services, with 70% of them are based outside America, with the largest number in India.

11.1 Define organizational structure

An organizational structureis to be grasped by members and outsiders of an organization for understanding the formal reporting relationships between the hob titles and how work is structured within the company. There are five key elements of an organization's structure. Those five key elements, summarized in Table 11 – 1, describe how work tasks, authority relationships, and decision-making responsibilities are organized within the company. These elements will be discussed in the next several sections.

Table 11 – 1 Elements of Organizational Structure

Organizational Structure Dimension	Definition
Work specialization	The degree to which tasks in an organization are divided into separate jobs
Chain of command	Answers the question of "who reports to whom?" and signifies formal authority relationships
Span of control	Represents how many employees each manager in the organization has responsibility for
Centralization	Refers to where decisions are formally made in organizations

Table 11 – 1(continued)

Organizational Structure Dimension	Definition
Formalization	The degree to which rules and procedures are used to standardize behaviors and decisions in an organization

11.2 Describe the major elements of an organizational structure

11.2.1 Work Specialization

Work specialization is the way in which tasks in an organization are divided into separate jobs. In some organizations, this categorization is referred to as a company's division of labor. How many tasks does any one employee perform? To some degree, work specialization is a never ending trade-off among productivity, flexibility, and worker motivation. Take an assembly-line worker at Ford as an example. Henry Ford was perhaps the earliest(and clearly most well-known) believer in high degrees of work specialization. He divided tasks among his manufacturing employees to such a degree that each employee might only perform one single task, over and over again, all day long. Having only one task to perform allowed those employees to be extremely productive at doing that one thing. It also meant that training new workers was much easier when replacements were needed.

However, there are trade-offs when organizations make jobs highly specialized. Organizations may struggle with employee job satisfaction when they make jobs highly specialized. If you recall Chapter 6 on Job Satisfaction, we discussed five core characteristics of jobs that significantly affect satisfaction. One of those characteristics was variety, or the degree to which the job requires a number of different activities involving a number of different skills and talents. Employees tend to be more satisfied with jobs that require them to perform a number of different kinds of activities. Even though you might be very efficient and productive performing a job with only one task, how happy would you be to perform that job on a daily basis?

11.2.2 Chain of Command

The chain of command within an organization essentially answers the question: "Who reports to whom?". Every employee in a traditional organizational structure has one person to whom he or she reports. That person then reports to someone else, and on and on, until the buck stops with the CEO(though, in a public company, even the CEO is responsible to the board of directors). The chain of command can be seen as the specific flow of authority down through the levels of an organization's structure. Organizations depend on this flow of authority to attain order, control, and predictable performance. Some newer organizational structures make this chain of command a bit more complex. It has become common to have positions that report to two or more different managers.

11.2.3 Span of Control

A manager's span of control represents how many employees he or she is responsible for in the organization. Differences in span of control exists among managers, some might be responsible in leading only two employees, which would be considered as a narrow span of control. In other cases, each manager could be responsible for 10 employees. Typically, this number would be considered a wide span of control. Of course, the key question in many organizations is how many employees one manager can supervise effectively. Answering that question requires a better understanding of the benefits of narrow and wide spans of control.

Narrow spans of control allow managers to be much more hands-on with employees, giving them the opportunity to use directive leadership styles while developing close mentoring relationships with employees. A narrow span of control is especially important if the manager has substantially more skill or expertise than the subordinates. Early writings on management assumed that the narrower the span of control, the more productive employees would become. However, a narrow span of control requires organizations to hire many managers, which can significantly increase labor costs. Moreover, if the span of control becomes too narrow, employees can become resentful of their close supervision and long for more latitude in their day-to-day decision making. In fact, current research suggests that a moderate span of control is best for an organization's productivity. Note that organizational performance increases as span of control increases, but only up to the point that managers no longer have the ability to coordinate and supervise the large numbers of employees underneath them. Most organizations work hard to try to find the right balance, and this balance differs for every organization, depending on its unique circumstances. However, there is no question that spans of control in organizations have increased significantly in recent years. Organizations such as Coca-Cola have vice presidents with up to 90 employees reporting to them!

11.2.4 Centralization

Centralization reflects where decisions are formally made in organizations. If only the top managers within a company have the authority to make final decisions, we would say that the organization has a highly "centralized" structure. In contrast, if decision-making authority is pushed down to lower-level employees and these employees feel empowered to make decisions on their own, an organization has a "decentralized" structure. Decentralization becomes necessary as a company grows larger. Sooner or later, the top management of an organization cannot make every single decision within the organization. Centralized organizational structures tend to concentrate power and authority within a relatively tight group of individuals in the firm because they are the ones who have formal authority over important decisions. Have the organizations where you have worked been largely centralized or decentralized? Lower level of authority encountered, and higher degree of participation in decision-making, constitutes as two facets driving our perceptions of higher autonomy and decentralization.

11.2.5 Formalization

A company is high in formalization when there are many specific rules and procedures used to standardize behaviors and decisions. Although not necessarily something as visible as the chain of command or the span of control, the impact of formalization is heavily felt throughout the organization. Rules and procedures are a necessary mechanism for control in every organization. Although the word "formalization" has a somewhat negative connotation, think about your reaction if every McDonald's made its French fries in different ways at each location. Or think about this: Would it bother you if every time you called Dell for technical support, you got an operator who treated you differently and gave you conflicting answers? Formalization is a necessary coordination mechanism that organizations rely on to get a standardized product or deliver a standardized service.

Alcoa's Michigan Casting Center, a leading automotive part supplier, was plagued by the fact that it could have two machine operators running the same machine on two different shifts and get up to a 50 percent performance difference in output and quality between the workers. The company conducted a study to identify the best practices for each machine in its plant. These best practices became standard operating procedures for each worker, and that formalization allowed the company to get a more predictable level of output. Companies such as W. L. Gore, the manufacturer of Gore-Tex and hundreds of other products, fall at the other extreme when it comes to formalization. Whereas most companies have titles for their jobs and job descriptions that specify the tasks each job is responsible for, Bill Gore (company founder) felt that such formalization stifles communication and creativity. After one of his employees mentioned that she needed to put some kind of job title on a business card to hand out at an outside conference, Gore replied that she could put "supreme commander" on the card for all he cared. She liked the title so much that she followed through on his suggestion, and it became a running joke throughout the company.

11.2.6 Elements in Combination

You might have noticed that some elements of an organization's structure seem to go hand-in-hand with other elements. For example, wide spans of control tend to be associated with decentralization in decision making. A high level of work specialization tends to bring about a high level of formalization. Moreover, if you take a closer look at the elements, you might notice that many of the elements capture the struggle between efficiency and flexibility. Mechanistic organizations are efficient, rigid, predictable, and standardized organizations that thrive in stable environments. Mechanistic organizations are typified by a structure that relies on high levels of formalization, a rigid and hierarchical chain of command, high degrees of work specialization, centralization of decision making, and narrow spans of control. In contrast, organic organizations are flexible, adaptive, outward-focused organizations that thrive in dynamic environments. Organic organizations are typified by a structure that relies on low levels of formalization, weak or multiple chains of command, low levels of work specialization, and wide spans of control.

If you think about the differences between the two types, it probably wouldn't be too difficult to come up with a few companies that fall more toward one end of the continuum or the other. However, it is important to remember that few organizations are perfect examples of either of these extremes. Most fall somewhere near the middle, with certain areas within the organization having mechanistic qualities and others being more organic in nature. Although it is tempting to label mechanistic as "bad" and organic as "good", this perception is not necessarily true. Being mechanistic is the only way for many organizations to survive, and it can be a highly appropriate and fruitful way to structure work functions. To find out why that's the case, we need to explore why organizations develop the kinds of structures they do.

11.3 Understand what organizational design is and what the organizational design process depends on

11.3.1 Organizational Design

Organizational design is the process of creating, selecting, or changing the structure of an organization. Ideally, organizations don't just "let" a structure develop on its own; they proactively design it to match their specific circumstances and needs. However, some organizations aren't that proactive and find themselves with a structure that has unintentionally developed on its own, without any careful planning. Those organizations may then be forced to change their structure to become more effective. A number of factors influence the process of organizational design. Those factors include the environment in which the organization does business, its strategy and technology, and the size of the firm.

An organization's business environment consists of its customers, competitors, suppliers, distributors, and other factors external to the firm, all of which have an impact on organizational design. One of the biggest factors in an environment's effect on structure is whether the outside environment is stable or dynamic. Stable environments do not change frequently, and any changes that do occur happen very slowly. Stable environments allow organizations to focus on efficiency and require little change over time. In contrast, dynamic environments change on a frequent basis and require organizations to have structures that are more adaptive. A company strategy describes an organization's objectives and goals and how it tries to capitalize on its assets to make money.

Although the myriad of organizational strategies is too cumbersome to discuss here, two common strategies revolve around being either a low-cost producer or a differentiator. Companies that focus on a low-cost producer strategy rely on selling products at the lowest possible cost. To do this well, they have to focus on being as efficient as they can be. Such companies are more likely to take a mechanistic approach to organizational design. Other companies might follow a differentiation strategy. Rather than focusing on supplying a product or service at the lowest cost, these companies believe that people will pay more for a product that is unique in some way. It could be that their product has a higher level of quality or offers features that a low-cost product doesn't. A differentiation strategy often hinges on adjusting to changing environments quickly, which often makes an organic structure more appropriate.

Very early on in the study of organizations, it was assumed that technology was the major determinant of an organization's structure. Since then, the picture has become less clear regarding the appropriate relationship between technology and structure. Although not completely conclusive, research suggests that the more routine a technology is, the more mechanistic a structure should be. In many ways, this suggestion makes perfect sense: if a company makes the exact same thing over and over, it should focus on creating that one thing as efficiently as possible by having high levels of specialization, formalization, and centralization. However, if technologies need to be changed or altered to suit the needs of various consumers, it follows that decisions would be more decentralized and the rules and procedures the organization relies on would need to be more flexible. There is no question that there is a significant relationship between company size, or total number of employees, and structure. As organizations become larger, they need to rely on some combination of specialization, formalization, and centralization to control their activities and thus become more mechanistic in nature. When it comes to organizational performance, however, there is no definite answer to "how big is too big". As many organizations get bigger, they attempt to create smaller units within the firm to create a "feeling of smallness". W. L. Gore did just that by attempting to prevent any one location in the company from having more than 150 employees. Top management was convinced that a size of 150 would still allow all the employees to talk to one another in the hallways. However, even W. L. Gore hasn't been able to keep that goal as it has grown to encompass 7, 300 employees in 45 locations.

11.3.2 Common Organizational Forms

Our discussion of organizational design describes how an organization's business environment, strategy, technology, and size conspire to make some organizational structures more effective than others. Now we turn our attention to a logical next question: "What structures do most organizations utilize?" The sections that follow describe some of the most common organizational forms. As you read their descriptions, think about whether these forms would fall on the mechanistic or organic side of the structure continuum. You might also consider what kinds of design factors would lead an organization to choose that particular form.

11.4 Describe some of the more common organizational forms that an organization might adopt for its structure

11.4.1 Simple Structures

are perhaps the most common form of organizational design, primarily because there are more small organizations than large ones. In fact, more than 80 percent of employing organizations have fewer than 19 employees. Small accounting and law firms, family-owned grocery stores, individual-owned retail outlets, independent churches, and landscaping services are all organizations that are likely to use a simple structure. Figure 11 – 1 shows a simple structure for a manager-owned restaurant via an organizational chart, a chart that represents every job in the organization and the formal reporting relationships among them. The figure reveals that simple structures are just that: simple. Simple structures are generally used by extremely small organizations in which the manager, president, and owner are all the same person. A simple structure is a flat organization with one person as the central decision-making figure; it is not large enough to have a high degree of formalization and will only have very basic differences in work specialization.

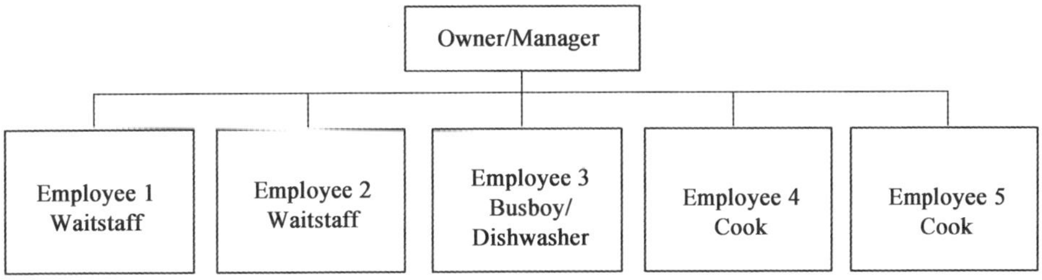

Figure 11 – 1 An Organizational Structure for a Small Restaurant

11.4.2 Bureaucratic structures

When you think of the word "bureaucracy", what thoughts come to mind? Stuffy, boring, restrictive, formal, hard to change, and needlessly complex are some of the terms that have a tendency to be associated with bureaucracies. Those unflattering adjectives aside, chances are very good that you either currently work in a bureaucracy or will after you graduate. A bureaucratic structure is an organizational form that exhibits many of the facets of the mechanistic organization. Bureaucracies are designed for efficiency and rely on high levels of work specialization, formalization, centralization of authority, rigid and well-defined chains of command, and relatively narrow spans of control. As mentioned previously, as an organization's size increases, it is incredibly difficult not to develop some form of bureaucracy.

There are numerous types of bureaucratic structures on which we might focus. The most basic of these is the functional structure. As shown in Figure 11 – 2, a functional structure groups employees by the functions they perform for the organization. For example, employees with marketing expertise are grouped together, those with finance duties are grouped together, and so on. The success of the functional structure is based on the efficiency advantages that come with having a high degree of work specialization that is centrally coordinated. Many small companies naturally evolve into functionally based structures as they grow larger.

Functional structures are extremely efficient when the organization as a whole has a relatively narrow focus, fewer product lines or services, and a stable environment. The biggest weaknesses of a functional structure tend to revolve around the fact that individuals within each function get so wrapped up in their own goals and viewpoints that they lose sight of the bigger organizational picture. In other words, employees don't communicate as well across functions as they do within functions.

11.4.3 Multidivisional structures

In contrast to functional structures, multidivisional structures are bureaucratic organizational forms in which employees are grouped into divisions around products, geographic regions, or clients (Figure 11 – 2). Each of these divisions operates relatively autonomously from the others and has its own functional groups. Multidivisional structures generally develop from companies with functional structures whose interests and goals become too diverse for that structure to handle. For example, if a company with a functional structure begins to add customers that require localized versions of its product, the company might adopt a geographic structure to handle the product variations. Which form a company chooses will likely depend on where the diversity in its business lies.

Product structures group business units around different products that the company produces. Each of those divisions becomes responsible for manufacturing, marketing, and doing research and development for the products in its own division. Boeing, Procter & Gamble, Hewlett – Packard, and Sony are companies that have developed product structures. Product structures make sense when firms diversify to the point that the products they sell are so different that managing them becomes overwhelming. Geographic structures are generally based around the different locations where the company does business. The functions required to serve a business are placed under a manager who is in charge of a specific location. Reasons for developing a geographic structure revolve around the different tastes of customers in different regions, the size of the locations that need to be covered by different salespeople, or the fact that the manufacturing and distribution of a product are better served by a geographic breakdown. One last form of multidivisional structure is the client structure. When organizations have a number of very large customers or groups of customers that all act in a similar way, they might organize their businesses around serving those customers. For example, small banks traditionally organize themselves into divisions such as personal banking, small business banking, personal lending, and commercial lending. Similarly, consulting firms often organize themselves into divisions that are responsible for small business clients, large business clients, and federal clients. For an example of how a merger affected two multinational firms and their structures, see OB Internationally feature in this chepter.

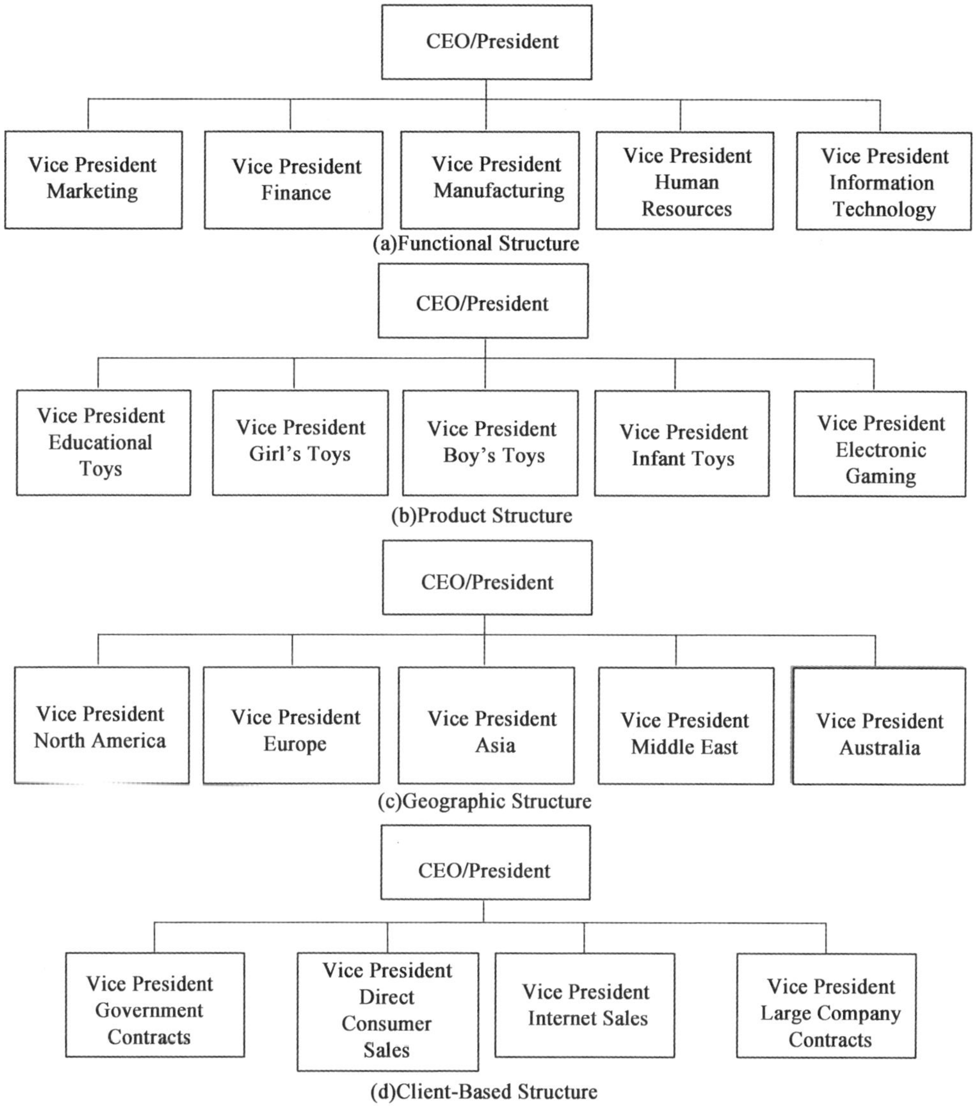

Figure 11 – 2 Functional and Multidivisional Structure

Matrix structures are more complex forms of organizational design that try to take advantage of two types of structures at the same time. Companies such as Xerox, General Electric, and Dow Corning were among the first to adopt this type of structure. Figure 11 – 3 provides an example of a matrix structure. In this example, employees are distributed into teams or projects within the organization on the basis of both their functional expertise and the product that they happen to be working on. Thus, the matrix represents a combination of a functional structure and a product structure. There are two important points to understand about the matrix structure. First, the matrix allows an organization to put together very flexible teams based on the experiences and skills of their employees. This flexibility enables the organization to adjust much more quickly to the environment than a traditional bureaucratic structure would.

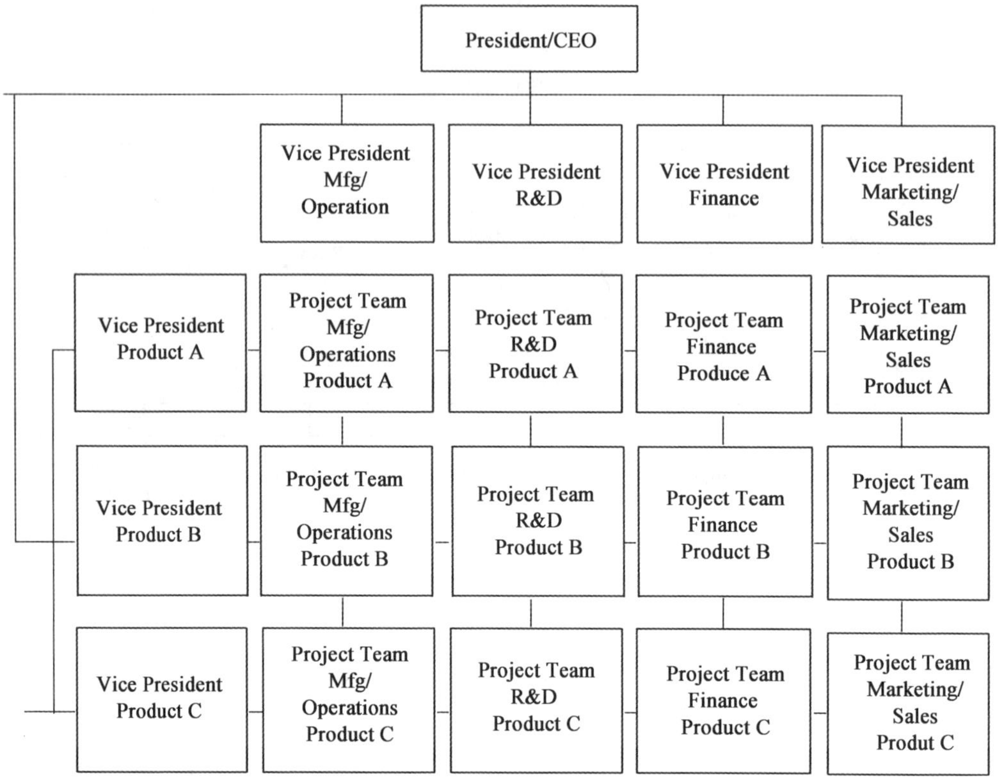

Figure 11 –3　Matrix Structure

Second, the matrix gives each employee two chains of command, two groups with which to interact, and two sources of information to consider. This doubling of traditional structural elements can create high stress levels for employees if the demands of their functional grouping are at odds with the demands of their product- or client-based grouping. The situation can become particularly stressful if one of the two groupings has more power than the other. For example, it may be that the functional manager assigns employees to teams, conducts performance evaluations, and decides raises—making that manager more powerful than the product-or client-based manager. Although matrix structures have been around for an extremely long time, the number of organizations using them is growing as teams become a more common form of organizing work. They also have become more common in global companies, with the functional grouping balanced by a geographic grouping. For example, Areva NP, a French company that designs and builds nuclear power plants, has a matrix structure based on products (plants, fuel, services, and equipment) and geographical locations (France, Germany, and North America).

Restructuring

As you have read through our discussion of organizational structure, you may have noticed how important it is for organizations to adapt to their environment. The first step in adapting is recognizing the need to change. The second (and sometimes much more problematic) step is actually doing it by restructuring. The process of changing an organization's structure is called restructuring. Organizations attempt to restructure all the time—in fact, it's difficult to pick up a copy of Business Week or Fortune without reading about some organization's restructuring initiatives. General Motors has undertaken a massive restructuring effort no less than six times over the past 20 years! Indeed, most of the examples we put into this chapter center on organizations that were restructuring.

11.5 Describe the steps organizations can take to reduce the negative effects of restructuring

When employees get a sense that their company might be getting ready to restructure, it causes a great deal of stress because they become worried that they will be one of those to lose their jobs (due to a possible "flattening" of the organization). When Hewlett-Packard recently decided to restructure, it caused widespread fear and panic among employees. For the 60 days prior to the actual restructuring announcement, work came to a standstill at the company—tales of high stress, low motivation, political battles, and power struggles abounded. It is estimated that Hewlett-Packard as a company lost an entire quarter's worth of productivity.

One of the ways in which managers can do their best to help a restructuring succeed is to help manage layoff survivors (employees that remain with the company following a layoff). Many layoff survivors are known to experience a great deal of guilt and remorse following an organization's decision to remove some employees from the company. Researchers and practitioners recently have been trying to understand layoff survivors better, as well as how to help them adjust more quickly. One of the major problems for layoff survivors is the increased job demands placed on them. After all, that coworker or boss the employee had was doing something. Layoff survivors are generally burdened with having to pick up the leftover tasks that used to be done by somebody else. This burden creates a sense of uncertainty and stress. Recent research suggests that one of the best ways to help layoff survivors adjust is to do things that give them a stronger sense of control. Allowing survivors to have a voice in how to move forward or help set the plans about how to accomplish future goals are two ways managers can help employees feel more in control. In addition, honest and frequent communication with layoff survivors greatly helps reduce their feelings of uncertainty and stress.

To some degree, an organization's structure provides the foundation for almost everything in organizational behavior. Think about some of the things that organizational structure affects:

communication patterns between employees, the tasks an employee performs, the types of groups an organization uses, the freedom employees have to innovate and try new things, how power and influence are divided up in the company... we could go on and on. Picture the walls of a house. The occupants within those walls can decorate or personalize the structure as best they can. They can make it more attractive according to their individual preferences by adding and taking away furniture, but at the end of the day, they are still stuck with that structure. They have to work within the confines that the builder envisioned (unless they are willing to tear down walls or build new ones at considerable time, effort, and expense!). Organizational structures operate in much the same way for employees and their managers. A given manager can do many things to try to motivate, inspire, and set up an effective work environment so that employees have high levels of performance and commitment; however, at the end of the day, a manager must work within the structure created by the organization.

11.6 Understand how organizational restructuring affects job performance and organizational commitment

Given how many organizational forms there are, it is almost impossible to give an accurate representation of the impact of organizational structure on job performance. In fact, we might even say that an organization's structure determines what job performance is supposed to look like! In addition, the elements of structure are not necessarily good or bad for performance. For example, a narrow span of control is not necessarily better than a broad one; rather, the organization must find the optimal "middle ground". One thing we can say, is that changes to an organization's structure can have negative effects on the employees who work for the company, at least in the short term. Research suggests that restructuring has a small negative effect on task performance, likely because changes in specialization, centralization, or formalization may lead to confusion about how exactly employees are supposed to do their jobs, which hinders learning and decision making. Restructuring has a more significant negative effect on organizational commitment, however. Restructuring efforts can increase stress and jeopardize employees' trust in the organization. There is some evidence that the end result is a lower level of affective commitment on the part of employees because they feel less emotionally attached to the firm.

11.7 Takeaways

1. An organization's structure formally dictates how jobs and tasks are divided and coordinated between individuals and groups within the organization. This structure, partially illustrated through the use of organizational charts, provides the foundation for organizing jobs, controlling employee behavior, shaping communication channels, and providing a lens through which employees view their work environment.

2. There are five major elements to an organization's structure: work specialization, chain of command, span of control, centralization of decision making, and formalization. These elements can be organized in such a way as to make an organization more mechanistic in nature, which allows it to be highly efficient in stable environments, or more organic in nature, which allows it to be flexible and adaptive in changing environments.

3. Organizational design is the process of creating, selecting, or changing the structure of an organization. Factors to be considered in organizational design include a company's business environment, its strategy, its technology, and its size.

4. There are literally thousands of organizational forms. The most common is the simple structure, which is used by most small companies. Larger companies adopt a more bureaucratic structure. This structure may be functional in nature, such that employees are grouped by job tasks, or multidivisional, such that employees are grouped by product, geography, or client. Organizations also may adopt a matrix structure that combines functional and multidivisional grouping.

5. To reduce the negative effects of restructuring, organizations should focus on managing the stress levels of the employees who remain after the restructuring. Providing employees with a sense of control can help them learn to navigate their new work environment.

6. Organizational restructuring efforts have a weak negative effect on job performance. They have a more significant negative effect on organizational commitment because employees tend to feel less emotional attachment to organizations that are restructuring.

11.8 Discussion questions

1. Is it possible to be a great leader of employees in a highly mechanistic organization? What special talents or abilities might be required?

2. Why do the elements of structure such as work specialization, formalization, span of control, chain of command, and centralization have a tendency to change together? Which of the five do you feel is the most important?

3. Which is more important for an organization: the ability to be efficient or the ability to adapt to its environment? What does this say about how an organization's structure should be set up?

4. Which of the organizational forms described in this chapter do you think leads to the highest levels of motivation among workers? Why?

5. If you worked in a matrix organization, what would be some of the career development challenges that you might face? Does the idea of working in a matrix structure appeal to you? Why or why not?

Chapter 12 Organizational Culture

12.1 Define organizational culture and describe its components

We have spent a great deal of time in this book talking about how employee attitudes and behaviors are shaped by group mechanisms such as teams and leaders, and individual characteristics such as personality and ability. In this chapter, we discuss how the organization as a whole affects employee attitudes and behavior. Instead of simply offering definitions of important topics, in this chapter, it is important for you to understand that there are just about as many definitions of organizational culture as there are people who study it. Sociologists study culture using a broad lens and anthropological research methods, like those applied to study tribes and civilizations. Psychologists tend to study culture and its effects on people using survey methods. In fact, many psychologists actually prefer the term "climate" as for "culture". But for us, we'll use the two terms interchangeably. In this chapter, we define organizational culture as the shared social knowledge within an organization regarding the rules, norms, and values that shape the attitudes and behaviors of its employees.

12.1.1 Why do Some Organizations Have Different Cultures Than Others?

One of the most common questions people ask when you tell them where you are employed is, "So, tell me... what's it like there?" The description you use in your response is likely to have a lot to do with what the organization's culture is all about. In calculating your response to the question, you might consider describing the kinds of people who work at your company. More than likely, you will do your best to describe the work atmosphere on a regular day. Perhaps you will painstakingly describe the facilities you work in or how you feel the employees are treated. You might even go as far as to describe what it is that defines "success" at your company. All of those answers give clues that help organizational outsiders understand what a company is actually like. To give you a feel for the full range of potential answers to the "what's it like there?" question, it's necessary to review the facets of culture in more detail.

12.2.2 Culture Components

There are three major components to any organization's culture: observable artifacts, espoused values, and basic underlying assumptions. You can understand the differences among these three components if you view culture like an onion. Some components of an organization's culture are readily apparent and observable, like the skin of an onion. However, other components are less observable to organizational outsiders or newcomers. Such outsiders can observe, interpret, and make conclusions based on what they see on the surface, but the inside remains a mystery until they can peel back the outside layers to gauge the values and assumptions that lie beneath. The sections that follow review the culture components in more detail.

Observable artifacts are the manifestations of an organization's culture that employees can easily see or talk about. They supply the signals that employees interpret to gauge how they should act during the workday. Artifacts supply the primary means of transmitting an organization's culture to its workforce. It is difficult to overestimate the importance of artifacts because they help show not only current employees but also potential employees, customers, shareholders, and investors what the organization is all about. There are six major types of artifacts: symbols, physical structures, language, stories, rituals, and ceremonies.

Symbols can be found throughout an organization, from its corporate logo to the images it places on its Web site to the uniforms its employees wear. Think about what Nike's "swoosh" represents: speed, movement, velocity. What might that symbol convey about Nike's culture? Or consider Apple Computer's "apple" logo. That symbol brings to mind Newton's discovery of gravity under the apple tree, conveying the importance of innovation within Apple's culture. Physical structures also say a lot about a culture. Is the workplace open? Does top management work in a separate section of the building? Is the setting devoid of anything unique, or can employees express their personalities? Bloomberg, an information services, news, and media company based in New York, built its new headquarters in Manhattan primarily out of steel and glass, resembling what workers call a "beehive". It has no private offices and no cubicles, and even the conference rooms have glass walls. CEO Lex Fenwick sits on the third floor, surrounded by his sales and customer service staff. He believes this setup leads to instantaneous communication among employees. IDEO, a creative think tank, also has an open office environment, though IDEO lets employees set up their offices however they like. When you walk around their work areas, you'll be walking underneath bicycles hanging over your head and crazy objects and toys in every direction.

Language reflects the jargon, slang, and slogans used within the walls of an organization. Do you know what a CTR, CPC, or Crawler is? Chances are you don't. If you worked for Yahoo!, however, those terms would be second nature to you: CTR stands for click-through rate, CPC stands for cost-per-click, and a Crawler is a computer program that gathers information from other Websites. Yum Brands Inc., which owns Pizza Hut, Taco Bell, KFC, and other fast-food restaurants, expects employees to be "customer maniacs"—language that conveys its culture for customer interaction. Stories consist of anecdotes, accounts, legends, and myths that are passed down from cohort to cohort within an organization. When the London-based, global conglomerate Unilever purchased Ben & Jerry's Homemade Inc. in 2001, the Unilever chairman first walked into the Vermont-based company to a sight he didn't often see: all the employees were wearing togas!

This story captures some of the cultural differences between Unilever and Ben & Jerry's and will likely be told over and over again within the organization.

Rituals are the daily or weekly planned routines that occur in an organization. Employees at New Belgium Brewing in Colorado, home of Fat Tire Ale, receive a case of beer a week after a year on the job, conveying the importance of both employees and the company's product. At UPS, every driver and package handler attends a mandatory "three-minute meeting" with their managers to help with communication. The 180-second time limit helps enforce the importance of punctuality in the UPS culture. The Men's Wearhouse pays managers quarterly bonuses when theft (referred to as "shrink") is kept low. That ritual sends a message that "when workers steal from you, they are stealing from themselves and their colleagues". Ceremonies are formal events, generally performed in front of an audience of organizational members. In the process of turning around the company, Continental Airlines held a ceremony to burn an employee-despised 800-page policy manual. Gordon Bethune, then CEO of Continental, put together a task force that came up with a new 80-page manual.

Espoused values are the beliefs, philosophies, and norms that an organization explicitly states. Espoused values can range from published documents such as a company's vision or mission statement to verbal statements made to employees by executives and managers. Examples of some of UPS's outward representations of espoused values can be found in Table 12 – 1. What do each of these statements tell you about UPS and what it cares about?

Table 12 – 1 The Espoused Values of UPS

Below includes some of the 37 values that spell out UPS's vision for managing its workforce. These values are spelled out in a "policy book" that is handed out to the company's management team.
· We build our organization around people
· We place great value on diversity
· We treat our people fairly and without favoritism
· We insist upon integrity in our people
· We promote from within
· We promote an open-door approach to managing people
· We expect our people to be neat in appearance

It is certainly important to draw a distinction between espoused values and enacted values. It is one thing for a company to outwardly say something is important; it is another thing for employees to consistently act in ways that support those espoused values. When a company holds to its espoused values over time and regardless of the situations it operates in, the values become more believable to both employees and outsiders. However, in times of economic downturns, staying true to espoused values is not always easy. One group that seemingly enacts their espoused values even in the face of adversity can be found in this chapter's OB in sports feature.

Basic underlying assumptions are taken for granted beliefs and philosophies that are so ingrained that employees simply act on them rather than questioning the validity of their behavior in a given situation. These assumptions represent the deepest and least observable part of a culture and may not be consciously apparent, even to organizational veterans. Edgar Schein, one of the preeminent scholars on the topic of organizational culture, uses the example of safety in an engineering firm. He states, "In an occupation such as engineering, it would be inconceivable to deliberately design something that is unsafe; it is a taken for granted assumption that things should be safe." Whatever a company's underlying assumptions are, its hidden beliefs are those that are the most likely to dictate employee behavior and affect employee attitudes. They are also the aspects of an organizational culture that are the most long-lasting and difficult to change.

12.2.3 General Culture Types

If we can consider the combination of an organization's observable artifacts, espoused values, and underlying assumptions, we can begin to classify its culture along various dimensions. Of course, there are many different types of organizational cultures, just like there are many different types of personalities. Many researchers have tried to create general typologies that can be used to describe the culture of any organization. For instance, one popular general typology divides organizational culture along two dimensions: solidarity and sociability. Solidarity is the degree to which group members think and act alike, and sociability represents how friendly employees are to one another. One typology describes organizations as communal, networked, fragmented, mercenary along the dimensions of sociability and solidarity. Organizations that are low on both dimensions have a fragmented culture in which employees are distant and disconnected from one another. Organizations that have cultures in which employees think alike but aren't friendly to one another can be considered mercenary cultures. These types of organizations are likely to be very political, "what's in it for me" environments. Cultures in which all employees are friendly to one another, but everyone thinks differently and does his or her own thing, are communal cultures. Many highly creative organizations have a communal culture. Organizations with friendly employees who all think alike are networked cultures.

12.2 Describe general and specific types of organizational cultures

12.2.1 Specific Culture Types

The typology described before is general enough to be applied to almost any organization. However, there are obviously other ways to classify an organization's culture. In fact, many organizations attempt to manipulate observable artifacts and espoused values to create specific cultures that help them achieve their organizational goals. Some of these specific cultures are more relevant in some industries than in others. Although the number of specific cultures an organization might strive for are virtually endless, we focus on three examples: customer service cultures, diversity cultures, and creativity cultures.

Many organizations try to create a customer service culture focused on service quality. After all, 65 percent of the gross domestic product in the United States is generated by service-based organizations. Organizations that have successfully created a service culture have been shown to change employee attitudes and behaviors toward customers. These changes in attitudes and behaviors then manifest themselves in higher levels of customer satisfaction and sales. Figure 12 – 1 illustrates the process of creating a service culture and the effects it has on company results. Numerous companies claim that the sole reason for their continued existence is their ability to create a service culture in their organization when it wasn't originally present. Other companies, such as Circuit City, have tried to reinvigorate customer service by recreating a service culture within their stores. After falling way behind rival Best Buy, the retailer has been inching its way back to respectability by making changes such as shifting its mostly commission – based workforce to an hourly pay rate.

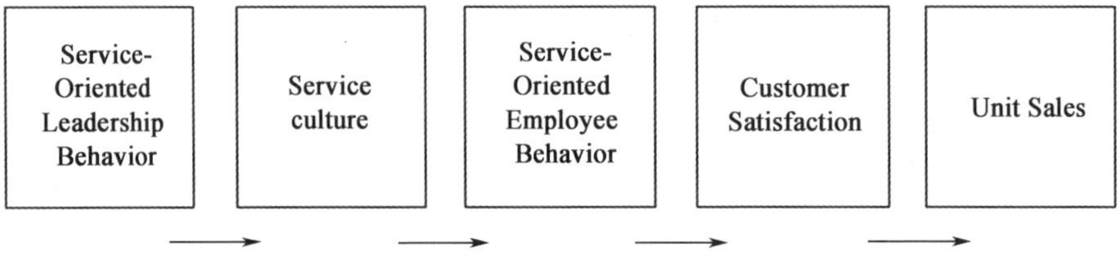

Figure 12 – 1 The Service Culture Process

There are a number of reasons why an organization might want to foster a diversity culture. What images come to mind when you think of Denny's? Do you think of the nation's largest family-style, full-service restaurant chain in the country and the Grand Slam breakfast, or do you think of race discrimination? Although the lawsuits that charged company discrimination against African Americans were settled back in 1994, the stigma of Denny's discrimination complaints still lingers. Since 1994, Denny's has maintained a position within the company of chief diversity officer whose sole responsibility is to help create a culture of diversity. Denny's has since become a prime example of how to aggressively lead a charge toward a diversity culture. Denny's has tried to transform itself by hiring a large number of new minority managers and franchise owners, replacing half of the all-male board of directors with women, conducting diversity sensitivity training sessions, and performing other symbolic actions. Many of the techniques used by Denny's are now recognized as key elements in successful corporate diversity initiatives.

Given the importance of new ideas and innovation in many industries, it is understandable that some organizations focus on fostering a creativity culture. Creativity cultures have been shown to affect both the quantity and quality of creative ideas within an organization. Google recently put policies in place that will allow its engineers to spend 20 percent of their working time pursuing projects that they feel passionate about to foster innovation at the organization. In part to foster a culture of creativity, Pfizer Canada has banned all e-mails and voice mails on weekends and after 6:00 p. m. on weekdays to keep their employees fresh while they are on the job. The company feels this 12-hour break has led to a higher-quality flow of ideas and provided a morale boost to go along with it.

12.2.2 Culture Strength

Although most organizations seem to strive for one, not all companies have a culture that creates a sense of definite norms and appropriate behaviors for their employees. If you've worked for a company and can't identify whether it has a strong culture or not, it probably doesn't. A high level of culture strength exists when employees definitively agree about the way things are supposed to happen within the organization (high consensus) and when their subsequent behaviors are consistent with those expectations (high intensity). A strong culture serves to unite and direct employees. Weak cultures exist when employees disagree about the way things are supposed to be or what is expected of them, meaning that there is nothing to unite or direct their attitudes and actions.

12.3 Describe a strong culture, and what makes a culture strong

Strong cultures take a long time to develop and are very difficult to change. Individuals working within strong cultures are typically very aware of it. However, this discussion brings us to an important point: "strong" cultures are not always "good" cultures. Strong cultures guide employee attitudes and behaviors, but that doesn't always mean that they guide them toward the most successful organizational outcomes. As such, it is useful to recognize some of the positive and negative aspects of having a strong organizational culture. Table 12 – 2 lists some of the advantages and disadvantages. You might have noticed that all of the advantages in the left-hand column of Table 12 – 2 allow the organization to become more efficient at whatever aspect of culture is strong within the organization. The right-hand column's disadvantages all lead toward all organization's inability to adapt.

Table 12 – 2 Pros and Cons of a Strong Culture

Advantages of a Strong Culture	Disadvantages of a Strong Culture
Differentiates the organization from others	Makes merging with another organization more difficult
Allows desired behaviors among employees	Attracts and retains similar kinds of employees, thereby limiting diversity of thought

Table 12 -2(continued)

Advantages of a Strong Culture	Disadvantages of a Strong Culture
Facilitates desired behaviors among employees	Can be "too much of a good thing" if it creates extreme behaviors among employees
Creates stability within the organization	Makes adapting to the environment more difficult

In some cases, the culture of an organization is not really strong or weak. Instead, there might be sub-cultures that unite a smaller subset of the organization's employees. These subgroups may be created because there is a strong leader in one area of the company that engenders different norms and values or because different divisions in a company act independently and create their own cultures. Subculture exist when the overall organizational culture is supplemented by another culture governing a more specific set of employees. Subcultures are more likely to exist in large organizations than they are in small companies. Most organizations don't mind having subcultures, to the degree that they do not interfere with the values of the overall culture. In fact, subcultures can be very useful for organizations if there are certain areas of the organization that have different demands and needs for their employees. However, when their values don't match those of the larger organization, we call subcultures countercultures. Countercultures can sometimes serve a useful purpose by challenging the values of the overall organization or signifying the need for change. In extreme cases, however, countercultures can split the organization's culture right down the middle, resulting in the differentiated culture.

12.4 Explain how organizations maintain their culture and describe how companies change their culture

12.4.1 Maintaining an Organizational Culture

Clearly an organization's culture can be described in many ways, from espoused values and underlying assumptions, to general dimensions such as solidarity or sociability, to more specific types such as service cultures or creativity cultures. No matter how we describe an organization's culture, however, that culture will be put to the test when an organization's founders and original employees begin to recruit and hire new members. If those new members do not fit the culture, then the culture may become weakened or differentiated. However, two processes can conspire to help keep cultures strong: attraction-selection-attrition and socialization.

12.4.2 Attraction – Selection – Attrition(ASA)

The ASA framework holds that potential employees will be attracted to organizations whose cultures match their own personality, meaning that some potential job applicants won't apply due to a perceived lack of fit. In addition, organizations will select candidates based on whether their personalities fit the culture, further weeding out potential "misfits". Finally, those people who still don't fit will either be unhappy or ineffective when working in the organization, which leads to attrition(i. e., voluntary or involuntary turnover).

Several companies can provide an example of ASA in action. FedEx has worked hard to create a culture of ethics. The executives at FedEx believe that a strong ethical culture will attract ethical employees who will strengthen moral behavior at FedEx. The Cheesecake Factory believes that selection is where maintaining a culture begins. Management suggests that its heavily service-oriented culture calls for certain types of employees. They believe that teaching people how to perform regular restaurant duties is possible, but teaching people to have the right personality and attitudes is not. As a company, it consistently tries to identify the traits that allow employees to thrive in a Cheesecake Factory environment. Of course, attraction and selection processes do not always align employees' personalities with organizational culture—one reason voluntary and involuntary turnover occur in every organization.

12.4.3 Socialization

In addition to taking advantage of attraction – selection – attrition, organizations also maintain an organizational culture by shaping and molding new employees. Starting a new job with a company is a stressful, complex, and challenging undertaking for both employees and organizations. In reality, no outsider can fully grasp or understand the culture of an organization simply by looking at artifacts visible from outside the company. A complete understanding of organizational culture is a process that happens over time. Socialization is the primary process by which employees learn the social knowledge that enables them to understand and adapt to the organization's culture. It is a process that begins before an employee starts work and doesn't end until an employee leaves the organization. What is it that an employee needs to learn and adapt to in order to be socialized into his or her new role within an organization? Most of the important information can be grouped into six dimensions, highlighted in Figure 12 – 2. Research shows that each of these six dimensions is an important area in the process of socialization. Each has unique contributions to job performance, organizational commitment, and person-organization fit.

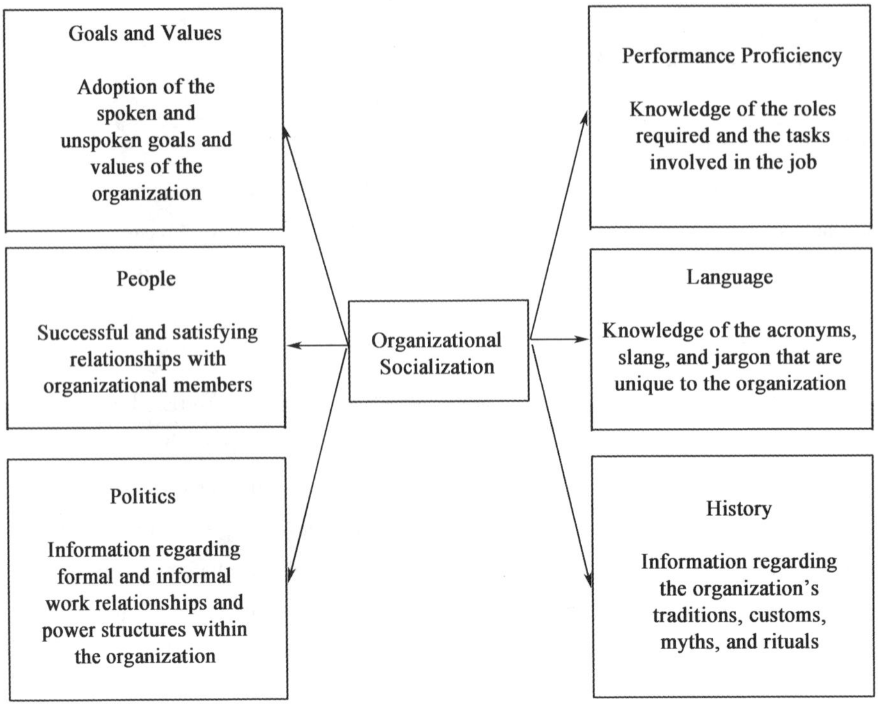

Figure 12 – 2 Dimensions Addressed in Most Socialization Effort

12.5 Describe two steps organizations can take to make sure that newcomers will fit with their culture

One of the most inexpensive and effective ways of socializing employees and thus reducing early turnover is the use of realistic job previews. Realistic job previews (RJPs) occur before an employee even starts working for the company! These RJPs involve making sure a potential employee has an accurate picture of what working for an organization is going to be like by providing both the positive and the negative aspects of the job. Kal Tire, a leading Canadian automotive retail outlet, allows job candidates to spend an entire day inside the company becoming familiar with the organization and the job they are applying for. By allowing applicants to see what the organizations'idea of customer service is and the job demands of road tire repairs, Kal Tire is effectively reducing the likelihood of employees being surprised by what they find when they start work and shortening the time it takes for employees to socialize.

Another way organizations try to speed up the socialization process is through mentoring. Mentoring is a process by which a junior-level employee (protege) develops a deep and long-lasting relationship with a more senior-level employee (mentor) within the organization. The mentor can provide social knowledge, resources, and psychological support to the protege both at the beginning of employment and as the protégé continues his or her career with the company. Mentoring has always existed in companies on an informal basis. However, as organizations continue to learn about the strong benefits of these relationships, they are more frequently instituting mentoring programs that formally match newcomers with mentors. This process has worked well for Budco, a marketing services and distribution firm that works with GM and Disney, which pairs four proteges with two mentors and has them meet twice a month. Group reentering at the 850-employee company has significantly reduced turnover among new hires.

12.5.1 Changing an Organizational Culture

Given all the effort it takes to create and maintain a culture, changing a culture once one has been established is perhaps even more difficult. In fact, estimates put the rate of successful major culture change at less than 20 percent. Mark Fields, head of Ford Motor Company's North and South American auto operations, knows how difficult it can be to change the culture at an organization. Prior CEOs at Ford have tried, unsuccessfully, to change a culture that current employees call "toxic" "cautious" "hierarchical" and "cliquish." To instigate a change, Fields took drastic measures, including purposefully creating a sense of stress and crisis among employees. Ford is calling its new attempt at major culture change the "Way Forward". In the "Way Forward" war room (where Fields and colleagues map out the drastic changes the company needs to make), big sheets of white paper hang on the wall reading, "Culture eats strategy for breakfast" and "Culture is unspoken, but powerful. It develops over time—difficult to change." Fields has gone to many extremes to create a climate for change among those responsible for helping him with the plans to overhaul Ford's culture. He has banned PowerPoint presentations, uses phrases such as "change or die" in meetings, and makes employees wear blue wristbands with "Red, White and Bold" inscripted on them, signifying a new Ford. In practice, there are two primary ways to change a culture: changes in leadership and mergers or acquisitions.

(1) Changes in Leadership. There is perhaps no bigger driver of culture than the leaders and top executives of organizations. Just as the founders and originators of organizations set the tone and develop the culture of a new company, subsequent CEOs and presidents leave their mark on the culture. Many times, leaders are expected simply to sustain the culture that has already been created. At other times, leaders have to be the driving force for change as the environment around the organization shifts. This expectation is one of the biggest reasons that organizations change their top leadership. For example, Nortel Networks recently hired two former Cisco executives into the roles of chief operating officer and chief technology officer. It is Nortel's hope that these executives will help bring some of Cisco's culture of aggressiveness to Nortel and thus allow it to compete more effectively in the high-technology industry environment.

(2) Mergers and Acquisitions. Merging two companies with two distinct cultures is a surefire way to change the culture in an organization. The problem is that there is just no way to know what the culture will look like after the merger takes place. What the new culture will resemble is a function of both the strength of the two cultures involved in the merger and how similar they are to each other. Ideally, a new culture would be created out of a compromise in which the best of both

companies is represented by the new culture. There are many stories that have arisen from the mergers of companies with very different cultures: AOL/Time Warner, Exxon/Mobil, HP/Compaq, and RJR/Nabisco, to name a few. Unfortunately, very few of these stories are good ones. Mergers rarely result in the strong culture that managers hope will appear when they make the decision to merge. In fact, most merged companies operate under a differentiated culture for an extended period of time. Some of them never really adopt a new identity, and when they do, many of them are seen as failures by the outside world. This perception is especially true in global mergers, in which each of the companies not only has a different organizational culture but is from a different country as well.

Merging two different cultures has major effects on the attitudes and behaviors of organizational employees. Companies merge for many different strategic reasons, and though many managers and executives may realize its importance, whether the cultures will match is rarely the deciding criterion. Slightly less troublesome but still a major hurdle to overcome are acquisitions. In most instances, and as evidenced by the chapter's opening example, the company doing the acquiring has a dominant culture to which the other is expected to adapt. We've noted how difficult it is just to get one person to adapt to an established culture through the socialization process. Can you imagine how difficult it is to change an entire organization at the same time? See our OB on Screen feature for one potential answer.

12.5.2 How Important is Organizational Culture?

Normally, this section is where we summarize the importance of organizational culture by describing how it affects job performance and organizational commitment, the two outcomes in our integrative model of OB. However (similar to organizational structure in Chapter 11), it's difficult to summarize the importance of culture in this way because there are so many different types and dimensions of the concept. High solidarity cultures, high sociability cultures, diversity cultures, creativity cultures, and so forth all have different effects on performance and commitment—effects that likely vary across different types of organizations and industries.

12.6 Culture maintenance and culture change

Regardless of the type of culture we're talking about, however, one concept remains important for any employee in any business: fit. Think for a moment about working for an organization whose culture doesn't match your own values. Maybe you work for an organization that produces a product that you don't believe in or that might be harmful to others, such as Phillip Morris, Budweiser, or Harrah's casinos. Maybe your employer is an organization that expects you to perform questionable behaviors from an ethical standpoint or produces a product that is of poor quality. Person-organization fit is the degree to which a person's personality and values match the culture of an organization. Employees judge fit by thinking about the values they prioritize the most, then judging whether the organization shares those values. Which values would you say are the most important to you?

A recent meta-analysis illustrates the importance of person-organization fit to employees. When employees feel that their values and personality match those of the organization, they experience higher levels of job satisfaction and feel less stress about their day-to-day tasks. They also feel higher levels of trust toward their managers. Taken together, those results illustrate why person-organization fit is so highly correlated with organizational commitment, one of the two outcomes in our integrative model of OB. When employees feel they fit with their organization's culture, they are much more likely to develop an emotional attachment to the company. The effects of fit on job performance are weaker, however. In general, person-organization fit is more related to citizenship behaviors than task performance. Employees who sense a good fit are therefore more likely to help their colleagues and "go the extra mile" to benefit the company.

12.7 Takeaways

1. Organizational culture is the shared social knowledge within an organization regarding the rules, norms, and values that shape the attitudes and behaviors of its employees. There are three components of organizational culture: observable artifacts, espoused values, and basic underlying assumptions. Observable artifacts include symbols, physical structures, language, stories, rituals, and ceremonies.

2. An organization's culture can be described on dimensions such as solidarity and sociability to create four general culture types: networked, communal, fragmented, and mercenary. Organizations often strive to create a more specific cultural emphasis, as in customer service cultures, diversity cultures, and creativity cultures.

3. Strong cultures have the ability to influence employee behaviors and attitudes. Strong cultures exist when employees agree on the way things are supposed to happen and their behaviors are consistent with those expectations. Strong cultures are not necessarily good or bad. Generally, a culture's effectiveness depends on how well it matches the company's outside environment. To this degree, adaptive cultures can be very useful.

4. Organizations maintain their cultures through attraction, selection, and attrition processes and socialization practices. Organizations change their cultures by changing their leadership or through mergers and acquisitions.

5. There are a number of practices organizations can utilize to improve the socialization of new employees, including realistic job previews and mentoring.

6. Person – organization fit is the degree to which a person's values and personality match the culture of the organization. Person – organization fit has a weak positive effect on job performance and a strong positive effect on organizational commitment.

12.8 Discussion Questions

1. Have you or a family member worked for an organization that you would consider to have a strong culture? If so, what made the culture strong? Did you or they enjoy working there? What do you think led to that conclusion?

2. Is it possible for an employee to have personal values that are inconsistent with the values of the organization? If so, how is this inconsistency likely to affect the employee's behavior and attitudes while at work?

3. If you had to describe the culture of your university, what would it be like? What observable artifacts are present to be perceived by students? Are there any underlying assumptions that guide your behavior at your university?

4. How can two companies with very different cultures that operate in the same industry both be successful? Shouldn't one company's culture automatically be a better fit for the environment?

5. If an organization wanted to foster a diversity culture, what steps might management take to ensure that employees will support the new culture? What observable artifacts might a company change to instill this culture?

6. When you think of the U. S. Postal Service's culture, what kinds of words come to mind? Where do these impressions come from? Do you think your impressions are accurate? What has the potential to make them inaccurate?

7. Think about the last job you started. What are some unique things that companies might do to reduce the amount of reality shock that new employees encounter? Are these methods likely to be expensive?

References

[1] FRIEDMAN T L. The world is flat:a brief history of the twenty-first century[M]. New York: Farrar,Straus,& Giroux,2005.

[2] WELBOURNE T M,ANDREWS A O. Predicting the performance of initial public offerings: should human resource management be in the equation [J]. Academy of Management Journal,1996,39:891 –919.

[3] FULMER I S,GERHART B,SCOTT K S. Are the 100 best better? An Empricial investigation of the relationship between being a great place to work'and firm performance[J]. Personnel Psychology,2003,56:965 –993.

[4] PFEFFER J, VEIGA J f. Putting people first for organizational success[J]. Academy of Management Executive,1999,13:37 –48.

[5] LOCKE E A,LATHAM G P. What should we do about motivation theory? six recommendations for the twenty-first century[J]. Academy of Management Review,2004,29: 388 –403.

[6] PETERSON S J, LUTHANS F. The impact of financial and non-financial incentives on business unit outcomes over[J]. Journal of Applied Psychology,2006,91:156 –165.

[7] STAJKOVIC A D, LUTHANS F. A Meta-analysis of the effects of organizational behavior modification on task performance,1975 –1995[J]. Academy of Management Journal,1997, 40:1122 –1149.

[8] VAN DYNE L,LEPINE J A. Helping and voice extra role behavior:evidence of construct and predictive validity[J]. Academy of Management Journal,1998,41:25 –44.

[9] ROBINSON S L,BENNETT R L. A typology of deviant workplace behaviors; a multidimensional scaling study[J]. Academy of Management Journal,1995,38:555 –572.

[10] HOFSTEDE G. Cultures and organizations:software of the mind[M]. New York:McGraw – Hill,1991.

[11] HARPER D. Spotlight abuse-save profits[J]. Industrial Distribution,1990,79:47 –51.

[12] ANDERSON L M, PEARSON C M. Tit for tat? The spiraling effect of incivility in the workplace[J]. Academy of Management Review 1999,24:452 –471.

[13] HAMPER R B. Tales from the assembly line[M]. New York:Warner Books,1991.

[14] PORTER L W, STEERS R M. Organizational, work, and personal factors in employee turnover and absenteeism[J]. Psychological Bulletin,1973,80:151 –176.

[15] MARQUEZ J. Home depot slashes hr staff by half; 1000 will go workforce[EB/OL]. [2008 – 04 –07]. http://www. worforce. com/section/00/articale/25/46/42. html.

[16] LAWLER E E. Pay and organizational effectiveness:a psychological view[M]. New York: McGraw – Hill,1971.

[17] HACKMAN J R,OLDHAM G R. Work redesign[M]. MA:Addison – Wesley,1980.

[18] FRIED Y,FERRIS G R. The validity of the job characteristics model:a review and meta-

analysis[J]. Personnel Psychology, 1987, 40: 287 – 322.

[19] CAMPION M A, MCCLELLAN C L. Interdisciplinary examination of the costs and benefits of enlarged jobs: a job design quasi-experiment[J]. Journal of Applied Psychology, 1991, 76: 186 – 198.

[20] ASHKANASY N M, HARTEL C J, DAUS C S. Diversity and emotion: the new frontiers in organizational behavior research[J]. Journal of management, 2002, 28: 307 – 338.

[21] LAYARD R. Happiness[M]. New York: Penguin Press, 2005.

[22] PERKINS A. Medical costs: saving money by reducing stress[J]. Harvard Business Review, 1994, 72(6): 12.

[23] DEFRANK R S, FOLKMAN S. Stress on the job: an executive update[J]. Academy of Management Executive, 1998, 12: 55 – 56.

[24] GOLDSTEIN D L. Stress, catecholamines, and cardiovascular disease[M]. New York: Oxford University Press, 1995.

[25] CANNON W B. Stresses and strains of homeostasis[J]. American Journal of Medical Science, 1935, 189: 1 – 14.

[26] FRIEDMAN M, ROSENMAN R H. Type a behavior and your heart[M]. New York: Knops, 1974.

[27] COHEN S. After effects of stress on human performance and social behavior: a review of research and theory[J]. Psychological Bulletin, 1980, 88: 82 – 108.

[28] CAVANAUGH M A, BOSWELL W R, ROEHLING M V, et al. An empirical examination of self-reported work stress among U. S. managers[J]. Journal of Applied Psychology, 2000, 85: 65 – 74.

[29] LATHAM G P, PINDER C C. Work motivation theory and research at the dawn of the twenty-first century[J]. Annual Review of Psychology, 2005, 56: 485 – 516.

[30] MASLOW A H. A theory of human motivation[J]. Psychological Review, 1943, 50: 370 – 396.

[31] TANG T L. The meaning of money revisited[J]. Journal of Organizational Behavior, 1992, 13: 197 – 202.

[32] ADAMS J S, ROSENBAUM W B. The relationship of worker productivity to cognitive dissonance about wage inequities[J]. Journal of Applied Psychology, 1962, 46: 161 – 164.

[33] SCULLEN S E, BERGEY P K, AIMAN – SMITH L. Forced distribution rating systems and the improvement of workforce potential: a baseline simulation[J]. Personnel Psychology, 2005, 58: 1 – 32.

[34] VAN EERDE W, THIERRY H. Vroom's expectancy models and work-related criteria: a meta-analysis[J]. Journal of Applied Psychology, 1996, 81: 575 – 586.

[35] MAYER R C, DAVIS J H, SCHOORMAN F D. An integrative model of organizational trust [J]. Academy of Management Review, 1995, 20: 709 – 734.

[36] RUOSSEAU D M, SITKIN S B, BURT R S, et al. Not so different after all: a cross-discipline view of trust[J]. Academy of Management Review, 1998, 23: 393 – 404.

[37] SCHWEITZER M E, ORDONEZ L, DOUMA B. Goal setting as a motivator of unethical behavior[J]. Academy of Management Journal, 2004, 47: 422 – 432.

[38] MCCABE D L. Academic dishonesty in graduate business programs: prevalence, causes, and proposed action[J]. Academy of management Learning and Education, 2006, 5: 294 – 305.

[39] WAGNER R K, STERNBERG R J. Practical intelligence in real-world pursuits: the role of tacit knowledge[J]. Journal of Personality and Social Psychology, 1985, 4: 436 – 458.

[40] EUCKER T R. Understanding the impact of tacit knowledge, and regional innovative capacity [J]. Regional Studies, 1999, 21: 487 – 513.

[41] BANDURA A. Social foundations of thought and action: a social cognitive theory [M]. Englewood Cliffs, NJ: Prentice Hall, 1986.

[42] VANDEWALLE D. Development and validation of a work domain goal orientation instrument [J]. Education and Psychological Measurement, 1997, 8: 995 – 1015.

[43] MARCH J G, SIMON H A. Organizations[M]. New York: Wiley, 1958.

[44] Kahneman D, Tversky A. On the psychology of prediction[J]. Psychological Review, 1973, 80: 237 – 251.

[45] MENON T, MORRIS M W, CHIU C, et al. Culture and the construal of agency: attribution to individual versus group dispositions[J]. Journal of Personality and Social Psychology, 1999, 76: 701 – 717.

[46] BARRICK M R, MOUNT M K, STRAUSS J P. Personality and job performance: test of the mediating effects of goal setting[J]. Journal of Applied Psychology, 1993, 78: 715 – 722.

[47] HOGAN J, HOLLAND B. Using theory to evaluate personality and job – performance relations: a socioanalytic perspective[J]. Journal of Applied Psychology 2003, 88: 100 – 112.

[48] SHALLEY C E, ZHOU J, OLDHAM G R. The effects of personal and contextual characteristics on creativity: where should we go from here[J]. Journal of Management, 2004, 30: 933 – 958.

[49] MCCRAE R R, TERRACCIANO A. Personality profiles of cultures: aggregate personality traits[J]. Journal of Personality and Social Psychology, 2005, 89: 407 – 425.

[50] TRIANDIS H C, SUH E M. Cultural influences on personality [J]. Annual Review of Psychology, 2002, 53: 133 – 160.

[51] MOTOWIDLO S J, BORMAN W S, SCHMIT M J. A theory of individual differences in task and contextual performance[J]. Human Performance, 1997, 10: 71 – 83.

[52] JUDGE T A, ILIES R. Relation between measures of typical and maximum job performance [J]. Journal of Applied Psychology, 1988, 73: 482 – 486.

[53] GRANT S, LANGAN – FOX J. Personality and occupational stressor-strain relationships: the role of the big five[J]. Journal of Occupational Health Psychology, 2007, 12: 20 – 33.

[54] COHEN S G, BAILEY D E. What makes teams work: group effectiveness research from the shop floor to the executive suite[J]. Journal of Management, 1997, 23: 239 – 290.

[55] TUCKMAN B W. Developmental sequence in small groups [J]. Psychological Bulletin, 1965, 63: 44 – 67.

[56] BENNE K, SHEATS P. Functional roles of group members [J]. Journal of Social Issues, 1948, 4: 41 – 49.

[57] LEPINE J A, VAN DYNE L. An attributional model of helping in the context of work groups [J]. Academy of Management Review, 2001, 26: 67 – 84.

[58] BARRY B, STEWART G L. Composition, process, and performance in self-managed groups: the role of personality[J]. Journal of Applied Psychology, 1997, 82: 62 – 78.
[59] STEINER I D. Group processes and productivity[J]. New York: Academic Press, 1972.
[60] MULLEN B, COPPER C. The relation between group cohesiveness and performance: an integration[J]. Psychological Bulletin, 1994, 115: 210 – 227.
[61] THOMAS K W. Toward multi-dimensional values in teaching: the example of conflict behaviors[J]. Academy of Management Review, 1977, 2: 484 – 490.
[62] DE DREU C K, BEERSMA B, KLUWER E S, et al. A theory-based measure of conflict management strategies in the workplace[J]. Journal of Organizational Behavior, 2001, 22: 645 – 668.
[63] HOUSE R J, HANGES P J, JAVIDAN M, et al. Culture, leadership, and organizations[M]. Thousand Oaks, CA: Sage, 2004.
[64] KERR S, JERMIER J M. Substitutes for leadership: their meaning and measurement[J]. Organizational Behavior and Human Performance, 1986, 22: 88 – 102.
[65] HOWELL J P, DORFMAN P W, KERR S. Moderator variables in leadership research[J]. Academy of Management Review, 1986, 11: 88 – 102.
[66] CHILD J, MCGRATH M. Organizations unfettered: organizational forms in an information-intensive economy[J]. Academy of Management Journal, 2001, 44: 1135 – 1148.
[67] PORTER M. Competitive strategy[M]. New York: Free Press, 1980.
[68] CHATMAN J A. Matching people and organizations: selection and socialization in public accounting firms[J]. Administrative Science Quarterly, 1991, 36: 459 – 484.
[69] O'REILLY C A. Corporations, culture, and commitment: motivation and social control in organizations[J]. California Management Review, 1989, 31: 9 – 25.
[70] GRAVELLE M. The five most common hiring mistakes and how to avoid them[J]. The Canadian Manager, 2004, 29: 11 – 13.
[71] PLATT G. Global merger activity sets record pace[J]. Global Finance, 2006, 20: 60.
[72] HAMM S. A passion for the planet[J]. BusinessWeek, 2005, 8(21): 92 – 94.
[73] LASHINSKY A. Where does Google go next[J]. Fortune, 2008, 5(26): 104 – 110.
[74] FISHER A. Turning clock-watchers into stars[J]. Fortune, 2004, 3(22): 60.